MW00576308

Historical Fiction Now

Historical Fiction Now

Edited by

MARK EATON
AND
BRUCE HOLSINGER

With an afterword by

HILARY MANTEL

OXFORD
UNIVERSITY PRESS

OXFORD
UNIVERSITY PRESS

Great Clarendon Street, Oxford, OX2 6DP,
United Kingdom

Oxford University Press is a department of the University of Oxford.
It furthers the University's objective of excellence in research, scholarship,
and education by publishing worldwide. Oxford is a registered trade mark of
Oxford University Press in the UK and in certain other countries

Published in the United States of America by Oxford University Press
198 Madison Avenue, New York, NY 10016, United States of America

British Library Cataloguing in Publication Data
Data available

Library of Congress Control Number: 2023934727

ISBN 978–0–19–887703–5

DOI: 10.1093/oso/9780198877035.001.0001

Printed and bound by
CPI Group (UK) Ltd, Croydon, CR0 4YY

Contents

Acknowledgments

In 2017, on a magical May evening at the Huntington Library, the late Hilary Mantel read publicly for the first time from the third and final book in her Wolf Hall trilogy. Those of us who were fortunate enough to be in attendance listened, rapt, as the author shared pages that would soon make their way into her manuscript and, ultimately, the novel. *The Mirror and the Light* was then a work in progress, the culmination of a decade-long process of research, reflection, and writing that had already resulted in two Booker Prize-winning works of historical fiction. Two days later, also at the Huntington, Mantel discussed the evolution of the trilogy in conversation with Mary Robertson, a Tudor historian and the dedicatee of *Wolf Hall* who had been instrumental in Mantel's early research on Cromwell's life and work.

The two events bookended an international conference held over those three days at the Huntington, which has housed Mantel's growing literary archive since 2001. "Fictive Histories, Historical Fiction," organized by Sophie Coulombeau, convened a gathering of novelists, literary historians, and critics to think together about history and fiction, their commonalities and intersections, as well as the nature of historical fiction as a form of writing that has brought these modes of thought together in complex and often contradictory ways. The afterword to *Historical Fiction Now* is the full text of Hilary Mantel's keynote address, published here for the first time alongside other papers presented at the conference as well as several essays commissioned or reprinted for this volume.

We are grateful to Sophie Coulombeau for organizing a wonderful event. Thanks to Steve Hindle, then W.M. Keck Foundation Director of Research at the Huntington Library, along with his staff for hosting the conference with such efficiency, generosity, and warmth. Special thanks to our fellow participants who contributed chapters to this book. Finally, we are grateful to Jacqueline Norton, Karen Raith, and Aimee Wright at Oxford University Press, as well as the anonymous readers who made many helpful suggestions for the volume's improvement.

List of Illustrations

List of Contributors

Geraldine Brooks is the author of six novels and three works of nonfiction. Her most recent novel is *Horse* (2022). Her novel *The Secret Chord* (2015) is about the life of David. She is also the author of the Pulitzer Prize-winning *March* (2008), and the international bestsellers *Caleb's Crossing* (2011), *People of the Book* (2009), and *Year of Wonders* (2001). *Caleb's Crossing* was the winner of the New England Book Award for Fiction and the Christianity Today Book Award, and it was a finalist for the Langum Prize in American Historical Fiction. *People of the Book* was named the Australian Book Industry Book of the Year in 2009. In 2010, she received the Dayton Literary Peace Prize for Lifetime Achievement. In 2016, she was appointed an Officer in the Order of Australia. She was Centennial Writer in Residence at the American Library in Paris in 2020. She is a Visiting Lecturer of English at Harvard University.

Jessie Burton is the author of four novels: *The Miniaturist* (2014), *The Muse* (2016), *The Confession* (2019), and *The House of Fortune* (2022). *The Miniaturist* and *The Muse* were both *Sunday Times* no. 1 bestsellers, *New York Times* bestsellers, and Radio 4's *Book at Bedtime*. *The Confession* was an instant *Sunday Times* bestseller and Radio 4's *Book at Bedtime*. *The House of Fortune* is a *Sunday Times* no. 1 bestseller. *The Miniaturist* went on to sell over a million copies in its year of publication, and it was Christmas no. 1 in the United Kingdom, National Book Awards Book of the Year, and Waterstones Book of the Year 2014. *The Miniaturist* was shown as a two-part miniseries on BBC One in 2017, starring Anya Taylor-Joy, Alex Hassell, and Romola Garai. Jessie Burton's first novel for children, *The Restless Girls*, was published in 2018, and *Medusa*, her second, in 2021.

Kirstin Chen is the award-winning author of three novels. Her debut novel, *Soy Sauce for Beginners* (2014), was an Amazon bestseller and an *Oprah Magazine* editor's pick. Her second novel, *Bury What We Cannot Take* (2018), was named a best book of the season by *Electric Literature*, *The Millions*, *The Rumpus*, *Harper's Bazaar*, and *InStyle*. The book was also shortlisted for the Singapore Literature Prize. Her third novel, *Counterfeit* (2022), is a Reese Witherspoon book club pick, a Roxane Gay book club pick, and a *New York Times* Editors' Choice. Her writing has appeared in *Real Simple*, *Literary Hub*, *Writer's Digest*, *Zyzzyva*, and the *Best New Singaporean Short Stories*. She holds an MFA from

Emerson College and a BA from Stanford University. Born and raised in Singapore, she lives in New York City. She teaches creative writing at the University of San Francisco and in Ashland University's Low-Residency MFA Program.

Sophie Coulombeau is a Lecturer in the Department of English and Related Literature at the University of York. She is the author of the novel *Rites* (2012) and is currently finishing her second novel, which has received grants from Arts Council England and the Society of Authors. She has also made numerous programs for BBC Radio, and has written for publications including *The Guardian*, *History Today*, and the *Times Literary Supplement*. Her scholarly work has appeared in *Nineteenth-Century Prose*, *Huntington Library Quarterly*, and *Eighteenth-Century Life*. Dr. Coulombeau is currently working on a monograph titled *Romantic Onomastics: Naming and Identity in Britain 1779–1814*. She is co-investigator on the AHRC-funded project, Unlocking the Mary Hamilton Papers, which is based at the John Rylands Library, Manchester.

Mark Eaton is a Professor of English at Azusa Pacific University and an Associate Research Professor at Claremont Graduate University. He is the author of *Religion and American Literature since 1950* (2020). He is a contributor to *A Companion to the Modern American Novel, 1900–1950* (2009); *A Companion to Film Comedy* (2012); *Screenwriting* (2014); *The Routledge Companion to Literature & Religion* (2015); and *A Companion to the Multi-Ethnic Literature of the United States* (2023). He is Editor of the journal *Christianity & Literature*.

David Ebershoff's novels include *The Danish Girl* (2000), which won the Lambda Literary Award and was adapted into an Oscar-winning film, and the no. 1 bestseller, *The 19th Wife* (2008), which was adapted for television. His books have been translated into more than thirty languages to critical acclaim. Ebershoff is currently Vice President and Editor-in-Chief at Hogarth Books and an Executive Editor at Random House.

Bruce Holsinger is Linden Kent Memorial Professor of English at the University of Virginia. He is the author of several nonfiction books, including *Music, Body, and Desire in Medieval Culture: Hildegard of Bingen to Chaucer* (2001), winner of the Modern Language Association Prize for a First Book, the John Nicholas Brown Prize from the Medieval Academy of America, and the Philip Brett Award from the American Musicological Society; *The Premodern Condition: Medievalism and the Making of Theory* (2005); *Neomedievalism, Neoconservatism, and the War on Terror* (2007); and, most recently, *On Parchment: Animals, Archives, and the Making of Culture from Herodotus to the Digital Age* (2023). He is also the author of four novels, most recently *The Displacements* (2022). He is Editor of the journal *New Literary History*.

Katherine Howe is a *New York Times* bestselling and award-winning writer of historical fiction. Her adult novels are *The Daughters of Temperance Hobbs* (2019), *The Physick Book of Deliverance Dane* (2009), which debuted at no. 2 on the *New York Times* bestseller list, and *The House of Velvet and Glass* (2012), which was a *USA Today* bestseller. Her latest novel, *A True Account of Hannah Masury's Sojourn Amongst the Pyrates, Written by Herself*, will be published in 2023. For young adults, she has written *Conversion* (2014), which received the 2015 Massachusetts Book Award in young adult literature, and *The Appearance of Annie van Sinderen* (2015), which was named a "Must Read" by the Massachusetts Center for the Book. She edited *The Penguin Book of Witches* (2014), a primary source reader on the history of witchcraft in England and North America. Her fiction has been translated into over twenty languages. In 2015, she was the visiting writer in residence at Lenoir-Rhyne University in North Carolina, and she spent 2016 as a visiting scholar at the Center for Advanced Study in the Behavioral Sciences at Stanford University.

Gavin Jones is the Frederick P. Rehmus Family Professor of the Humanities at Stanford University. He is the author of four books: *Strange Talk: The Politics of Dialect Literature in Gilded Age America* (1999); *American Hungers: The Problem of Poverty in U.S. Literature, 1840–1945* (2007); *Failure and the American Writer: A Literary History* (2014); and *Reclaiming John Steinbeck: Writing for the Future of Humanity* (2021). He has edited a new edition of Sylvester Judd's novel *Margaret: A Tale of the Real and Ideal, Blight and Bloom* (1845), and is coediting (with Michael Collins) *The Cambridge Companion to the American Short Story* (2022). He is currently writing a book about Zora Neale Hurston.

Jane Kamensky earned her BA (1985) and Ph.D. (1993) in history from Yale University. She is Jonathan Trumbull Professor of American History at Harvard University and Pforzheimer Foundation Director of the Schlesinger Library on the History of Women in America at Harvard Radcliffe Institute. A historian of British America and the United States, she is the author of numerous books, including *A Revolution in Color: The World of John Singleton Copley* (2016), which won four major prizes and was a finalist for several others. With Jill Lepore, she jointly wrote the historical novel *Blindspot* (2008). A former Commissioner of the Smithsonian National Portrait Gallery, she serves as a Trustee of the Museum of the American Revolution, and as one of the principal investigators on the NEH/ Department of Education-funded initiative, Educating for American Democracy.

Michael Lackey is the Distinguished McKnight University Professor at the University of Minnesota Morris. He is the author of *Biofiction: An Introduction* (2021); *Ireland, the Irish, and the Rise of Biofiction* (2021); *Conversations with*

Biographical Novelists: Truthful Fictions Across the Globe (2019); *The American Biographical Novel* (2016); *Truthful Fictions: Conversations with American Biographical Novelists* (2014); *The Modernist God State: A Literary Study of the Nazis' Christian Reich* (2012); and *African American Atheists and Political Liberation* (2007). He is also editor of *Biographical Fiction: A Reader* (2016).

The late **Hilary Mantel** was the author of sixteen books, including *A Place of Greater Safety* (1993), Beyond Black (2005), *The Assassination of Margaret Thatcher: Stories* (2014), and the memoir *Giving up the Ghost* (2017). Her best-selling novels *Wolf Hall* (2009) and its sequel *Bring Up the Bodies* (2012) won the Man Booker prize. *The Mirror and the Light*, the final part of her Wolf Hall trilogy, was published in 2020 and, like *Wolf Hall*, won the Walter Scott Prize for historical fiction. The Royal Shakespeare Company/Playful Productions adapted *Wolf Hall* and *Bring Up the Bodies*, and Hilary Mantel and Ben Miles, working with the same producers, brought *The Mirror and the Light* to the stage in 2021. A BBC/Masterpiece six-part adaption of the first two Thomas Cromwell novels was broadcast in 2015, and an adaptation of the third is in progress.

Maaza Mengiste is a novelist and essayist. She is the author of the novel, *The Shadow King* (2019), which was shortlisted for the Man Booker Prize and was a finalist for the 2020 LA Times Book Prize. It was named best book of the year by the *New York Times, NPR, Elle, Time*, and more. Her debut novel, *Beneath the Lion's Gaze* (2010) was selected by *The Guardian* as one of the ten best contemporary African books and named one of the best books of 2010 by *Christian Science Monitor, Boston Globe*, and more. She is the recipient of an American Academy of Arts and Letters Award in Literature, the Premio il ponte, and fellowships from the Fulbright Scholar Program, the National Endowment for the Arts, and the Dorothy and Lewis B. Cullman Center for Scholars and Writers at New York Public Library. Her work can be found in the *New Yorker*, the *New York Review of Books, Granta, The Guardian*, the *New York Times, Rolling Stone*, and the BBC, among other places. She is the Assistant Director of the Queens College MFA Program in Creative Writing.

Tiya Miles is the author of *All That She Carried: The Journey of Ashley's Sack, a Black Family Keepsake* (2021), winner of the National Book Award, the Frederick Douglass Book Prize, and many other awards, as well as a *New York Times* bestseller. She is also the author of *Dawn of Detroit: A Chronicle of Slavery and Freedom in the City of the Straits* (2017), winner of the Frederick Douglass Book Prize, the American Book Award, and the Hurston/ Wright Foundation Legacy Award; *Ties That Bind: The Story of an Afro-Cherokee Family in Slavery and Freedom* (2015), winner of the Frederick Jackson Turner Award from the Organization of American Historians and the Lora Romero Prize from the American Studies Association; *Tales from the Haunted South: Dark Tourism and Memories of Slavery from the Civil War Era* (2015); and *The House on Diamond Hill: A Cherokee Plantation Story* (2010). With Sharon P. Holland, she coedited a collection of essays, *Crossing Waters, Crossing Worlds: The African Diaspora in Indian Country* (2006). Her first novel, *The Cherokee Rose: A Novel of Gardens and Ghosts* (2015), was a finalist for the Lambda Literary Award. Random House is publishing a new edition of the novel in 2023. She received a MacArthur Foundation Fellowship in 2011. She is a Professor of History at Harvard University.

Téa Obreht was born in Belgrade, in the former Yugoslavia, and grew up in Cyprus and Egypt before eventually immigrating to the United States. Her debut novel, *The Tiger's Wife*, won the 2011 Orange Prize for Fiction and was a 2011 National Book Award finalist. Her second novel, *Inland*, was published by Random House in 2019. Her work has appeared in the *New Yorker, Harper's, The Atlantic, Vogue, Esquire, Zoetrope: All-Story*, and *The Best American Short Stories*. She was the recipient of the Rona Jaffe fellowship from the Dorothy and Lewis B. Cullman Center for Scholars and Writers at the New York Public Library, and a 2016 fellowship from the National Endowment for the Arts. She was a National Book Foundation 5 Under 35 honoree, and was named by the *New Yorker* as one of the twenty best American fiction writers under forty.

George Saunders is the author of *Liberation Day* (2022); *Fox 8: A Story* (2018); *Lincoln in the Bardo* (2017), winner of the Man Booker Prize; *Pastoralia* (2001); *Tenth of December* (2013), a finalist for the National Book Award; and *CivilWarLand in Bad Decline* (1996). He is also the author of the nonfiction book, *A Swim in a Pond in the Rain: In Which Four Russians Give a Master Class on Writing, Reading, and Life* (2021). He has received fellowships from the Lannan Foundation, the American Academy of Arts and Letters, and the Guggenheim Foundation. In 2006, he was awarded a MacArthur Fellowship. In 2013, he was awarded the PEN/Malamud Award for Excellence in Short Fiction and was included in *Time*'s list of the 100 most influential people in the world. He teaches in the creative writing program at Syracuse University.

Namwali Serpell is a Zambian writer and a Professor of English at Harvard University. She received the 2020 Windham-Campbell Prize for fiction, the 2015 Caine Prize for African Writing, and the 2011 Rona Jaffe Foundation Writers' Award. Her first novel, *The Old Drift* (2019), won the Anisfield-Wolf Book prize for fiction, the Arthur C. Clarke Award for Science Fiction, the Grand Prix des Associations Littéraires Prize for Belles-Lettres, and the *L.A. Times*' Art Seidenbaum Award for First Fiction in 2020. It was named one of the year's 100

Notable Books by the *New York Times Book Review*. Her second novel, *The Furrows* (2022), was named one of the ten best books of the year by the *New York Times* and *Publisher's Weekly*, and it is longlisted for the Joyce Carol Oates Prize. Her nonfiction book, *Stranger Faces* (2020), was a finalist for the National Book Critics Circle Award for Criticism.

Naomi J. Williams is the author of the novel *Landfalls* (2015), long-listed for the Center for Fiction First Novel Prize and the National Book Critics Circle's John Leonard Award. Her short fiction and essays have appeared in numerous places, including *A Public Space*, *One Story*, the *Southern Review*, *LitHub*, and *The Rumpus*, garnering a Pushcart Prize and Best American Short Stories honorable mention. Educated at Princeton, Stanford, and UC Davis, Williams makes her home in Sacramento, California, and teaches fiction writing with the low-res MFA program at Ashland University in Ohio.

Introduction

Historical Fiction Now

Bruce Holsinger

At the opening of *I the Supreme* (*Y el Supremo*, 1974), Augusto Roa Bastos's sweeping historical novel of absolutism in nineteenth-century Paraguay, the reader encounters a decree, avowedly written by the "Supreme Dictator of the Republic" himself, ordering his own postmortem decapitation. His head must then be placed on a pike in the Plaza de la República, all of his servants hanged then buried in anonymous and unconsecrated graves outside the city walls; and then, "At the end of the aforementioned period, I order that my remains be burned and my ashes thrown into the river ..." The decree pauses here, the ellipsis indicating where its prose has been interrupted—whereupon we learn that we have been reading the proclamation through the eyes of its putative author, El Supremo himself. "Where was this found?" the dictator asks of the document of his own execution, dismemberment, and cremation. "Nailed to the door of the cathedral," a yet unnamed underling responds, and from there the opening exchange blossoms into a metatextual display of archival knowledge and bookish erudition. Was the decree torn out of a book? Did it come from the malevolent pen of a forger? Might it be found among the "thousands of documents, dossiers, and decrees in the archives"? For all I care, El Supremo avows, "they can manufacture their paper from consecrated rags. Write it, print it with consecrated letters on a consecrated press ... They're daring to parody my Supreme Decrees now. They imitate my language, my handwriting, trying to infiltrate by way of it."[1] In short, the novel slyly implies, we can trust nothing we read from here on in, and by now we are only on the second page.

The novel's self-consciousness about the deceptiveness and reliability of writing in its various forms gets at the essential dilemmas of historical fiction as genre and mode. Which voices are speaking from what particular pasts in

Bruce Holsinger, *Introduction: Historical Fiction Now*. In: *Historical Fiction Now*. Edited by Mark Eaton and Bruce Holsinger, Oxford University Press. © Bruce Holsinger (2023). DOI: 10.1093/oso/9780198877035.003.0001 the pages of the historical novel, and on whose authority and terms? How does the written form of the novel embody this authority, and with what consequences for diverse readerships and publics in a globalizing world? What is the writer's burden of responsibility to represent the past with accuracy, and what does accuracy even mean in the age of truthiness and alternative fact?

Historical Fiction Now: the title of this collection reflects an interest in the *present* of historical fiction, which our contributors explore from a number of perspectives: the current state of the genre across the English-speaking world, the perspectives taken by today's authors and scholars on archives and research, the epistemological challenges of writing in a mode that braids past, present, and future into compelling narrative, and so on. Gathering together the voices of novelists, critics, academics, and several authors writing across these categories, we explore the nature of reading, writing, and writing about historical fiction in the present moment while meditating on some of the myriad contexts of the genre. What inspires writers to choose particular moments, events, and personalities as the subjects of their fictional imaginings, and with what implications for their readers' understanding of the present? How do contemporary scholars approach the making and reception of historical fiction, and how do these approaches resonate with writers' own preoccupations in the process of invention? What might scholars of a genre with a long and complex history learn from its contemporary practitioners? Conversely, how do novelists understand their own historical fictions (if at all) in relation to the theoretical and critical traditions shaping the work of their academic colleagues?

One challenge shared by anyone who writes or writes about historical fiction today comes in the form of an enduring narrative about the genre's own history and, for lack of a better phrase, its uneven development. By the third decade of the twentieth century, this story goes, historical fiction had suffered something of a decline, no longer embraced by the gatekeepers of "serious" literary culture; or, as György Lukács put it in the preface to his enormously influential study *The Historical Novel* (1937), "the historical novel of our day, despite the great talent of its best exponents, still suffers in many respects from the remnants of the harmful and still not entirely vanquished legacy of bourgeois decadence."[2] Modernism was seemingly hostile to the historical novel given its penchant for realism, its epic pretensions, and its supposed resistance to formal experimentation. Much of historical fiction's energy was now directed toward the mass market, with novels such as Margaret Mitchell's *Gone with the Wind* (1936) topping the bestseller lists, lowering critical respect for the genre even while increasing its visibility among the general public. As Perry Anderson put it in an influential 2011 essay for the *London Review of Books*, "By the interwar period, the historical novel had become déclassé, falling precipitously out of the ranks of serious fiction."[3]

Yet the story Anderson and others have told about the development of the historical novel is only partially true. For one thing, this account overlooks the enormous popularity of mass market historical fiction already established as early as the late nineteenth century, as the work of scholars such as Alison Light and Diana Wallace has shown; and it obscures the role of gender as a shaping force in the development of the genre.[4] In the middle decades of the twentieth century, women readers transformed the audience and public of the historical novel, with the works of Daphne du Maurier, Philippa Gregory, and many others creating new readerships on both sides of the Atlantic. The era also saw the emergence of new schools of historical fiction around the world, from sub-Saharan Africa to East Asia. Even within European and American modernist schools, writers invigorated the form through an array of historical novels that pushed the boundaries of the form, including H.D.'s *Pilate's Wife* (1929), Virginia Woolf's *Orlando* (1928), Hermann Broch's *The Death of Virgil* (1945), and William Faulkner's *Absolom, Absolom!* (1936), a Civil War novel published the same year as *Gone with the Wind*. In their attempts to capture the here-and-now in novelistic form, writers of this era melded archaic styles and contemporary techniques and media to shape a new idiom of historical fiction.

In an age of belligerent nationalism and contested empire, historical fiction also played an important role in cultural conversations around the limits of state power in an era of increasingly global conflict. This in turn led to what Anderson calls "one of the most astonishing transformations in literary history": namely the "postmodern revival" of historical fiction, typified in the rise of the New Historical Novel in Latin America during the so-called Boom of the 1970s. Here and elsewhere, a resurgent realism converged with experimental modes of postmodernism to create what Linda Hutcheon has called "historiographic metafiction," a mode of fictional narrative that plays deliberately and self-consciously with the conventions of history writing in new and inventive ways.[5] The advent of postmodernism spawned numerous schools of historical fiction writing, from the work of Umberto Eco in Italy, Edouard Glissant in Martinique, and Paul Hazoume in Benin to the novels of Toni Morrison, whose Nobel Prize for Literature followed by one year the publication of her historical novel *Jazz* (1992).

Despite the flourishing of the historical novel across languages, nations, and literary avant-gardes for the last century and more, historical fiction continues to spark a peculiar kind of defensiveness from certain literary quarters. Burdened by a putative legacy of popularization, sentiment, anti-quarianism, and even irrelevance, the genre seems always required to argue for its own legitimacy, perhaps the result of selective reading and short memory on the part of its critics and practitioners alike. Writing in the *New York Times* just before this collection went into production, Jonathan Lee perfectly captures this self-abnegating stance. For the last twenty years, he writes, "the novels celebrated for defining our time have almost always been books set *within* our time, from Jonathan Franzen's voluminous social comedies to Sally Rooney's smartly self-knowing novels and the seam of contemporary autofiction that has run between them. Historical fiction, by contrast, has not been in fashion." Instead, the historical novel "has been seen as its own fusty fashion, relentlessly uncontemporary and easy to car-icature, filled with mothballed characters who wear costumes rather than clothes, use words like 'Prithee!' while having modern-day thoughts, and occasionally encounter villains immediately recognizable by their yellow teeth or suspicious smell."[6] As an accomplished contributor to the genre himself, Lee is writing at least partially tongue-in-cheek here, and the essay goes on to celebrate the success of the historical novel in anglophone fiction over the last two decades. But the argument grants the naysayers quite a lot of weight; as he asks, "What light could such novels possibly shed on the present day?"

A sassier take on the same question comes from Fran Lebowitz: "Con-tempt would be the word that best defines my feelings for the historical novel," she has bluntly said, adding that the "outstanding example of middle-brow literature would be the historical novel. ... I don't like historical novels for a number of reasons ... they're in the province of the third rate. Peo-ple read them to learn things, as in James Michener. I think a real writer writes about his own life."[7] Such aspersions come not solely from critics or academics but from within contemporary literary culture, or at least certain quarters of it. In a pair of acerbic assessments of the genre (both cited by Michael Lackey in his contribution to this volume), Nobel Prize-winning novelist Olga Tokarczuk—author of the historical novel *The Books of Jacob* (2014)—declares herself "not really a fan of historical novels," while Henry James, at least as imagined by Colm Tóibín in his historical novel *The Mas-ter*, views the historical novel as tainted by "a fatal cheapness"—a phrase James himself used in a 1901 letter to Sarah Orne Jewett.

One other factor that explains the oddly self-defeating gestures on the part of contemporary writers and critics is the gatekeeping around particular subgenres of historical fiction—for instance, the distinction between the biographical novel and the historical novel proper. Lackey takes as an indicative example of this heuristic contrast *The Danish Girl* (2000), a biographical novel by David Ebershoff that imagines the life of Lili Elbe, a transgender woman and one of the first known subjects to receive gender confirmation surgery. Rather than striving for accuracy in all of its historical movements and details, Lackey argues, what the biographical historical novel (or "biofiction") attempts instead is a form of self-fashioning on the part of the reader, a guide to "activate agential and meaningful living in the present and the future" and a more reflective avenue of becoming. Ebershoff's own contribution to this volume, a short meditation titled "Looking for the Danish Girl," finds such agential force along the streets of Dresden, where he begins to understand the central questions posed in the novel: "whose memory informs our own," and how "the past, seemingly obliterated, infuse[s] our vision of the world at hand, and of ourselves." The merging of the biographical and the historical in the form of the novel will always be contingent, Lackey suggests, resistant to easy categorization and generic specification.

Though the novel has been the privileged form of historical fiction, it is not the only one. As Gavin Jones puts it in his contribution, citing Yi-Ping Ong, "novels tend to assume a totality and autonomy, a completeness of readerly experience that is related to the free, inward subject of liberalism and to the novel's ability to make knowable (and hence to sanction) the larger classes and institutions of which it is part." Yet as Jones asks, "What kind of history do we receive within the spatial and temporal limitations of the short story?" The short story's relation to history and historical change is not "horizontally developmental and encompassing (even welcoming)," like the novel's, "but instead vertically layered and discomforting." Such jarring discomforts suffuse as well recent modes of speculative writing that enlist historical fiction in partial or provisional ways: as discrete sections in novels that work on multiple time scales, as moments of documentary authority lending weight to present-day narration, as ephemeral flashbacks ghosting up from the past in the forms of parable, chronicle, fragment.

The *now* of historical fiction is also a grammatical now, marking the proliferation of present-tense narration in the genre over the last twenty years. This stylistic choice may speak to "the transience of the digital world," as Richard Lea has put it, though some contemporary writers have explained this turn to the present tense as an attempt to capture or replicate a lost immediacy.[8] Hilary Mantel's Wolf Hall trilogy is written in a vivid present tense that came to her the instant she decided to write the first installment: "*Wolf Hall* attempts to duplicate not the historian's chronology but the way memory works: in leaps, loops, flashes. The basic decision about the book was taken seconds before I began writing. 'So now get up': the person on the ground was Cromwell and the camera was behind his eyes." This delightful anachronism places film technology in Tudor England as a machine of perspectival transparency; the present tense becomes a lens, capable of focusing and zooming out at will, able to convey "the jitter and flux of events, the texture of them and their ungraspable speed." The mode, Mantel says, is "humble and realistic—the author is not claiming superior knowledge—she is inside or very close by her character, and sharing their focus, their limited perceptions. It doesn't suit authors who want to boss the reader around and like being God."[9]

Such a posture of humility, as Mantel is surely aware, sets her Wolf Hall trilogy apart from the great historical novels of the nineteenth century, which tend to favor omniscient and indeed God-like points of view, as in the majestic opening pages of George Eliot's *Romola*, in which the narrator gazes across centuries and over mountains to convey in a hortatory third person the deep continuities of the human condition: "As our thought follows close in the slow wake of the dawn, we are impressed with the broad sameness of the human lot, which never alters in the main headings of its history—hunger and labour, seed-time and harvest, love and death."[10] If *Romola* begins at 30,000 feet, *Wolf Hall* begins at ground level, inside the just-struck head of its protagonist, beaten by his father: "Felled, dazed, silent, he has fallen; knocked full length on the cobbles of the yard. His head turns sideways; his eyes are turned toward the gate, as if someone might arrive to help him out. One blow, properly placed, could kill him now."[11] This *now* signals and performs the immanent: death may be universal to the "human lot," in Eliot's words, but here it is proximate, individualized, a hale presence in the readerly now.

Yet novelists are rarely as in control of their narratives as they imagine themselves to be, and writers of historical fiction are no different. As George Saunders puts it, speaking for a number of authors represented in this collection, "We buy into some version of the intentional fallacy: the notion that art is about having a clear-cut intention and then confidently executing same. The actual process, in my experience, is much more mysterious and more of a pain in the ass to discuss truthfully." In much the same spirit, Jesse Burton describes the act of remembrance in fiction as something of a

double-edged sword; the historical novelist's attempts at responsible representation are always at risk of being undercut by the destabilizing passions
of art:

> Seeking to re-present the past is an impossible act, and not just because
> physics forbids it. The fact is, as soon as you start writing a story set in the
> past in order to "get close" to that very same past, a paradoxical gap grows
> between the original material and the new presentation. Believing this, I
> suppose I've never come at my source material in a particularly respectful
> fashion. I've had a writer's hunger, and a reader's hunger too. Am I making a
> new past? Maybe; and one as equally unstable. I've been looking at the past
> to give me something. I've used it to get somewhere else—not somewhere
> higher, or better. Just somewhere different.

Another word for this making of a specific "somewhere different" is particularism, a term that might help distinguish modern and contemporary
historical fiction from the universalizing aspirations that Lukács found in
the nineteenth-century historical novel. These "artful maneuvers for marking cultural distance," as Doris Sommer explains, can have a salutary effect
on literary making: "Particularism's seductive and defensive tangle with uni-
versalism produces the formal experiments and aesthetic thrill that can be
lost on readers who rush toward one term or the other."[12] A useful distinction for critic and novelist alike: contemporary writers of historical fiction
aspire to speak beyond the limits of their immediate cultural sphere while
maintaining an intimate distance with their subjects.

Crucial to these oscillations between the particular and the universal is
the place of the archive—or rather "the archive," that elusive conceptual
edifice so central to the historical imagination. Working archivists in con-
servation, collections care, and user access will go rightly apoplectic when
theorists and novelists swoop in with abstractions about the archive as a
knowable let alone usable repository of knowledge, and it is a rare historical
novelist (or, for that matter, literary theorist) who spends time these days in
nondigital archives sifting through written material in manuscript or print.
Nevertheless, for novelists writing about the distant past, the archive functions as resource, wellspring, and, in some cases, fiction. Edward P. Jones,
in several interviews around the publication of his Pulitzer Prize-winning
novel *The Known World*, repeatedly claimed to have done little or no historical research. Though he had piles of books he would occasionally consult, his
characters came alive only in his imagination: "Had I done research, it might

have been a different story. Maybe I would have focused on something that explained them, but I didn't do research." Whenever pressed on the subject, he has stuck to his guns: "There was no research. No. I didn't do any research ... The creative part of my brain told me, 'you really don't need that.' ... Forget the research. It's overrated."[13] Quite a flex, and an instructive note of caution for novelists tempted to burden their scenes with over-researched descriptions of wall tapestries or wardrobes past. As Burton warns here, "historical novelists can sometimes be *more* respectful to their sources than historians are, because they are afraid of the accusation of sub-intellectual understanding, of misinterpreting their research. Thus, psychological acuity can give way to fetishized historical detail; obsessive historical recreation outweighs lightness of touch and nuance."

Jones's case is especially ironic given his access to the kinds of primary and secondary sources many novelists can only dream of. Geraldine Brooks, in her contribution here, writes of the challenges posed by the writing of *The Secret Chord*, set during the life of the biblical David: "how do you research the life of a man who shimmers between history and myth in the Second Iron Age, 3,000 years ago? Archives, letters, journals, court documents—the usual staples of my craft—aren't available in this case. Outside the Bible, there is no written record of David." Brooks seeks the matter of her novel instead in scripture, in the resonance of locality and landscape, in the smell and taste of ancient plants and the hollowed-out chambers of archaeological digs. Yet even quite recent archival finds hardly lend themselves to transparency. Maaza Mengiste, for *The Shadow King* (2019), collected numerous wartime photographs of Ethiopian girls and women, not as unproblematic sources of representation but as politically charged documents of atrocity, redolent with militarism, conquest, and sexual violence. The photographs helped Mengiste build the story of the novel "in increments, folding archival research into my own readings of the photographs I was collecting," showing in the process that history is a "shape-shifting collection of memories and data replete with gaps." Such gaps, of course, are the very stuff of historical fiction.

***

We have organized this collection with the aim of juxtaposing the voices of fiction writers and literary scholars, historians and novelists, allowing each contributor to speak from a specific viewpoint while identifying some areas of resonance among smaller clusters of essays. We have grouped these clusters thematically, with the aim of bringing together diverse perspectives on particular subjects: literary invention, the archive, genre, epistemology. While each piece can profitably be read in isolation, the groupings have helped orient us during our own editorial work of assemblage and synthesis, and we hope they will help the curious through-reader in turn.

Part I, "Inventions," takes up the sources of inspiration and provocation that make up the creative process: those twinned modes of deliberation and mishap, inclusion and exclusion, forethought and surrender that historical fiction requires of its authors in the process of making this peculiar form of art. Thus George Saunders writes of the "beautiful, mysterious experience" of writing *Lincoln in the Bardo*, a novel that required a sort of capitulation to the many voices clamoring, often beyond the grave, for his attention. Sophie Coulombeau takes up the problem of character names in historical fiction, with particular attention to the work of Hilary Mantel, arguing that Mantel's inventive experiments with the fracturing and mutating of historical names suggests the fictiveness of history writ large. David Ebershoff explores the tensions between "internal memory" and "organic creation" in historical fiction, finding inspiration precisely in a willed estrangement from the putative interior life of his protagonist. Ebershoff's novel *The Danish Girl* is one of the subjects of Michael Lackey's essay on biofiction, which offers a helpful distinction between the historical novel broadly understood and the biographical novel, "a literary form that seeks to illuminate and safeguard human agency" through its resistance to the determinism and fatalism that can accrue around conventional understandings of historical fiction.

The five essays in Part II, "Archives," take up in different ways the sources of historical fiction: not the supposedly transparent historical records and primary sources drawn on by writers in the genre, but the archival provocations and phantoms that help give shape to fictive imaginings. Katherine Howe considers the structures of belief and veracity that gave rise to the Salem witch trials, structures knowable only through the handwritten documents, trial transcripts, and digital images she consulted in the course of writing *The Physick Book of Deliverance Dane*. The subtitle of a contribution by Tiya Miles, "Ghosts, Grounds, and the Archives," evokes the image of the memory garden, a site of memory and translation between the dead and the living that Miles takes as a compelling figuration of her own work of translation in *The Cherokee Rose*. Geraldine Brooks wrote *The Secret Chord* without an archive to speak of, relying on myth and scripture to limn the contours of an ancient past recoverable through the reconstructive detail and empathetic impetus of historical fiction. Namwali Serpell details her work with what she calls "the Afronaut archives," a constellation

of pamphlets, interviews, clips, reports, notes, photographs, and other matter that present research as "an ongoing process that both interrupts and
feeds the writing": as Serpell puts it, "My historical research is a way to create a textural reality that undergirds the flights of fancy and philosophy in my
writing." Research and fancy converge in a different way in Bruce Holsinger's
essay, which explores the role of error and anachronism in the writing,
reception, and criticism of historical fiction, suggesting that the avoidance
of error has become something of an aesthetic impulse in its own right.

Part III, "Genres," begins with Gavin Jones's meditation on the difficult
subgenre of historical short fiction, which resists the totalizations of the classic historical novel with a more contingent and perhaps unsettling approach
to a layered past. In order to write *The Shadow King*, her novel of women and
war in 1930s Ethiopia, Maaza Mengiste had to grapple with the form and
genre of history itself as she assembled its variegated fragments into the form
of her historical novel. Mark Eaton contends with alternate-history novels in
the context of a broader category of counterfactual fictions, in which writers might use anachronism to scramble the historical record or transpose
actual events to different times and places. One such place, the American
West, is the enchanted setting of Téa Obreht's *Inland*, which rewrites the
genre of the Western in a spectral reckoning with a blistering and unfamiliar America, a place whose "ghosts seem to haunt from both the past and the
future."

Part IV, "Epistemologies," considers the many ways of knowing (and
unknowing) afforded by historical fiction as genre and mode. Jessie Burton
explores the paradoxical but productive gap between historical sources and
novelistic invention, evoking the phrase "historical impressionism" to connote the pointillist approach to fiction adapted in *The Miniaturist* (2000).
Jane Kamensky, along with her colleague Jill Lepore, found herself writing
a historical novel set in the eighteenth century almost on a lark—though
the project soon turned urgent, opening up "a different way of knowing and
telling the past" than either had experienced or explored through the nonfiction idiom of historical prose. Naomi Williams begins her epistemological
journey with the deceptive certainties of maps, going on to suggest that strict
historical accuracy can be as much a "stylistic choice" on the novelist's part
as an ethical obligation to the past. Kirstin Chen finds an epistemological
challenge to the writing of historical fiction in the contingencies of national
and racial identity, exploring the responsibilities of the writer and the perils
of cultural appropriation while remaining alert to the differing expectations
of audiences in a globalized literary sphere.

The afterword by the late Hilary Mantel was first delivered as a lecture in a hushed auditorium at the Huntington Library, and it preserves the original idiom of its spoken delivery. "I Met a Man Who Wasn't There" marks an appropriately reflective epilogue to this book, as Mantel describes the thrill of discovery as she came to meet and know Thomas Cromwell; her own archive fever as she delved into the "archetypal force" of her subject's documented life, and conjured those parts requiring the novelist's inventions; her self-reflections about writing within the established genre of historical fiction yet in a new and breathless mode; and the epistemological uncertainties that continued to haunt her even very late into the making of her trilogy. Those of us who were fortunate enough to be in the audience that evening remain haunted (in the best way) by the power of her voice and her art, and grateful for the inspiration they have given us to imagine the new potentials of historical fiction now.

PART I

INVENTIONS

1

Ghosts in the Graveyard

George Saunders

Many years ago, during a visit to Washington DC, my wife's cousin pointed out to us a crypt on a hill and mentioned that, in 1862, while Abraham Lincoln was president, his beloved son, Willie, died, and was temporarily interred in that crypt, and that the grief-stricken Lincoln had, according to the newspapers of the day, entered the crypt "on several occasions" to hold the boy's body. An image spontaneously leapt into my mind—a melding of the Lincoln Memorial and the *Pietà*. I carried that image around for the next twenty-odd years, too scared to try something that seemed so profound, and then finally, in 2012, noticing that I wasn't getting any younger, not wanting to be the guy whose own gravestone would read "Afraid to Embark on Scary Artistic Project He Desperately Longed to Attempt," I decided to take a run at it, in exploratory fashion, no commitments. My novel, *Lincoln in the Bardo*, is the result of that attempt, and now I find myself in the familiar writerly fix of trying to talk about that process as if I were in control of it.

We often discuss art this way: the artist had something he "wanted to express," and then he just, you know … expressed it. We buy into some version of the intentional fallacy: the notion that art is about having a clear-cut intention and then confidently executing same.

The actual process, in my experience, is much more mysterious and more of a pain in the ass to discuss truthfully.

***

A guy (Stan) constructs a model railroad town in his basement. Stan acquires a small hobo, places him under a plastic railroad bridge, near that fake campfire, then notices he's arranged his hobo into a certain posture—the hobo seems to be gazing back at the town. Why is he looking over there? At that little blue Victorian house? Stan notes a plastic woman in the window, then turns her a little, so she's gazing out. Over at the railroad bridge, actually. Huh. Suddenly, Stan has made a love story. Oh, why can't they be together? If only "Little Jack" would just go home. To his wife. To Linda.

George Saunders, *Ghosts in the Graveyard*. In: *Historical Fiction Now*. Edited by Mark Eaton and Bruce Holsinger, Oxford University Press. © George Saunders (2023). DOI: 10.1093/oso/9780198877035.003.0002

What did Stan (the artist) just do? Well, first, surveying his little domain, he noticed which way his hobo was looking. Then he chose to change that little universe, by turning the plastic woman. Now, Stan didn't exactly decide to turn her. It might be more accurate to say that it occurred to him to do so; in a split-second, with no accompanying language, except maybe a very quiet internal "Yes."

He just liked it better that way, for reasons he couldn't articulate, and before he'd had the time or inclination to articulate them.

An artist works outside the realm of strict logic. Simply knowing one's intention and then executing it does not make good art. Artists know this. According to Donald Barthelme: "The writer is that person who, embarking upon her task, does not know what to do." Gerald Stern put it this way: "If you start out to write a poem about two dogs fucking, and you write a poem about two dogs fucking—then you wrote a poem about two dogs fucking." Einstein, always the smarty-pants, outdid them both: "No worthy problem is ever solved in the plane of its original conception."

How, then, to proceed? My method is: I imagine a meter mounted in my forehead, with "P" on this side ("Positive") and "N" on this side ("Negative"). I try to read what I've written uninflectedly, the way a first-time reader might ("without hope and without despair"). Where's the needle? Accept the result without whining. Then edit, so as to move the needle into the "P" zone. Enact a repetitive, obsessive, iterative application of preference: watch the needle, adjust the prose, watch the needle, adjust the prose (rinse, lather, repeat), through (sometimes) hundreds of drafts. Like a cruise ship slowly turning, the story will start to alter course via those thousands of incremental adjustments.

The artist, in this model, is like the optometrist, always asking: Is it better like this? Or like this?

The interesting thing, in my experience, is that the result of this laborious and slightly obsessive process is a story that is better than I am in "real life"— funnier, kinder, less full of crap, more empathetic, with a clearer sense of virtue, both wiser and more entertaining.

And what a pleasure that is; to be, on the page, less of a dope than usual.

***

Revising by the method described is a form of increasing the ambient intelligence of a piece of writing. This, in turn, communicates a sense of respect for your reader. As text is revised, it becomes more specific and embodied in the particular. It becomes more sane. It becomes less hyperbolic, sentimental, and misleading. It loses its ability to create a propagandistic fog. Falsehoods get squeezed out of it, lazy assertions stand up, naked and blushing, and rush out of the room.

Is any of this relevant to our current political moment?

Hoo, boy.

When I write, "Bob was an asshole," and then, feeling this perhaps somewhat lacking in specificity, revise it to read, "Bob snapped impatiently at the barista," then ask myself, seeking yet more specificity, why Bob might have done that, and revise to, "Bob snapped impatiently at the young barista, who reminded him of his dead wife," and then pause and add, "who he missed so much, especially now, at Christmas,"—I didn't make that series of changes because I wanted the story to be more compassionate. I did it because I wanted it to be less lame.

But it is more compassionate. Bob has gone from "pure asshole" to "grieving widower, so overcome with grief that he has behaved ungraciously to a young person, to whom, normally, he would have been nice." Bob has changed. He started out a cartoon, on which we could heap scorn, but now he is closer to "me, on a different day."

How was this done? Via pursuit of specificity. I turned my attention to Bob and, under the pressure of trying not to suck, my prose moved in the direction of specificity, and in the process my gaze became more loving toward him (i.e., more gentle, nuanced, complex), and you, dear reader, witnessing my gaze become more loving, might have found your own gaze becoming slightly more loving, and together (the two of us, assisted by that imaginary grouch) reminded ourselves that it is possible for one's gaze to become more loving.

Or we could just stick with "Bob was an asshole," and post it, and wait for the "likes," and for the pro-Bob forces to rally, and the anti-barista trolls to anonymously weigh in—but, meanwhile, there's poor Bob, grieving and misunderstood, and there's our poor abused barista, feeling crappy and not exactly knowing why, incrementally more convinced that the world is irrationally cruel.

**

What does an artist do, mostly? She tweaks that which she's already done. There are those moments when we sit before a blank page, but mostly we're adjusting that which is already there. The writer revises, the painter touches up, the director edits, the musician overdubs. I write, "Jane came into the room and sat down on the blue couch," read that, wince, cross out "came into the room" and "down" and "blue" (Why does she have to come into the room? Can someone sit UP on a couch? Why do we care if it's blue?) and the sentence becomes "Jane sat on the couch," and suddenly, it's better (Hemingwayesque, even!), although ... why is it meaningful for Jane to sit on a couch? Do we really need that? And soon we have arrived, simply, at "Jane," which at least doesn't suck, and has the virtue of brevity.

But why did I make those changes? On what basis?

On the basis that, if it's better this new way for me, over here, now, it will be better for you, later, over there, when you read it. When I pull on this rope here, you lurch forward over there.

This is a hopeful notion, because it implies that our minds are built on common architecture—that whatever is present in me might also be present in you. "I" might be a nineteenth-century Russian count, "you" a part-time Walmart clerk in 2017, in Boise, Idaho, but when you start crying at the end of my (Tolstoy's) story "Master and Man," you have proved that we have something in common, communicable across language and miles and time, and despite the fact that one of us is dead.

Another reason you're crying: you've just realized that Tolstoy thought well of you—he believed that his own notions about life here on earth would be discernible to you, and would move you.

Tolstoy imagined you generously, you rose to the occasion.

We often think that the empathetic function in fiction is accomplished via the writer's relation to his characters, but it's also accomplished via the writer's relation to his reader. You make a rarefied place (rarefied in language, in form; perfected in many inarticulable beauties—the way two scenes abut; a certain formal device that self-escalates; the perfect place at which a chapter cuts off); and then welcome the reader in. She can't believe that you believe in her that much; that you are so confident that the subtle nuances of the place will speak to her; she is flattered. And they do speak to her. This mode of revision, then, is ultimately about imagining that your reader is as humane, bright, witty, experienced, and well intentioned as you, and that, to communicate intimately with her, you have to maintain the state, through revision, of generously imagining her. You revise your reader up, in your imagination, with every pass. You keep saying to yourself: "No, she's smarter than that. Don't dishonor her with that lazy prose or that easy notion."

And in revising your reader up, you revise yourself up too.

***

I had written short stories by this method for the last twenty years, always assuming that an entirely new method (more planning, more overt intention, big messy charts, elaborate systems of numerology underlying the letters in the characters' names, say) would be required for a novel. But, no. My novel proceeded by essentially the same principles as my stories always have: somehow get to the writing desk, read what you've got so far, watch that forehead needle, adjust accordingly. The whole thing was being done on a slightly larger frame, admittedly, but there was a moment when I finally realized that, if one is going to do something artistically intense at 55 years old, he is probably going to use the same skills he's been obsessively honing all of those years; the trick might be to destabilize oneself enough that the skills come to the table fresh-eyed and a little confused. A bandleader used to working with three accordionists is granted a symphony orchestra; what he's been developing all of those years, he may find, runs deeper than mere instrumentation—his take on melody and harmony should be transferable to this new group, and he might even find himself looking anew at himself, so to speak: reinvigorated by his own sudden strangeness in that new domain.

It was as if, over the years, I'd become adept at setting up tents and then a very large tent showed up: bigger frame, more fabric, same procedure. Or, to be more precise (yet stay within my "temporary housing" motif): it was as if I'd spent my life designing custom yurts and then got a commission to build a mansion. At first I thought, "Not sure I can do that." But then it occurred to me that a mansion of sorts might be constructed from a series of connected yurts—each small unit built by the usual rules of construction, their interconnection creating new opportunities for beauty.

***

Any work of art quickly reveals itself to be a linked system of problems. A book has personality, and personality, as anyone burdened with one will attest, is a mixed blessing. This guy has great energy—but never sits still. This girl is sensitive—maybe too much; she weeps when the wrong type of pasta is served. Almost from the first paragraph, the writer becomes aware that a work's strengths and weaknesses are bound together, and that, sadly, his great idea has baggage.

For example: I loved the idea of Lincoln, alone at night in the graveyard. But how is a novel made from one guy in a graveyard at night? Unless we want to write a 300-page monologue in the voice of Lincoln ("Four score and seven minutes ago, I did enter this ghastly place") or inject a really long-winded and omniscient gravedigger into the book (we don't, trust me, I tried), we need some other presences there in the graveyard. Is this a problem? Well, it sure felt like one, back in 2012. But, as new age gurus are always assuring us, a "problem" is actually an "opportunity." In art, this is true. The reader will sense the impending problem at about the same moment the writer does, and part of what we call artistic satisfaction is the reader's feeling that just the right cavalry has arrived, at just the right moment. Another wave of artistic satisfaction occurs if she feels that the cavalry is not only arriving efficiently, but is a cool, interesting cavalry—that is, an opportunity for added fun/beauty, a broadening-out of the aesthetic terms.

In this case, the solution was pretty simple—contained, joke-like, in the very statement of the problem ("Who else might be in a graveyard late at night?").

I remembered an earlier, abandoned novel, set in a New York State graveyard that featured—wait for it—talking ghosts. I also remembered a conversation with a brilliant former student of mine, who said that if I ever wrote a novel, it should be a series of monologues, as in a story of mine called "Four Institutional Monologues."

So: the book would be narrated by a group of monologuing ghosts stuck in that graveyard.

And suddenly what was a problem really did become an opportunity: someone who loves doing voices, and thinking about death, now had the opportunity to spend four years trying to make a group of talking ghosts be charming, spooky, substantial, moving, and, well, human.

***

A work of fiction can be understood as a three-beat movement: a juggler gathers bowling pins; throws them in the air; catches them. This intuitive approach I've been discussing is most essential, I think, during the first phase: the gathering of the pins. This gathering phase really is: conjuring up the pins. Somehow the best pins are the ones made inadvertently, through this system of radical, iterative preference I've described. Concentrating on the line-to-line sound of the prose, or some matter of internal logic, or describing a certain swath of nature in the most evocative way (that is, by doing whatever gives us delight, and about which we have a strong opinion), we suddenly find that we've made a pin. Which pin? Better not to name it. To name it is to reduce it. Often "pin" exists simply as some form of imperative, or a thing about which we're curious; a threat, a promise, a pattern, a vow we feel must soon be broken. Scrooge says it would be best if Tiny Tim died and eliminated the surplus population; Romeo loves Juliet; Akaky

Akakievich needs a new overcoat; Gatsby really wants Daisy. (The color grey keeps showing up; everything that occurs in the story does so in pairs.)

Then: up go the pins. The reader knows they are up there and waits for them to come down and be caught. If they don't come down (Romeo decides not to date Juliet after all, but to go to law school; the weather in St Petersburg suddenly gets tropical, and the overcoat will not be needed; Gatsby sours on Daisy, falls for Betty; the writer seems to have forgotten about his grey motif), the reader cries foul, and her forehead needle plummets into the "N" zone and she throws down the book and wanders away to get on to Facebook, or rob a store.

The writer, having tossed up some suitably interesting pins, knows they have to come down, and, in my experience, the greatest pleasure in writing fiction is when they come down in a surprising way that conveys more and better meaning than you'd had any idea was possible. One of the new pleasures I experienced writing this, my first novel, was simply that the pins were more numerous, stayed in the air longer, and landed in ways that were more unforeseen and complexly instructive to me than has happened in shorter works.

Without giving anything away, let me say this: I made a bunch of ghosts. They were sort of cynical; they were stuck in this realm, called the *bardo* (from the Tibetan notion of a sort of transitional purgatory between rebirths), stuck because they'd been unhappy or unsatisfied in life. The greatest part of their penance is that they feel utterly inessential—incapable of influencing the living. Enter Willie Lincoln, just dead, in imminent danger (children don't fare well in that realm). In the last third of the book, the bowling pins started raining down. Certain decisions I'd made early on forced certain actions to fulfillment. The rules of the universe created certain compulsions, as did the formal and structural conventions I'd put in motion. Slowly, without any volition from me (I was, always, focused on my forehead needle), the characters started to do certain things, each on his or her own, the sum total of which resulted, in the end, in a broad, cooperative pattern that seemed to be arguing for what I'd call a viral theory of goodness. All of these imaginary beings started working together, without me having decided they should do so (each simply doing that which produced the best prose), and they were, it seemed, working together to save young Willie Lincoln, in a complex pattern seemingly being dictated from ... elsewhere. (It wasn't me, it was them.)

Something like this had happened in stories before, but never on this scale, and never so unrelated to my intention. It was a beautiful, mysterious experience and I find myself craving it while, at the same time, flinching at the thousands of hours of work it will take to set such a machine in motion again.

Why do I feel this to be a hopeful thing? The way this pattern thrillingly completed itself? It may just be—almost surely is—a feature of the brain, the byproduct of any rigorous, iterative engagement in a thought system. But there is something wonderful in watching a figure emerge from the stone unsummoned, feeling the presence of something within you, the writer, and also beyond you—something consistent, willful, and benevolent, that seems to have a plan, which seems to be: to lead you to your own higher ground.

2

Naming Names

Reflections on Referentiality in Hilary Mantel's Wolf Hall Trilogy

Sophie Coulombeau

Hilary Mantel's reader is a third of the way through *The Mirror and the Light* (2020), and Thomas Cromwell is at Windsor, when:

> ... Somewhere out of sight a man is singing, voice echoing around the stones:
>> "Now God defend and make an end
>> Their crimes to mend:
>> From Crum and Cram and Cramuel
>> St Luke deliver such to Hell.
>> God send me well!"
>
> He thinks, I believe that's Sexton. I thought the pest was crushed. "Who is Cromwell?" he asks the messengers. "What manner of man do you take him to be?"
>
> Sir, they say, do you not know him? He is the devil in guise of a knave. He wears a hat and under it his horns.[1]

Who is Thomas Cromwell? The messengers, blissfully unaware of whom they're addressing, think they've got the size of him. He's the devil. But Sexton the fool knows it's a bit more complex than that—and so does Mantel's reader. Who *is* Thomas Cromwell? He is Crum, and Cram, and Cramuel. He is singular and plural. He's "a mystery, like the Trinity."[2] He's a hero and a villain of Tudor history. He is fact, and fiction. He's a courtier, a fixer, a lover. He's a father, a friend, an enemy. In the final installment of Mantel's trilogy, his pronouns flicker like strobe lighting. He's I, you, he, and we.

As with the pronouns, so with the names he uses. In fact, throughout Mantel's trilogy, her protagonist is barely called "Thomas Cromwell" at all.

Sophie Coulombeau, *Naming Names: Reflections on Referentiality in Hilary Mantel's Wolf Hall Trilogy*. In: *Historical Fiction Now*. Edited by Mark Eaton and Bruce Holsinger, Oxford University Press. © Sophie Coulombeau (2023). DOI: 10.1093/oso/9780198877035.003.0003

Instead, he appears as Thomas, Tom, Master Thos. Cromwell, Tomos, Tommaso, Thomaes, Hercules, Ercole, Cremuel, Crumb, Dr Chramuel, Cremuello, Lord Cromwell, Master Secretary, Sir Cromwell, Baron Cromwell, Privy seal, Put-an-edge-on-it, Tom Thumb, Jolly Tom, the king's Viceregent, Cromwell of Wimbledon, Lord Keeper of the Privy Seal, Knight of the Garter, Harry Smith, Thomas Craphead, Crummel, and Thomas Essex. "Unless," the narrator challenges the reader, at one point, "you have a better idea?"[3]

This dizzying proliferation of names can tell us something important, about Mantel's trilogy and about the claim it makes for truth. Not that it's an easy task, to pin down what that "something" might be. The personal name is one of those concepts so charged with feeling, and so intrinsic to our understanding of ourselves, that it seems to shatter under scrutiny. When we look at a name for long enough, it loses its meaning. It's only after the scrutineer gives up, and their glance moves on, that the pieces slyly reform themselves, in the margins of vision. We suspect that the name could reveal secrets—if we could only get a good look at it.

The aim of this series of reflections is to get the name to give up some of those secrets. I try to do this—taking my cue from Mantel, who excels at optical imagery—by looking at the personal name from very far away, and then very close up, in rapid succession. A sort of cognitive palaeography, if you like. The specific sort of name that interests me is the referential charactonym—the kind that occurs in a declared work of fiction but refers to a "real" person. To put this as bluntly as possible, there's clearly a difference between a character called "Thomas Cromwell" and one called "Martin"— but what, precisely, is that difference? Mantel labels one explicitly "fictional" in her third Cast of Characters[4]—but is that the beginning and end of its significance? What sorts of truth do these two characters' names seek to convey? What different claims on behalf of "history" and of "fiction" might they foster?[5]

I approach these questions from two discrete perspectives. I'm a scholar of the act of personal naming, and its relationship to identity formation, in late eighteenth-century British literature. I'm also an avid reader—for pleasure— of Mantel's novels. These two positions correspond to the two ways in which I approach names in this essay: analytical, and emotional. In switching between the two perspectives, and between broad-brush onomastic theory and close textual analysis, I hope I can create some sort of productive blurring and sharpening. Some sort of frictional trickery, in which we might glimpse the referential charactonym as it really is.

1. Naming and the Critics

Referentiality has always been a pressure point in literary mediations of the past. Long ago, Sir Philip Sidney—defending poets from the charge of dishonesty—pleaded, "Their naming of men is but to make their picture the more lively, and not to build any history: painting men, they cannot leave men nameless."[6] Four hundred years later, Georg Lukács, in his landmark study *The Historical Novel*, drew an influential contrast between "historically authenticated and well-known representative figures" and "historically unknown, semi-historical or entirely non-historical persons."[7] Both Sidney and Lukács recognize that the interplay between history and art often hangs on the nail of a referential name. Today, the dichotomy still stands—the literary scholar Ann Rigney, for example, remarks that "the interplay between invented story elements and historical ones" defines the historical novel as a genre.[8] But Rigney only engages the referential name in a tantalizing digression. Considering the "flesh-and-blood individual(s)" behind Walter Scott's characters, she remarks that "Andrew Gemmels and 'Edie Ochiltree,' are clearly linked, but they are patently not identical because they have a different name."[9]

Such sharp sideways glances can only take us so far. In this essay, I try to look squarely at the role that the referential charactonym plays in making a claim for truth in historical fiction. I attempt to pin down what sort of an ethical contract a writer enters when there's a real-world referent for their character's name, and a certain level of public recognition attached to it. I consider the uniqueness of the historical novel in this respect—and the artistic opportunities the referential charactonym offers its writer, even as it confines them. I hope that thinking carefully about these issues might help us account for both the popularity of the historical novel at the present moment, and some of the suspicion it generates.

My case study, Mantel's record-breaking trilogy, requires little introduction. Literary criticism is still scrabbling to catch up with its success, but the last few years have given us a few valuable studies. Eileen Pollard and Ginette Carpenter's recent edited collection, for example, contains several insightful essays on the trilogy, in which themes of "ambiguity, ghosts, trauma, childhood and memory" are particularly prevalent.[10] However, for the most part, such studies seem curiously reluctant to engage the obvious question of how Mantel's Tudor novels stand in relation to the historical record—that is, how her fiction grows from a factual root.

Perhaps this is because concerns about "accuracy" have dominated *main-stream* coverage of the trilogy—sometimes in unhelpful ways. In 2015, the historian David Starkey, incensed by Mantel's depiction of Cromwell as a family man, called *Wolf Hall* a "deliberate perversion of fact."[11] Her depiction of (St.) Thomas More has also incurred spirited disagreement from more than one bishop.[12] And in 2017 John Guy (More's biographer) complained that candidates interviewing to read history at Cambridge University were citing Mantel's novels as if they were historical sources.[13] Unfortunately, insightful analyses such as Mark Eaton's essay exploring Mantel's mediation of the Protestant Reformation, or Peter Iver Kaufman's defense of More, don't receive as much publicity as these outbursts of indignation.[14]

At heart, I think that these critics are objecting to Mantel's deployment of the referential charactonym. At the risk of stating the obvious, if she'd called her characters, say, "John Blacksmith" and "Sir Matthew Less"—and the king they served "Reginald the Third"—then nobody would care, no matter how transparent the veil. But the names "Thomas Cromwell" and "Thomas More"—at least in the eyes of Starkey, Guy, and the bishops—indicate that Mantel is saying, *This is how it was.* She's staking a claim to a kind of truth—and they don't see any place for that, in fiction. She's muddling disciplinary conventions that they think should stay distinct, and blurring lines that they'd prefer to stay solid. But what if this muddling is productive, and this blurring is beneficial? If it not only widens the scope of fiction, but also calls us to consider "history" itself in a useful and enlightening way?

2. The Long View

I want to start by exploring—in very broad strokes—why the personal name rakes up such strong feelings when it is used in the print-based public sphere. I look here at the living and the dead, in both "life" and "fiction." And I frequently use examples from the world of litigation to illustrate my points, because it seems to me that nothing underlines the performative power of a referential name quite as clearly as getting hit with a financial penalty if you use it irresponsibly. We get to Hilary Mantel, then, via sociolinguistic theory, Jonathan Swift's "gutted" eighteenth-century names, the warning example set by David Peace's novel *The Damned United*, and the question of why you can't defame the dead.

Naming in Life

In the "real world," what do personal names *do*? The answer, according to many sociolinguistic experts in naming (onomasticians) is that they exist purely to mark out a particular person. Unlike most other nouns, they have no meaning of their own. In the words of one scholar: "[N]ames do not have meaning, names only have reference ... It is only the identifying function of the names—their reference—that is important, not the lexical meaning of the words they are based on."[15] So, if we have a friend called "April White," we aren't primarily thinking of either the month or the color when we use her name. We think only of *her*. (She may, for all we know, have been born in April. And, long ago in her ancestral chain, somebody may have acquired that surname because of a pale complexion. But this is incidental when we refer to April herself. These meanings are dead, trapped like a prehistoric fly in amber.)

At least in England and Wales, referential names are nowhere more powerful than in the field of defamation law. People living in this juris-diction have long borne a heavy responsibility when they use another person's name in public print. As Richard Steele put it in 1709, to "attack ... a Man by Name" is "no venial Fault, no trivial Flaw," but "offending against *ev'ry* Law."[16] Indeed, some scholars believe that the visually dis-tinctive "gutted" name in eighteenth-century texts started life as a strategy to avoid being sued for defamation. As Jonathan Swift tells us, "[W]e are careful never to print a man's name out at length; but as I do that of Mr. St—le: So that although every body alive knows who I mean, the plaintiff can have no redress in any court of justice."[17] As usual, Swift's tongue was creeping into his cheek—using a gutted name was no iron-clad protection against legal action.[18] But if *not* using a name wasn't quite enough to evade prosecution, then using one was still the best way to invite it.

In fact, this remains the case today. An alleged defamation must still be understood "by a reasonable reader" to refer to the claimant as an individual—when the "words used would lead the pursuer to believe that the pursuer was the person referred to."[19] Dropping heavy hints about occu-pation or appearance still might be enough to prove defamation (and this is why British tabloids have made a fine art of describing celebrity scandals in a manner that walks a fine line between libel and incomprehensibility). But to name a particular person is still by far the easiest way to get yourself into legal trouble.

The thing I want to emphasize about how the personal name works in life, then, is that it holds us to account. It pins us to our pronouncements. It drills us to our declarations. It makes sure that we're *responsible* about naming names. Or, at least, it does when the people we name are alive. Conversely, the dead have no cause of action for defamation (and neither do their survivors.) The reason for this is wonderfully matter-of-fact. Name conflicts not only need a legal basis, but also a nominal plaintiff. In other words, the squeaky wheel gets the grease—and the dead don't squeak.

To name and shame the dead is, then, an ethical rather than a legal act. Does that mean that such an act is less emotionally significant? I'd argue the opposite. Look at the outrage triggered whenever a revisionist biography is published. We invest a lot of feeling in the "real" dead, and when they're attacked, our fury is so intense precisely because it's so impotent. The poor dead can't defend themselves in a court of law—and we can't do it for them, either. The only court of appeal is emotional. And so, we go in with all guns blazing.

Naming in Fiction

So, that's "life"—and death. But what about fiction? When we encounter a person's name in a novel (a character name, or charactonym), surely it performs a different function to the one I've just outlined? Because the person to whom the name alludes doesn't really exist. They're a figment of the author's imagination, and their name reflects that. Or are they? And does it?

Literary onomastics is the academic study of charactonyms. Experts in this field generally presume that names are made up by the author, and that they're intended to carry meaning rather than reference. That is, the charactonym is selected or constructed primarily to create a particular effect in a reader's mind. Back in 1970, the medievalist Gerhard Eis put it succinctly: "Names [in literature] are instruments by which to characterize persons … and are mostly used after careful consideration by the authors."[20] Eis's view still underlies the practice of literary onomastics today. For example, the case studies in Alastair Fowler's 2012 study of literary names—the mythological mash-ups in Edmund Spenser's *Faerie Queen*, "characteristic" names such as Ben Jonson's "Sir Voluptuous Beast," and Dickens's quirky charactonyms—largely hang on the same assumption.[21]

Literary onomasticians do sometimes consider that charactonyms might be found rather than invented. "Shakespeare drew on William Camden's essays on names in *Remains*," Fowler tells us, while "Irvine Welsh gets his names from the Edinburgh phone book."[22] But is the original reference attached to these names? In Shakespeare's play, or Welsh's novel, do they refer to the *same people* indicated in Camden's text, or the phone book? Of course not. Rather, they're used for the general associations that the author attaches to them—the feel of a particular era, the regional flavor, or the ono-matopoeic twang. When the name is transferred to a new text, the reference is emptied out. Only the meaning (and sometimes not even that) is retained.

Of course, there's always the odd novelist who *will* deliberately use a ref-erential name as a charactonym. That is, they'll name a character "after" somebody who really exists. This gesture rather depends on how the char-acter is portrayed. Where a novelist runs a competition for a reader to have a character named in their honor, for example, consent is established by the reader's entering the competition, and furthermore the character is unlikely to be unpleasant. Nothing wrong with that, then. But under different cir-cumstances, a novelist can get into just as much trouble as a journalist. That disclaimer at the beginning of many contemporary novels—"Any resem-blance to actual persons, living or dead, events or localities, is entirely coincidental"? It's a nice try—but, legally speaking, it's as flimsy as the paper on which it's printed. Ever since 1910—when a judge awarded enormous damages to a Welsh barrister called Thomas Artemus Jones who objected to a fictional portrayal of a London church warden with the same name—publishers have been extremely careful about such things.[23] (Of course, such incidents are rare, precisely because coming forward as complainant invites speculation about the truth of the libel. You might be unfortunate to be called Patrick Bateman, like the protagonist of Brett Easton Ellis's *American Psycho*. But you probably wouldn't take him to court over it.)

Names used in "life," then, have reference but no meaning, whereas names used in "fiction" have meaning but no reference. Only, when the histor-ical novel comes along, this neat binary is blown to bits. For there's a certain kind of historical novel that deals, in Lukács's words, with "histori-cally authenticated and well-known representative figures." These novels use charactonyms with clear real-world referents. They induce a certain level of public recognition. To appropriate the terminology of the literary critic Catherine Gallagher, they concern "Somebody" rather than "Nobody."[24]

Where a person named and defamed is still alive, "historical" novelists are subject to just the same risks as anybody else. (The novelist David Peace found this to his cost in 2010, when the former Leeds United footballer Johnny Giles took him to court over Peace's novel *The Damned United*.[25])

But most historical novelists respect Walter Scott's famous rule of thumb, by setting their narratives seventy years or more in the past. One advantage to this approach, of course, is that you're almost guaranteed to be dealing only with the undefameable dead.

And so, to Hilary Mantel. Here, we have a novelist who uses names that have the freedom of charactonyms, but the force of libels. And perhaps we can understand a little better just why her critics rage—over Thomas Cromwell and Thomas More, as well as her more recently deceased referents.[26] But it would be a serious error to let those critics fully define the character of Mantel's enterprise. Her trilogy is no hit-and-run biography hiding behind a disclaimer. Her naming *is* acutely referential, but it's also meaningful. As I indicated in my introduction, her Cromwell is a creature of multiple names, each indicating a different place, time, relationship. If we put our eyes close to the page, we can trace the patterns of those names, and how they shape the reader's understanding of a hinterland between "history" and "fiction."

3. The Close-up

Wolf Hall (2009)

"Felled, dazed, silent, he has fallen." We begin with the pronoun that has become the most famous aspect of Mantel's prose style.[27] "He" is Cromwell, in his childhood—but we don't know that yet; "he" is "silent" indeed. It's a few pages later that we first get a name, when Kat and Morgan Williams are putting the object of the kicking back together: "'Just stand back,' Kat advises. 'You don't want bits of Thomas on your London jacket ... what were you doing, Tom, to set him off?'"[28] And now we know. It's Thomas Cromwell. But a younger version. Softer. Affectionately nicknamed, Tom. This is his private self. We hope to know it better.

But he won't always be Tom. Far from it. Soon we've been whisked forward to 1527, when it's an older referent who's "coming in," as Stephen Gardiner is "going out." Once again, "he" is an innuendo—like Swift's gutted name, or the pronoun insisting upon its own mystery. "He" is "bland," according to the narrator, just as before, as a boy, he was "silent."[29] This scene, though, is a little more giving than the Putney bloodbath. We're told the reason for Gardiner's sullen chagrin: he knows that "if they met on a dark night, Master Thos. Cromwell would be the one who walked away dusting off his hands and smiling."[30] This is his public self, then. This is the Cromwell we expected.

But, as the narrative accelerates, more mutations emerge. Cardinal Wolsey is entitled to use the familiar "Thomas"—although, since "half the world is called Thomas," an eavesdropper like Boleyn "will never be sure if it was him" when the cardinal calls the name into the shadows.[31] Like Boleyn, the reader is being invited, on some level, to ask, *Can we be sure it is him? The real him?* This anxiety stands at the core of referentiality. And it takes its most potent form when Boleyn has departed—and the cardinal, raising his hand, causes multiple selves to emerge:

> He, Thomas, also Tomos, Tommaso and Thomaes Cromwell, withdraws his past selves into his present body and edges back to where he was before. His single shadow slides against the wall, a visitor not sure of his welcome. Which of these Thomases saw the blow coming?[32]

Cromwell's past, especially his time on the Continent, has wrought not one referent but several. He's not only the English Thomas, he's also the Welsh Tomos, the Italian Tommaso, the Flemish Thomaes (and later on, we'll learn that he was also Hercules, or Ercole). At this moment, his multiple pasts possess him, and one of them, reading the cardinal's raised hand as a threat, makes him spring backwards. After a few seconds, he's able to collect his selves. But the reader can never look at him the same way again. If it wasn't obvious earlier, then it should be by now. We're dealing with not one stable referent, but a palimpsest of identities.

As we progress deeper into the narrative, these identities only multiply. In Cromwell's first meeting with Anne Boleyn, she confers upon him a new name: the Franglish *Cremuel*.

> "*Alors*," Anne says softly, "suddenly everything is about you. The king does not cease to quote Master Cromwell." She pronounces it as if she can't manage the English: *Cremuel*. "He is so right, he is in all points correct ... Also, let us not forget, Maître Cremuel makes us laugh."[33]

This nicknaming, of course, says as much about Anne as it does about her referent. Once her star begins to descend, her Frenchified sophistication becomes a burden rather than a blessing. She can't "manage" Cromwell as a political force, any more than she can as a series of phonemes. And yet, in a sense he's just who she wants him to be—for just as long as it suits him.

When he leaves her, he reflects, "A world where Anne can be queen is a world where Cromwell can be Cromwell. He sees it; then he doesn't."[34] The reader, too, both sees Cromwell as Cromwell, and doesn't. It's this tension that distinguishes him from the other characters. It feels like the quality that connects him with the reader. Some sort of a mark of modernity.

Before I read *Wolf Hall*, I'd seen various reviewers try to pin down what it was about this historical novel that felt different. Once I'd finished it, I thought I knew. It was the flickering referent. The way that the strobing names demanded I both follow Cromwell with my eyes and, every few pages, make him anew. There's something to that paradox of the way we process the past. But, of course, I didn't put it to myself quite in those words. To do so, I'd need to read the second installment three years later. To see what could have been a mere tic, solidified into a tendency.

Bring Up the Bodies (2014)

In *Wolf Hall*, Mantel's Cast of Characters contained two separate iterations of the protagonist—"Thomas, [Walter's] son" and "Thomas Cromwell, a lawyer."[35] In *Bring Up the Bodies*, he's entered once: "Thomas Cromwell, a blacksmith's son: now Secretary to the king, Master of the Rolls, Chancellor of Cambridge University, and deputy to the king as head of the church in England."[36] From the very frontal paratext of the trilogy's second installment, then, the close relation between names and jobs is brought sharply into focus. In this book, chummy nicknames will characterize both Cromwell and his fellow courtiers, drawing attention to the homosocial bonds that weave ladders to power. Yet, one form of naming eludes Cromwell—those aristocratic titles that not only signify rank but confer access to the highest level of diplomatic negotiations.

Barely fifty pages in, the reader learns that Cromwell has a new name. Henry and his privy counselors have squashed him into "Crumb." On one level "Crumb" is an affectionate diminutive, of course. But it's also a way to make a big man small. To remind him of his lowly and derivative status. Cromwell himself is aware, it seems, of the double edge of the moniker. He advises Thomas Wriothesley to use this name, if he must, only behind his back—demonstrating again his own awareness of his multiple identities.[37]

Cromwell also observes, at this same moment, that he's far from the only character to have a nickname. In fact, they're catching like a contagion. Thomas Boleyn is "Monseigneur." William Fitzwilliam is "Fitz."

Richard Riche is "Sir Purse." And Thomas Wriothesley himself is "Call-Me-Risley" or "Call-Me." Henry, who veers so wildly between formality and neediness, is sometimes "Henricus Rex," and other times plain "Harry." Anne—"La Ana," "Anna Regina," and "Ana Bolena"—is a conspicuous exception to the chummy fashion. Her variations gesture toward her cosmopolitan past and her hard-won royal persona, rather than any sort of private self. Anne knows a lot, but she doesn't know how to play the nickname game. She still has "a skittish slur in her speech, the odd French intonation, her inability to say [Cromwell's] name."[38]

Well might Eustache Chapuys complain that in England, "Anyone may say his name any way he likes, different on different days."[39] In its insistence that many actors have many names, the second book in the trilogy shows Cromwell leaving his mark. It constructs a court mimicking the fashion that he's set, that of the fractured charactonym. And yet, at the heart of Crumb, there's an absence. The title *my lord*, that onomastic bridge between being and doing, is withheld from the blacksmith's son. "Cremuel remains a nobody ... plain Master Cromwell goes out at morning, plain Master Cromwell comes in at night." Somewhat to his own surprise, Master Cromwell finds that this irks him. When the contemptible Charles Brandon tells him he is "not fit to talk to princes" due to his lack of a title, he "knows Brandon's words will go round in his head when that head touches the pillow."[40]

He might be careful what he wishes for. In the final part of the trilogy, Henry will grant all the titles Cromwell's heart could desire. But, almost instantly, it will become outré to have many names—or at least to believe in them too fervently. Cromwell's inability to understand that names derive their power from the giver, not the holder, will prove crucial to his undoing.

The Mirror and the Light (2020)

Anne Boleyn is out of the picture, but the French are still struggling. "No Frenchman can ever pronounce [Cromwell's] name," the reader is told, as the Calais headsman wipes his sword.[41] Among other things, of course, *The Mirror and the Light* will be the story of Cromwell attempting to "reconfigure the map," to break out of the "old, worn-out games that have lasted [his] lifetime" and create "the new Europe."[42] The continued inability of the French to name him correctly is one indication that the old powers, the old belief systems, are on their way out. The new world order, emblematized in the Bavarian delegation, is (however briefly) on its way in. Anna of Cleves and her entourage will have no problem saying Cromwell's name.

Perhaps more importantly, the irritation Cromwell displays at the heads-man's mangling of his name is also a sign that he's starting to care about a thing like pronunciation. This is a further hint of a shift in his outlook, from a nonchalant indifference toward names to a fatal investment in their prop-erties. Once father to a son, Henry's grip on a clutch of titles suddenly relaxes, and Cromwell finds himself ennobled beyond all precedent. Vicegerent, Sir Thomas, Lord Cromwell.[43] To have "so many posts and titles," Jane Seymour notes, is "a thing never seen before."[44] Cromwell's unique configuration of names makes him special, and he takes it very seriously. Jane Rochford, let-ting a "Master Secretary" slip, is admonished, "You must learn to use my new title."[45] Margaret Pole is told, "if you could learn to think the Tudors rightful kings of England—and you say you could—I am sure you can come to think of me as Lord Privy Seal."[46] When Norfolk taunts him that northern children are frightened by the name of Cromwell, the response is uncharacteristically petulant: "*Lord* Cromwell would be more polite."[47]

Cromwell of Wimbledon. Lord Keeper of the Privy Seal. Knight of the Garter. Lord Chamberlain. Thomas Essex.[48] The names pile up like snow-drifts. And they all come from Henry, who insists that they bear meaning as well as reference: "If I say Cromwell is a lord, he is a lord."[49] What is curious is that Cromwell himself, so used to interpreting Henry expansively, takes these words literally. Like the Cornish blacksmith An Gol, he starts to fancy "that his name might 'tell you what he [i]s.'"[50]

This, of course, is Cromwell's fundamental error. Alarm bells should have started to ring early in the narrative, when other characters begin to draw back from the notion that names have meaning. Gregory gently mocks Richard Riche, for equating his name with his destiny.[51] Surrey warns Cromwell that while he "note[s his] title," "it does not change what you are."[52] And Norfolk scoffs at the notion that northern children will ever need to get accustomed to the name Lord Cromwell. "Their view is, the fellow will be dead before we have to use it."[53]

There's a parallel here between Cromwell and Anne, who both make the same error when they begin to forget that the names the king has lent them can be taken back. Indeed, it's in *The Mirror and the Light* that the homosocial note of Cromwell's relationship to Henry is most forcibly struck:

> Sometimes, sitting beside the king—it is late, they are tired, he has been working, since first light—he allows his body to confuse with that of Henry,

so that their arms, lying contiguous, lose their form and become cloudy like thaw water. He imagines their fingertips graze, his mind meets the royal will: ink dribbles onto the paper. Sometimes the king nods into sleep. He sits by him scarcely breathing, careful as a nursemaid with a fractious brat. Then Henry starts, wakes, yawns; he says, as if he were to blame, "It is midnight, master!" The past peels away: the king forgets he is "my lord"; he forgets what he has made him.[54]

Henry's momentary confiscation of Cromwell's title punishes the presumption of his fantasy—both pseudo-sexual and treasonous—of a bodily blurring between them. Cromwell's observation that "women are to be named and renamed, it is their nature, and they have no country of their own"[55] is at least as applicable to himself as to Anna of Cleves.

Ultimately, of course, *The Mirror and the Light* hinges on Henry's ability to change his mind—or perhaps more accurately, to think two opposing thoughts, simultaneously and seriously. Having piled a dozen names on his friend's head, for example, he can still maintain that he "would not trust a man with two names, even if he were my own brother" as he sentences John Lambert (aka Nicholson) to an excruciating death.[56] The parallels with Cromwell, who sits silently in the gallery, are clear enough. And if they weren't, the narrator takes care to remind us that the man who watches Lambert die is not only "my lord Privy Seal," but also "Thomas Cromwell, alias Harry Smith."[57]

The abruptness of Cromwell's final fall is Mantel's best proof that she really works from the historical record. No mere maker-up would ever truncate the narrative so sharply, squishing the denouement like a cartoon character run into a wall. But these final seventy pages of the novel do possess a certain internal equilibrium, and one of the motifs that provide it is the presence of Stephen Gardiner. Gardiner's fall and rise has seemed to repeat Cromwell's own metaphor of Anne and Jane's teeter-totter, and now he is "coming in" as Cromwell "goes out."[58] Tellingly, Gardiner loses no opportunity to hit Cromwell where it hurts when he's asked to address his old foe by the names he's earned. "You have no title. It's gone, Cromwell. You are no more than God made you."[59] This memo, however, hasn't reached the redoubtable Kingston: "you are Essex until I am told otherwise."[60] The two opposing views lead Cromwell to reflect, in his final few pages, on the size of an earldom and the nature of a name.

He is not sure if his earldom is a little thing. In the sight of God, perhaps it is. But he had felt it, this last two months, as protection, a wall the king had built around him.[61]

Is the name a big thing or a little thing? Does it have meaning, or only reference? Did Henry make "Thomas Cromwell," aka "Thomas Essex," any more than God did? What's the good of a wall that can't repel the enemy? The reader never receives answers to these questions, just as she never receives any firm confirmation whether Cromwell is Earl of Essex when he lays his head on the block. The question *Who is he?*—first raised almost 2,000 pages previously—receives no definitive answer. Yet this, I think, is precisely the point.

Mantel's cumulative attention to names throughout the trilogy amounts to more than the sum of its parts. It works to produce in the reader an enlightened frustration—a certain uncertainty. By taking the referential charactonym and then fracturing, mutating, and decentering it, Mantel makes her historical fiction a way of reflecting back on the fictiveness of history. Hayden White famously said that historical narratives are "verbal fictions, the contents of which are as much invented as found, the forms of which have more in common with their counterparts in literature than they have with those in the sciences."[62] And much literary scholarship in recent years has put the historical novel in dialogue with White's statement, showing how it works through self-reflexive techniques to destabilize the very notion of "fact." Mantel's trilogy, by using the referential charactonym to thicken and enliven our sense of how historical knowledge works, contributes toward this project.

4. Conclusions: More and More

In 2017, I presented an early version of this paper at a conference held at the Huntington Library in Pasadena, called "Fictive Histories, Historical Fictions." Hilary Mantel herself was presenting the keynote lecture, giving a reading from *The Mirror and the Light*, and holding a public conversation with the eminent historian (and dedicatee of all three Cromwell books) Mary Robertson. As if this wasn't enough, when her commitments were fulfilled, instead of going off to have fun in sunny Pasadena she actually sat through all the academic papers and listened to what we had to say. For those presenting on her work, this was extremely flattering, but also a bit nerve-wracking.

When I finished my paper, her hand crept upward. The moderator, of course, called on her straight away. She stood up. When she spoke, it was in careful and complete sentences (she's the only person I've ever met who doesn't say "Um," or leave thoughts trailing away). She told me that my paper had reminded her that Thomas More was fond of punning on his own name. Then she sat down again.

I nodded, and grinned, and gibbered my thanks. I was both relieved and crestfallen. I don't know what I'd expected. That she'd tell me that I'd got her novels wrong? Or that she'd pat me on the head and tell me that I'd found out her true meaning where so many others had failed? Either way, I wasn't sure quite what to do with her response. So, I filed it away in my mind, and flew home to the United Kingdom, where, for several years, I got distracted by several other projects and life events.

It took the publication of *The Mirror and The Light*, and the patient encouragement of Mark Eaton, to spur me to revisit this essay. At which point, I remembered Mantel's remark, and started to read into Thomas More's puns on his name. He and his friend Erasmus liked to play on the Greek *moriae*, which means "fool." He was also fond of his name's shared root with the Latin "mori"—"death."[63] It was tempting to plot these meanings against various narratives of More's career. Even to wonder (when I read that he was still punning away while in the Tower awaiting execution) whether his *decisions* might have been inflected by his consciousness of his name's etymological richness. Was he, perhaps, able to look death more squarely in the eye because he'd always seen it in his very name?

Then, something else struck me. More's addiction to punning on his name was no isolated idiosyncrasy. It was an instance of a widespread habit of early modern thought—the investment of meaning, as well as reference, in personal names. Despite what sociolinguists presume today, in sixteenth-century Europe, many people believed that their names had meaning.[64] The Vatican declared at the Council of Trent (1545–63) that children should be given the names of canonized saints, so that those saints might act as advocates before God. Surnames, though inherited rather than bestowed at birth, also seemed closer to their point of origin, whether rooted in appearance, achievement, trade or place.[65] Names had an important place in the popular practice of divination, and early modern dictionaries often gave the "meaning" of proper nouns alongside common ones, or else included proper names as appendices.[66] Once placed in this context, the onomastic pun takes on a certain sort of weight that is more than *only* playful. Trying to connect the name to its (etymological) root is an attempt to find meaning—whether, in More's case, in folly or in death.

This realization casts Mantel's fictional enterprise into something of a new and brilliant light. She doesn't place such emphasis on Cromwell's name only in order to generate readerly suspicion of a stable historical subject. By doing so, she actually *inhabits*—rather than merely describing—*an early modern mindset.* This makes it possible to read Cromwell's trajectory that I've traced over the trilogy, from onomastic sceptic to believer, in a slightly different way. It now looks like the story of a man who was modern, but not quite modern enough. Who was clawed back, eventually, and destroyed, by the mindset of his moment.

In this context, Mantel's remark in that Pasadena auditorium looks like a gentle reminder that meanings are multiple. That even the most referential historical novel is more about introducing possibilities than making arguments. In directing me from Cromwell to More—and suggesting a shift from grand historiography to minute wordplay—she was opening up the potential for pluralities. Of course, one must always be careful about putting words in the mouth (or thoughts in the head) of any writer. But I suspect it's safe to say that she was interested in puns during the final stage of her career. The title of her last single-authored publication—an essay collection released shortly after *The Mirror and the Light*—was *Mantel Pieces*.

In common with Sexton—who, like any good fool, has a dash of wisdom in his folly—when we look at "Thomas Cromwell" we must be willing also to contemplate Crum and Cram and Cramuel. Referentiality does for the historical novel what the pun does for the personal name—it exposes its plural modes and its palimpsest of meanings. It's in the sudden switch of focus, from one to the next, that the truth of fiction, and the fiction of truth, can be most clearly glimpsed.

3

Looking for the Danish Girl

David Ebershoff

On a gray April day in Dresden many years ago, I climbed the forty-one steps to the Brühlsche Terrace to have a look at the view. The river Elbe was running dark and fast, and the city, a ghost of its former self, sat sternly beneath a sky sagging with a late snow. The city bustled—electric trams and sub-compact cars and bicycles with wicker baskets and a police van in a chase with its blue light flashing. Across the river were stucco apartment complexes with washing tubs on the terraces and slab-concrete shopping arcades where garbage blew in a cold wind.

A city shaking itself alive after a century of terrible history, it seemed to me that day. From that view it was nearly impossible to imagine the former Dresden, once called the Teutonic Florence, and the terrace where I sat in the chill was known as the Balcony of Europe. "The most beautiful city on the Continent," proclaimed a 1909 English guidebook, *Romantic Germany*, the sort of book with hand-tinted illustrations of half-timber houses and water wells with little thatched roofs. And now this, a city bombed and burned and then choked for more than fifty years by the grip of the Communist East, startled by its recent freedom and the early green shoots of prosperity. Little remained to remind one of Dresden circa 1930. The view from the terrace only spoke of the air raids of February 1945; of the quartering of the German nation a few months later; of the long haul through the Soviet reign; of the wall a few hours to the north crumbling in November 1989. But I was there to research the beautiful past, the history through which Lili Elbe walked, first as Einar Wegener, then as herself.

The wind was sharp and I sealed my eyes against its bite, and there, in the half-instant of a blink, lay the old Dresden where Lili arrived one cold day in 1930 to complete her transition. My job was to imagine the past, to hunt through the remnants that lay in the streets and in the library archives that could suggest a world, and a mood, that once was. I was in Germany alone, and other than the librarian at the Dresden Hygiene Museum and my hired translator who scrolled through the microfiche, I spoke to no one during my

David Ebershoff, *Looking for the Danish Girl*. In: *Historical Fiction Now*. Edited by Mark Eaton and Bruce Holsinger, Oxford University Press. © David Ebershoff (2023). DOI: 10.1093/oso/9780198877035.003.0004

stay. I did not want to be in the present. I wanted my mind and the materials of research to take me back to the time Lili walked these streets, herself
lonely, but more excited than afraid. And it was that day on the Brühlsche
Terrace that I came to recognize one of the fundamental tasks of writing a
novel such as *The Danish Girl.*

Every novel has its own internal memory, the organic creation that the
reader and the writer recall, directly or indirectly, as the story propels itself
along. But, as I sorted out the story of Lili Elbe and Gerda Gottlieb, whom I
would call Greta, I began to wonder whose memory was relevant to my role
as novelist. For Lili Elbe, that beautiful Danish woman whom Gerda first
welcomed into their studio, had a history and a memory that belonged to
someone else—but did it? Lili spoke of her past as if it belonged to someone
else, as if Einar's memories were not her own. But can we jettison the parts of
our past that we no longer feel represent us? A novelist mines the emotional
interior of his or her characters. But what was I to do with a historical figure
who claimed her early life was not hers? A figure from history who believed
the person she had once been was now deceased. On that gray day I began to
understand some of the novel's questions: whose memory informs our own;
how does the past, seemingly obliterated, infuse our vision of the world at
hand, and of ourselves.

Dresden was gone, razed by an impressively American combination of
firepower and efficiency, and yet the city, all of it, lay at my feet, beneath
the terrace where lovers rented paddle boats, in the square outside the Sem-
peroper, in the young grass growing along the banks of the Elbe, the river
that gave Lili her new last name. 1930 was within my grasp, and so was Lili
Elbe conjuring memories of a person she claimed was gone—her own person gone; but not really. It led me to this: on the day Lili Elbe emerged from
the Dresden Municipal Women's Clinic, Einar Wegener fully, finally disappeared; yet where did Einar go? From that point, who would house those
memories? Einar was dead, Lili claimed, but also unburied. Einar was gone,
she said, but Lili failed to reconcile that Einar had no grave. Lili, who very
much believed she was a different soul than Einar, had to live with a history
that was and was not her own.

But don't we all?

I asked myself if this is any different than what humanity shoves upon all
of us? Each of us is defined by our own past, but also by that of our family
and lovers and friends and enemies, as well as our country and civilization,
and the forces of history that bring us to our own particular present. On
that April day the wind crossed the terrace with an iciness that stung the

eyes, and the novel which I was writing about Lili Elbe, still untitled and far from complete, took shape.

Identity—the loss and acquisition of it, the borrowing, the stealing, the rejection, the embrace; we grow up and declare ourselves yet the beautiful and awful past lingers forever. Beneath the rubble and the char, inside the pre-fab concrete and the asbestos tiles, swirling amid the factory belch and the cough of the car, rising in the wind, in the face of a daffodil bending beneath the last snow of the year, history and memory are held aloft by imagination and the sun as bright as a white kite above the river. Nothing is lost, I told myself that day in Dresden. A novel is written so nothing can be lost.

4

Using versus Doing History in the Contemporary Biographical Novel

Michael Lackey

Contemporary biographical novelists are not fond of historical fiction. This is not mere speculation. In a recent interview, Olga Tokarczuk, winner of the Nobel Prize in Literature and author of a biographical novel about Jacob Frank, an eighteenth-century Jewish religious leader, said: "I'm not really a fan of historical novels."[1] For those who treat the biographical novel as a subgenre or version of the historical novel, this comment must seem strange. How is it possible for an author to write a work set in the past, to name the protagonist after an actual historical figure, but then to claim that the work is somehow different from or not historical fiction? But Tokarczuk is not the only contemporary biographical novelist to distance herself from historical fiction.

In 2004 Colm Tóibín published *The Master*, which is now considered a canonical biographical novel. In that work, Tóibín's protagonist, Henry James, explicitly rejects and even condemns the historical novel. Late in the novel, Henry's brother William expresses concern about his sibling's work. He encourages his younger brother to abandon the novel of manners about the superficial and materialistic English and to turn his attention to a "novel which would deal with our American history," specifically "about the Puritan Fathers." Henry not only rejects William's proposal, but also uses the occasion to express his contempt for the historical novel: "'May I put an end to this conversation,' Henry said, 'by stating clearly to you that I view the historical novel as tainted by a fatal cheapness.'" To punctuate his point, Henry ends the discussion by dismissing William's proposal with a single word, "humbug."[2] The significance of these remarks is staggering. In one of the most celebrated biographical novels, the protagonist denounces the historical novel, which clearly suggests that *The Master* should not be considered a historical novel.

Michael Lackey, *Using versus Doing History in the Contemporary Biographical Novel*. In: *Historical Fiction Now*. Edited by Mark Eaton and Bruce Holsinger, Oxford University Press. © Michael Lackey (2023). DOI: 10.1093/oso/9780198877035.003.0005

In fact, Tóibín makes this point directly in a recent interview with Bethany Layne. When asked if there is a difference between the historical and biographical novel, Tóibín says there is. He then provides an example. Tóibín notes that James's apartment in Kensington was wired for electricity in 1896. A historical novelist, Tóibín claims, would incorporate such a detail in his or her work: "If you're writing a historical novel this is a marvelous scene for you where you're actually getting a key moment in history and you're integrating it into lives and you're seeing what the next day will be like." Tóibín does not write such novels, because "it would ruin my novel. It would be the end of the novel." By stark contrast, he writes biographical novels, which means that he "must be in James's mind all the time."[3]

Readers get additional insight into this critical view of the historical novel through a brief analysis of Tóibín's source text for his construction of this scene with William. Sarah Orne Jewett sent James a copy of her historical novel *The Tory Lover*, and in 1901 James responded, but instead of using the occasion to discuss the quality of Jewett's work, he uses it to reflect on the irredeemable vices of the historical novel. For James, this is an aesthetic form that is characterized by "a fatal cheapness," the same phrase Tóibín's James uses. The historical novelist gives readers a multitude of "little facts that can be got from pictures and documents, relics and prints," but what it lacks is "the real thing," which consists of "the invention, the representation of the old consciousness, the soul, the sense, the horizon, the vision of individuals in whose minds half the things that make ours, that make the modern world." All of these are "non-existent" in the historical novel, an aesthetic form that James calls "humbug." Of crucial importance for James is the mysterious, indefinable, semi-autonomous dimension of human consciousness, which is not just different from but diametrically opposed to the "conditioned"[4] consciousness represented in the historical novel.

The suggestion that the historical novel is "tainted by a fatal cheapness" is of crucial importance. For both James and Tóibín, there is a fatalistic dimension to the historical novel, because it underscores how humans are at the mercy of ("conditioned" by) external forces—the wiring of the house will have necessary and discernible consequences for the inner life of characters. But the historical novel is also a cheap literary form because it lacks the richness of creativity—the historical "novel" merely copies what is. James and Tóibín hold that there is something in the nature of the historical novel that is in irreconcilable conflict with the creative impulse in art, and that something is the deterministic dimension of history.

Other prominent biographical novelists are just as adamant as Tokarczuk and Tóibín in distancing themselves from the historical novel. Author
of three spectacular biographical novels, Colum McCann actually claims
to hate the idea of the historical novel. As he says in an interview with
Robert Birnbaum: "I hate the term 'historical novel.'"[5] He provides more
insight into the reasons why in his interview with Synne Rifbjerg: "I hate the
idea of the term 'the historical novel,' not that I hate history and not that I
hate the novel, but I hate the way those two words match each other and
plunge themselves down into an aspic, a softness; it almost wears a bodice
of sorts."[6] McCann's metaphors (aspic and bodice) suggest that the historical novel contains and straitjackets the human, thus inhibiting expansion,
development, and growth. In essence, the historical novel is a contradiction in terms, because the historical defines, confines, and restrains, while
the novel imagines, liberates, and creates. In a recent interview about his
biographical novels, the award-winning, Spanish writer Javier Cercas told
Virginia Rademacher: "Sometimes they [critics] say I write historical novels.
I don't really like that label. I write novels in which history has a role, but
they are not historical novels."[7] Joanna Scott has authored numerous biographical novels and short stories, and in a recent public forum about her
biographical novel *Careers for Women*, she said: "I'm not alone in sharing
some deep skepticism in terms of what we used to call the historical novel."[8]
These are not just the casual, off-the-cuff remarks of a few authors of biofiction. They are part of a comprehensive and coherent aesthetic vision, and
in the following pages I clarify why it is a mistake to treat biographical fiction as a form of historical fiction. But I also indicate that history is of vital
importance in biofiction. Therefore, the objective in this essay is to clarify
the way biographical novelists deploy history in their fiction.

1. Biofiction

... only if history can endure to be transformed into a work of art
will it perhaps be able to preserve instincts or even evoke them.[9]

Stated simply, authors of biofiction use rather than do history. Margaret
Atwood gives us a productive way of thinking about this distinction. In 1996,
Atwood authored *Alias Grace*, a biographical novel about the Irish servant
Grace Marks who was convicted in Canada of murdering her employer. In a
lecture about this work, Atwood told her audience that "such stories are not

about this or that slice of the past," a claim that certainly disqualifies the work as a historical novel. To the contrary, "they are about human nature," they are "about truth and lies, and disguises and revelations."[10] To conclude the lecture, Atwood references a scene from a then-contemporary film to express not just what she does but what biographical novelists do more generally:

> In the recent film *Il Postino*, the great poet Pablo Neruda upbraids his friend, a lowly postman, for having filched one of Neruda's poems to use in his courtship of a local girl. "But," replies the postman, "poems do not belong to those who write them. Poems belong to those who need them." And so it is with stories about the past. The past no longer belongs only to those who once lived in it; the past belongs to those who claim it, and are willing to explore it, and to infuse it with meaning for those alive today. The past belongs to us, because we are the ones who need it.[11]

As a creative writer, Atwood unapologetically lays claim to history in order to give life meaning for readers in the present and the future. Implicit in Atwood's apologia is a distinction between doing and using history. For those who do history, giving readers established facts about the past is of crucial importance, so altering them is unacceptable. But biographical novelists use rather than do history, so taking liberties with the facts is not just acceptable but also sometimes necessary. Malcolm Bradbury, author of a biographical novel about Denis Diderot, takes this idea to its most logical extreme in his wonderfully comical preface to *To the Hermitage*. Describing himself as a "wee postmodern Haussman," Bradbury says that he has drawn "a great deal on history," but he confesses that when history seems "dull or inaccurate," he decided to improve on it. As he claims: "I have quietly corrected errors in the calendar, adjusted flaws in world geography, now and then budged the border of a country, or changed the constitution of a nation."[12] In biofiction, history and biography take their cue from the vision of the creative writer rather than from the reality of the external world.

In an interview, Russell Banks clarifies why authors feel the need to subordinate history to their aesthetic vision. Banks has authored a spectacular biographical novel titled *Cloudsplitter*, which is about the son of John Brown, Owen. Banks is clear about his writing agenda in relation to history: "I'm using history in order to tell a story."[13] Therefore, what he as a novelist gives readers "is different from the character invented by the biographer or historian."[14] Banks specifies: the "novelist is trying to present, in a sense I suppose, a higher truth, a truth of what it is to be a human

being."[15] The historical and/or biographical truth about Owen is less important than the "higher truth." As Banks goes on to explain: the author "uses
the data of this character's life and embellishes it sufficiently and reorganizes
it and restructures it in such a way that it can both be data and a portrait of
human beings who are very different from John Brown. It could be a portrait of the reader."[16] For example, the real Owen Brown died in 1889, but
Banks's Brown narrates his story in 1903. Banks made this change because
he wanted Owen's "story" to "lose some of the antique quality it might have
had otherwise and would point toward the twentieth century, to our own
time."[17] What readers get in the novel, then, is not so much an accurate representation of Owen's life as a vivid picture of a particular type of person.
As Banks says, *Cloudsplitter* is "now being read as a portrait of the terrorist
that can be applied to our understanding of our present time."[18] To illustrate, Banks tells the story of his "best fan letter." After the publication of the
novel, he received a response from "a woman who had served twenty-four
years of a life sentence in Bedford Hills prison for women for crimes she
committed as a member of the Weather Underground in the sixties and sev-
enties."[19] What gratified Banks so much was her belief "that Owen Brown's
life and story were her life and her story."[20] By his own admission, Banks
was not trying to give his readers an accurate picture of his biographical
subject or the historical record. He fictionalized both to give readers a way
to think about and understand themselves and their world, and the letter
from the former member of the Weather Underground indicates that he
succeeded.

That authors of biofiction subordinate history and biography to their own
aesthetic vision is not as important as why they do this. According to Georg
Lukács, the historical novel, a logical product of Enlightenment rationalism,
came into being in order to foreground how historical forces, which operate according to the scientific laws of cause and effect, shape and determine
human subjectivity. Developments in the works of Friedrich Nietzsche and
Oscar Wilde indicate why certain writers rejected the axioms on which the
historical novel were premised and made the case for a counter-aesthetic
form like biofiction. In 1874, Nietzsche published "On the Uses and Disadvantages of History for Life," a work in which he argues that history,
when treated as an unassailable science, does irreparable damage to society,
because it subordinates human agency to the mechanistic laws of natural necessity. To counter the culture's fetishization of historical knowledge,
Nietzsche admonishes his readers to prioritize the biographical subject,
because, to vitalize society, human autonomy is of ultimate importance. But

Nietzsche did not just favor a turn to any type of biography. He specifies a particular kind: "if you want biographies, do not desire those which bear the legend 'Herr So-and-So and his age', but those upon whose title-page there would stand 'a fighter against his age.'"[21] For Lukács, the protagonist of a historical novel should function as a representative symbol of "the age,"[22] what he refers to as a historical-social type.[23] This figure symbolically represents the dominant forces that contributed to the making of representative people of the time. But for Nietzsche, needed is a turn to the biographical subject, specifically a figure that transcends the culture and environment, what he refers to as a "fighter against his age."

The ideas in Nietzsche's 1874 essay mandated the formation of a corresponding aesthetic form. *Thus Spoke Zarathustra* (1883–5) is that work, and it qualifies as biofiction. Instead of accurately representing the biographical subject, instead of doing history or biography, Nietzsche uses the life of Zarathustra to give readers the will-to-power, the death of God, the eternal recurrence, and the *Übermensch*, ideas that are not to be found in Zarathustra's *Zend-Avesta*. In other words, what readers get in *Zarathustra* is more Nietzsche than the Persian prophet, which Nietzsche makes clear in *Ecce Homo*: "I have not been asked, as I should have been asked, what the name of Zarathustra means in my mouth."[24] His answer is surprising. Nietzsche freely admits that the Zarathustra in his book is the opposite of the actual historical person, and as such, his protagonist is actually Nietzsche. To be more specific, the real Zarathustra invented morality, but Nietzsche's character overcomes and overturns the simplistic good-and-evil model: "the self-overcoming of the moralist, into his opposite—into me—that is what the name of Zarathustra means in my mouth."[25] Nietzsche fictionalizes the historical person in order to give his readers himself and his own vision of life, a vision that underscores the human ability to generate a new way of thinking and being.

A similar pattern can be found in Wilde's work. In 1879, a 24-year-old Wilde authored an essay about history, one that enthusiastically embraces the Enlightenment rationalist approach, which holds: "For the very first requisite for any scientific conception of History is the Doctrine of uniform sequence, in other words that certain events having happened certain other events corresponding to them will happen also."[26] Deterministic in nature, this model foregrounds "the empirical connection of cause and effect"[27] as well as "complete knowledge of the Laws of Human nature,"[28] thereby enabling historians to predict the future: "the past is the key of the future."[29] Wilde developed these ideas in "Historical Criticism," an essay he submitted "for the Chancellor's English Essay Prize at the University of Oxford in 1879."[30] Given the positive nature of his views about the scientific approach to history, it would seem that Wilde would have formulated an aesthetic model similar to Lukács. But in the late 1880s and early 1890s, when he did his most important theorizing about aesthetics ("The Decay of Lying," "The Critic as Artist," and "The Soul of Man"), Wilde came to the conclusion that the scientific approach that he applied to history was not only unsuitable for but also in irreconcilable conflict with the world of art. Therefore, instead of formulating an aesthetic model similar to Lukács, which uses the Enlightenment's scientific method to define art, he seeks to expose why subordinating art to history (increasingly defined over the course of the nineteenth century as a hard science) would damage aesthetics, the human, and even life.

The figure of Gilbert from "The Critic as Artist" incisively articulates one of the key ideas in Wilde's works, and this idea stands in direct opposition to the nineteenth century's dominant philosophy of history and its concomitant aesthetic form, the historical novel: "The longer one studies life and literature, the more strongly one feels that behind everything that is wonderful stands the individual, and that it is not the moment that makes the man, but the man who creates the age."[31] Literature should not be about the way the moment (history) creates the human, as we see in what Lukács refers to as the classical historical novel, but the way the human shapes "reality," which is the central axiom on which the biographical novel is premised. So while Lukács favors literature that gives "living human embodiment to historical-social types,"[32] Wilde, like Nietzsche, draws the exact opposite conclusion: "We are no longer in art concerned with the type. It is with the exception that we have to do."[33] According to this model, a work would succeed only insofar as it brings into existence a new way ("exception") of seeing or being. Wilde makes this point when he offers what is perhaps the first theoretical reflection about biofiction. As the character Vivian says in "The Decay of Lying": "if a novelist is base enough to go to life for his personages he should at least pretend that they are creations, and not boast of them as copies. The justification of a character in a novel is not that other persons are what they are, but that the author is what he is."[34] The justification of a person in a history or a biography is that the paper figure is an accurate representation of what the real person was. But the justification of a historical figure in fiction is much different. Specifically, for the author of biofiction, of utmost importance is the artist and his or her creative vision, and not the historical past or the biographical subject, because, as Vivian says: "Literature always anticipates life. It does not copy it, but moulds it to its purpose."[35] Therefore, in the realm of art, the aesthetic object should be judged a success insofar as it invents something new, which will subsequently give birth to a new reality in life, so accurate representation of the biographical subject and therewith history is not the author's aesthetic objective. And this is exactly what Wilde does in his biographical short story, "The Portrait of Mr. W.H." Based on the dedicatee and sometime-subject of Shakespeare's sonnets, who is simply referred to as Mr. W.H., Wilde uses Shakespeare's dedicatee to create a new reality, specifically an original way of thinking about women and homosexuality. For both Nietzsche and Wilde, the rise of a deterministic model of history mandated a new aesthetic form, one that would prize human autonomy over historical determinism.

What historical novelists get aesthetically wrong is their subordination of the human to history. Bruce Duffy has authored two spectacular biographical novels, one about Ludwig Wittgenstein (*The World as I Found It*), another about Arthur Rimbaud (*Disaster Was My God*), and in an interview about these works he explains why the historical novel is such a problem. History is the foreground of the historical novel, while the protagonist is of secondary importance. But this is backwards, argues Duffy, because the "hero of the novel should be the foreground, and the history should be the background."[36] Author of a biographical novel about Roger Casement (*Valiant Gentlemen*), Sabina Murray clarifies why creative writers privilege the human over history. In an interview about biofiction, she makes a distinction between the biographical novel and the historical novel. She says that "the biographical novel's embracing of personal psychologies offers an alternative to the historical novel's performance of understood notions."[37] The embedded and uncertain personal psychology stands in stark contrast to history's "understood notions." As an author of biofiction, what concerns Murray is the condition of being epistemologically and socially overdetermined. However, instead of identifying history or science as the primary deterministic culprit, she first targets technology:

Why this interest in biographical novels now? Perhaps as we deal with the onslaught of technology, we forget that life is determined by people. There is not a moment in time where one doesn't interact with some dehumanizing element of technology. In the midst of all this, we wonder what it is to be a person.[38]

For Murray, personhood is defined by that ability to evade being determined, which is why she decided to write specifically about Casement:

> I wanted to look at colonialism, the Belgian Congo, the First World War, and to question what it is to be alive in the present of those situations. Decisions are made by people. I said to myself: "This is what's important here, human psychology. Important here are interactions." And I was lucky to find someone like Casement, who was dealing with massive historical movements: the opening up of Africa, the First World War, the Barings Bank Crisis, emerging gay identities.[39]

What makes Casement so extraordinary is his ability to construct new realities in a time of so much upheaval and confusion, which is why he was the perfect protagonist of a biographical novel.

In essence, we could say that the real protagonist of the historical novel is history, while the real protagonist of the biographical novel is, not the biographical subject, but human agency, the ability that enables a human to create one's environment. The Nigerian-Belgian author Chika Unigwe has published a biographical novel about Olaudah Equiano (*De Zwarte Messias*), and she has also authored a short story about Equiano's daughter, Joanna, about whom almost nothing is known. In an interview, I asked Unigwe if it is possible to do a biographical novel about someone when there is almost no historical record. Her response is illuminating, as it offers readers an excellent way to think about the differences between historical and biographical fiction:

> In a historical novel, the author is invested in being true to the realities of that time, so there is little space to create characters that transcend their time in a very radical way, which you can do with biofiction. So in that way I think that Joanna is certainly more biofiction than historical fiction. There are things that Joanna does that I doubt that she would have been able to do if I were writing historical fiction. So I think in biofiction you are able to dream a lot more, a lot wider. Your dreams are more expansive, as a writer, than in historical fiction.[40]

Given the differences between the historical and biographical novel, readers come to the works for very different things. As Unigwe concludes: "Readers don't come to biographical fiction for truth. They come to biographical fiction for possibilities."[41] What readers want from the historical novel is an accurate representation of "the realities of that time," but what they want from the biographical novel is a model of a figure that transcends the deterministic forces of history and the environment, and this is something that places the protagonist of the biographical novel in irreconcilable conflict with the protagonist of the historical novel.

Spanish novelist Rosa Montero usefully clarifies what readers get from biographical novels. For Montero, the goal of the biographical novel should not so much be to depict a real life as to use the life "to try to better understand the world in its greater complexity." This, she explains, is what Robert Graves achieves in his novel *I, Claudius*: "He wasn't telling us the story of Emperor Claudius, but rather making an impressive fresco of the human condition."[42] Montero specifies exactly what fiction writers give readers in a discussion about the human "capacity for symbolic understanding."[43] Biography is of crucial importance, because it provides humans with an "existential map," which is a framework about "how to live."[44] This has direct relevance for understanding the function of a particular life in the biographical novel. In Montero's case, it would be incorrect to say that her goal was simply to give readers a picture of Marie Curie in her biographical novel about the famous Polish scientist. Montero is a novelist, not a biographer. Therefore, Montero unapologetically says that she "used Marie Curie as an enormous screen on which to project [...] possibilities."[45] Like Unigwe, the biographical subject is a figure that the author uses in order to imagine into existence possible ways of thinking and being for readers in the present and the future.

2. The Danish Girl

The truth must be spoken with a view to the results it will produce in the sphere of action.[46]

To bring into sharp focus the central ideas in this essay, let me conclude with a brief discussion of David Ebershoff's *The Danish Girl*, a biographical novel of Einar Wegener/Lili Elbe, one of the first people to undergo sex confirmation surgery. Historically and biographically speaking, the novel is an unmitigated disaster. The actual Einar was born in 1882, while Ebershoff's character was born in either 1890 or 1891. The actual Einar married in 1904 an artist named Gerda, who hailed from Fredricksburg, Denmark, and was the daughter of a clergyman. Ebershoff's Einar married after World War I an artist named Greta, who hailed from Pasadena, California, and was the daughter of a wealthy American family. The actual Gerda had never been married before wedding Einar, while Ebershoff's Greta was a widow when she married Einar. I can list a dozen other biographical and historical discrepancies. But it would be unfair and inaccurate to fault Ebershoff for making these changes, because Ebershoff is not doing history or biography. It would be more accurate to say that Ebershoff found something of major symbolic significance in the story of Lili, and he then used that story in order to give readers what Banks refers to as a "higher truth."

Within this aesthetic framework, biographical novelists alter biography and history in order to convert the main character into a symbol, which is why Ebershoff says: "*The Danish Girl* is a metaphor."[47] Ebershoff is clear about the nature of his objectives. As he says, he found "some important facts about Einar's actual transformation,"[48] and he then used those details in order to craft a narrative that would underscore the degree to which "there is universality to Einar's question of identity."[49] Given this fact, why did Ebershoff convert Einar's Danish-born wife into a wealthy American woman? The answer: she underscores and reinforces the novel's central theme, that humans have the ability to create themselves. Einar was born into an identity with which he was uncomfortable, and through an act of heroic agency, he transitioned from a male to a female, from being a Danish man into being a Danish woman. In like manner, Greta was born into an identity with which she was uncomfortable, and through an act of heroic agency, she transitioned from an American to a Dane, from being an American woman into being a Danish woman. In short, Ebershoff used rather than represented Einar/Lili, and he did this to express his own views about the link between a constructed identity and human agency. In an interview, Ebershoff clarifies the symbolic function of Lili within the novel:

> I believe that she was a great artist, even after she transitioned, and her greatest creation was herself. Artists are visionaries; they see something that does not yet exist. They can bring into creation something that is not yet there. And in many ways this is what Lili is doing: she is envisioning her future self, she is seeing a version of herself that is not yet there, and she is creating it.[50]

As Montero claims, biographical novelists do not give readers an accurate picture of the biographical subject. They use an actual life to give readers an "existential map" for new and creative possibilities for human living. So what readers get in *The Danish Girl* is not an accurate representation of history or biography. Rather, Ebershoff uses both to communicate to readers what they could possibly become, which is creative artists of their own lives and life more generally. The human ability to create life and a self is of ultimate importance, and biographical novelists, who value and respect history, use figures and stories from the past to activate agential and meaningful living in the present and for the future.

PART II

ARCHIVES

5

Real Witches, Real Life

Katherine Howe

The Salem witch trials of 1692 are hardly new territory, for either a historian or a novelist. However, when the trials appear in literature or in history, it is generally assumed that they are acting as a proxy for something else. Either the trials exploded out of social rivalries in Salem and present-day Danvers (the former Salem Village), or else they articulated tensions around the changing role of women in colonial culture, or else the afflicted little girls had all eaten moldy bread, which caused them to hallucinate. What is usually overlooked in these accounts is that, to the people who experienced the Salem panic, the trials were *really about witchcraft*. Everyone involved—judges, jury, clergymen, accusers, and defendants—lived in a religious system that held no doubt whatsoever that witches existed, and that the Devil could make mischief on earth through human interlocutors. When I started thinking about the story in *The Physick Book of Deliverance Dane* (2009), I decided to take the Salem villagers at their word for once: what if witchcraft was real?

And to some extent, witchcraft *was* real, though not in the ways that we think of it today. Medieval and early modern England held a long tradition of so-called cunning folk, local wise people who sold occult services ranging from basic divination, to the location of lost property, to the healing of assorted illnesses. Specifically, the cunning person specialized in unbewitchment; if you suspected that a witch had cast a spell on you, the cunning person was your best hope of redress. They were usually canny businesspeople, and their reputations were always rather suspect; after all, anyone with the power to remove spells could be assumed to have the ability to cast them, too.

Most cunning folk came from the artisan, rather than the laboring, class, in part because tradespeople had more flexible time for seeing clients, but also because they were more likely to be literate. The charms on offer derived both from published grimoires, or spell books translated from Latin into English, and from practices dating from pre-Reformation Christianity. It is

Katherine Howe, *Real Witches, Real Life*. In: *Historical Fiction Now*. Edited by Mark Eaton and Bruce Holsinger, Oxford University Press. © Katherine Howe (2023). DOI: 10.1093/oso/9780198877035.003.0006 thought that the cunning folk tradition did not travel to New England with the colonists, both because of the extreme form of Protestantism that they practiced, in which even Christmas was considered too pagan, and because of the newness of the physical space of the New World. The tangible qualities of magic, derived from special objects, special prayers, and special places, were rooted inextricably in the haunted realms of the Old World.

Or were they? When the Salem panic first broke out, villager Mary Sibley suggested that the culprit might be revealed through a witch cake, a biscuit made of rye meal and urine from the afflicted girls that was baked and then fed to a dog. Though her personality in the story is a product of my imagination, her actions are not. The real Mary Sibley was chastised for resorting to diabolical means to ascertain diabolical actions, but she nevertheless was confident that this popular magic technique held real power to address Salem's witchcraft problem. Similarly, the mysterious charmed boundary marker in the story is based on a real charmed boundary stone, located in Newbury, Massachusetts. Magic still lurked in the daily lives of colonial New Englanders, though its face was hidden.

I have endeavored to be as accurate as possible in my rendition of the historical world of Deliverance and her family, paying special attention to details of dress and room interior. In addition, numerous real people pepper the narrative, though I hasten to add that they are used fictitiously and that some details of their lives have been embellished or changed. The judge and jurymen during Deliverance's 1682 slander trial are all real, as is Robert "King" Hooper, the wealthy Marblehead merchant. My description of Lieutenant Governor William Stoughton, who presided over the Salem witch trials, derives from an extant portrait of him.

The nature of the evidence entered against the accused witches is also accurate, including the so-called witch's teat for suckling imps and familiars. This phenomenon provided the only reliable form of physical evidence against an accused witch; almost all other evidence was "spectral," or claims by witnesses that they had seen the accused specter doing malefic work. Historians differ on what the witch's teat might have really been, arguing variously for anomalous third nipples, for skin tags, for moles, and most notoriously, for the clitoris. In a world lacking in artificial light, hand mirrors, private bedrooms, or bathrooms, the suggestion that women might have been somewhat alienated from their own bodies seems less incredible.

Most important, Deliverance's codefendants in the witchcraft trial— Sarah Wildes, Rebecca Nurse, Susannah Martin, Sarah Good, and Elizabeth Howe—together with the dates on which they were tried and executed, are

all correct. I have attempted to be true to these women's personalities insofar as they are known, though I took some liberties with Sarah Good. Other
real accused witches make passing appearances: Wilmot Redd of Marblehead; Sarah Osborne, who died in prison; and deposed minister George
Burroughs. Sarah Good really did threaten from the gallows that "*I* am no
more a witch than you are a wizard, and if you take away my life, God will
give you blood to drink." Interestingly, local tradition holds that the man
on the receiving end of this threat, Nicholas Noyes, died years later of a
hemorrhage, so in a sense Sarah's prediction came true.

Sarah Good's daughter Dorcas, meanwhile, inspired my illustration of
how the effects of the trial echoed years later for the families involved. The
real Dorcas, at about four or five years old, spent eight months imprisoned
in Boston, and her mother was hanged. As a result of these twin horrors, little Dorcas lost her mind. In 1710, her father, William Good, sued the town
for help with her support and maintenance, claiming that Dorcas "being
chain'd in the dungeon was so hardly used and terrfyed that she hath ever
since been very chargeable having little or no reason to govern herself." Association with the trials, even for those who were ultimately acquitted, caused
entire families to suffer economic and social aftershocks until well into the
eighteenth century, a harsh reality that informed the reduced circumstances
of Mercy and Prudence in the story.

The representation of Prudence Bartlett as an eighteenth-century Marblehead midwife who keeps a daily log I owe directly to the scholarship of
Laurel Thatcher Ulrich on Martha Ballard, an eighteenth-century Maine
midwife (though not a witch, it must be said) who kept a diary of her
quotidian activities.

The assorted magical elements woven throughout the story are based on
research into grimoires held at the British Museum, in particular a text of
disputed age and authorship called the *Key of Solomon*. (No North American
colonial-era grimoires have been found—at least, not yet.) The magical circle conjured on the door of the Milk Street house is based on a circle drawn
in a manuscript in the Bibliothèque de l'Arsenal in Paris, reproduced in a
contemporary book of occult history. Similarly, the "Abracadabra" healing
charm derives from a Roman talisman, the triangular shape of which was
thought to draw illness out of the body, and discussed in a different modern
source on vernacular magic. Urine and witch bottles were a common tool of
cunning folk, following the widespread logic that a small part of the body can
be made to stand in for the whole. And finally, the "key and Bible" and "sieve
and scissors" were both widespread, mainstream divination techniques in

use as late as the nineteenth century. Anyone who has flipped a coin or shaken a magic eight ball in the course of making a decision has touched the modern descendants of these techniques.

And what of Deliverance Dane herself? The real Deliverance Dane was accused near the end of the Salem panic, when the accusations were spreading deeper into the Essex County countryside. She lived with her husband, Nathaniel, in Andover, Massachusetts, and she was imprisoned on suspicion of witchcraft for thirteen weeks in 1692. Little is known about her, apart from the fact that she survived the trials, and unlike some of her contemporaries, there is no evidence that she was actually a cunning woman. The only record that I have been able to find is an account listing how much Nathaniel owed for her maintenance while she was in jail. This document, along with transcripts and digital images of the actual court documents, can be viewed in the Salem witchcraft papers digital archive maintained by the University of Virginia.

And then there is me. Family genealogical research by successive generations of Howe women indicates our connection both to condemned witch Elizabeth Howe, who appears briefly here, and to accused witch Elizabeth Proctor. The latter connection is thought to be more direct, as she survived the trials, while Elizabeth Howe, as you know, did not.

For a long while this knowledge was just one of those weird, amusing details about me that not many people knew. Then after a few years working and living in Cambridge, I arrived in Essex County, Massachusetts. As we settled into life on the North Shore, I was moved both by how fully the past in New England still haunts the present, especially in its small, long-memoried towns, and also by how the idiosyncratic personhood of early colonists seems to have been lost in nationalist myth. In the bedroom of our little antique rental house, my husband and I even found a tiny horseshoe, caked in paint, nailed over the rear door for luck, or to ward off evil, we were not sure which.

I began telling myself this story while studying for my own Ph.D. qualifying exams, in American and New England studies at Boston University, taking my own dog on rambles through the woods between Salem and Marblehead. I honed it further while teaching an introductory research and writing seminar on New England witchcraft to two groups of BU freshmen. (They especially liked the extra-credit assignment, which was to look up two different methods of un-bewitching a cow and explain the pros and cons of each.)

The narrative offered a unique opportunity to restore individuality, albeit fictional, to some of these distant people. I was also drawn to Deliverance's story by my sympathy with the New England legacy of difficult, and sometimes overly bookish, women. Did the knowledge of my distant ancestors' unconventional paths help steer me toward graduate work in American culture? I feel certain that it did. But even lacking that knowledge, I suspect that their witchiness, however we understand it, contributed to my being the kind of person I am. I am grateful to those vanished people for whatever fragments of them may persist within myself.

***

Almost immediately after the largest, most deadly, and most widespread witch hunt in North America—Salem—drew to an ignominious close in 1693, the crime of witchcraft ceased to be prosecuted. As the eighteenth century opened in what would become the United States of America, witchcraft stayed on the books as a crime but receded from the courts. Family members of those accused at Salem sued for restitution or to have their good names restored in the first decade of the 1700s. A few witch trials flickered to life in this decade, though their outcomes were wildly different from what had gone before. In Virginia, for instance, in 1706, Grace Sherwood was one of the last women actually convicted of witchcraft in the colonies. She was freed after a relatively short period of incarceration, even going on to reclaim her property from the state, and eventually died of old age in her eighties. A far cry indeed from the spectacle hangings of Salem a mere decade and a half previous. So where did all the witches go?

By 1735 the English anti-witchcraft statute had changed, as Connie notes in the novel, from outlawing witchcraft itself, to outlawing the pretense of witchcraft. Instead of addressing a perceived mortal risk to body or livelihood, the law instead attempted to control the small, persistent cultural practices of conjuring, charming, unbewitching, and finding lost objects that were often done for a fee, and in communities all over the Atlantic world. The stakes were lower for people thought to be witches. But that doesn't mean that belief in witchcraft went away. The phrasing of the 1735 law suggests that the courts felt that people had to be protected, not from felony maleficium wrought on their bodies or crops or farm animals, but from being conned.

The reason for the lowered stakes was that by the 1730s, a consumer revolution was well under way. As common households in Britain and the colonies found it easier to secure food and goods, adjudicating the bewitch-ment of calves or butter was no longer of the mortal import that it had been in the 1600s. Economics, rather than changed belief, pushed witchcraft off the legal docket. From there, witchcraft moved into the world of folklore, where it has lived comfortably ever since.

The need to exert control over uncontrollable forces didn't go away with the advent of the Scientific Revolution or the spread of relatively greater material prosperity, however. In coastal New England communities that drew their living from farming and the sea, a major area for seeking con-trol lay in the weather. Moll Pitcher, "the sole Pythoness of ancient Lynn," born Mary Diamond in Marblehead to a family with a reputation for weather charming, lived from around 1736—just after the change in the anti-witchcraft statutes—to 1813, and gained particular fame for her pur-ported ability to predict the outcome of voyages. In an earlier generation Moll Pitcher would have been an object of fear and derision, but by the late eighteenth and early nineteenth centuries Pitcher's seeming command of the occult no longer posed a threat to her community. Instead, it could be offered as a benefit. The description of her by the poet John Greenleaf Whittier, however, fixes Pitcher squarely in the mode of the fairy tale witch: "a wasted, gray, and meagre hag, / In features evil as her lot." Whittier even gives her a crooked nose. In real life Pitcher was merely plain-looking, and far from haggish, but her literary ugliness speaks to the disquiet concerning women with a witchy reputation even after they were no longer threatening enough to legislate against.

Moll Pitcher's counsel would have been keenly valued during the real year without a summer, which wreaked havoc around the world, but particularly in New England, beginning in May 1816. The temperature plunge described in Temperance's timeline really occurred, and for the rest of the year, sum-mer never came. Crops failed. The New England economy tanked, and some historians have argued that the hardship brought about by the anomalous weather pattern contributed to the migration from the coasts of the former colonies into the interior, to western New York State and to Ohio. Con-struction on the Erie Canal, which would eventually serve as the primary artery of travel and commerce from the coast to the expanding frontier, began the following July, in 1817. Many factors, of course, contributed to the shifting of population during the Jacksonian period, but the uncertainty of weather was part of that nexus of causality. We are seeing the unintended consequences play out today, as rising global temperatures force massive changes on coastal areas all over the world. Connie didn't cause that change in weather pattern by herself (fossil fuel dependence did) but she—and all of us—will feel the consequences soon enough.

The specific accounts of witchcraft in this story derive from disparate sources, all with their roots in American folklore. Witches have long been believed to fly, with airborne witches showing up in medieval European woodcuts and Tituba Indian's confessional testimony at Salem. The flying ointment recipe that Connie finds hidden in the wall of the Milk Street house comes from a rare book of collected European and American folklore and superstitions, first published in the late 1700s and held today at the New York Public Library, which also provided the three-knot sailor charm that Temperance sells. Interestingly, the poisonous ingredient in the flying ointment—henbane—supposedly provides a sensation of flight when consumed. Whether Connie and Temperance really flew, or merely felt themselves to fly, I leave to the reader to decide.

Grace's conjure spell to both protect Connie and also discern the source of her struggles comes from a different real grimoire called the *Sixth and Seventh Book of Moses*, which dates from sometime in the eighteenth or nineteenth century, and which is still available for sale. The text followed a path from Germany (probably) to German immigrants to the Americas, where it grew in popularity among African American hoodoo practitioners in the South. (Notably, it also contains instructions for how to influence the weather.) Zazi's point about folk-magical practices penetrating into different regions and in different cultural contexts derives from my own reading while researching a different project—the sieve-and-scissors divination method described in detail in *The Physick Book of Deliverance Dane* as an artifact of early modern English folk magic, and alluded to her, really does show up almost completely unchanged in an oral history collected by a folklorist working in the American South in the 1920s. (Of course, magical needs sometimes change with current events: that text also contains instructions for a charm to keep a secret liquor still from being raided by the police. Inquiries may be submitted via my website, for a very reasonable fee.)

Lastly, my apologies to the people of Easthorpe, England, for Livvy's dim view of their village, which I assure them I do not share. Their church, however, did contain a real Sheela-na-gig, the primitive carving of a grinning, naked older woman that reminds Livvy that female power takes many guises, not all of them welcome in the halls of patriarchy. Sheelas are not widely understood, but have been documented all over Ireland, parts of Scotland, and in England as far east as Easthorpe. Their iconography reminded me of the grinning figure on the charmed boundary stone still standing in Byfield, Massachusetts—another concrete example of the never-ending struggle by individuals to assert power, agency, and safety in an uncertain and heavily circumscribed world. May we all of us some day settle in a city named for peace, as Livvy's mother sought to do, even if that place lies not on a thickly forested faraway coast, but somewhere inside ourselves.

6

Gardens of Memory

Ghosts, Grounds, and the Archives

Tiya Miles

The Cherokee Rose turned out to be many things: a ghost story, a love story, a mystery, a teaching tool, and what I like to think of as a temporal bridge novel—a work of both historical and contemporary fiction that illuminates the meaning of the past for the present and future. It was the first and only one of my books that my women family members read all the way through, and that, for me, was among its highest achievements. I was, in fact, writing for them, for my sister, sisters-in-law, mother, stepmother, and aunts, and writing for the many women like them (including myself) who might be more inclined on some days to pick up a thoughtful romance about the history and legacy of racial and gender issues rather than a dense, historical tome. In other words, I aspired to write in the Black feminist literary tradition of Pauline Elizabeth Hopkins and Frances Ellen Watkins Harper. These were African American public intellectuals whose late-nineteenth/early-twentieth-century pedagogical genre fiction about Black women's difficult pasts, American racial and sexual politics, and Black community strategies for uplift I had analyzed in my undergraduate thesis in Afro-American Studies and in my master's thesis in Women's Studies.[1] To Hopkins's and Harper's exemplary models, I added the spectral fiction of science fiction writer Octavia Butler, whose 1970s time-travelling novel *Kindred* is set on an antebellum Maryland plantation and features Black women and white men embroiled in a tangle of complex and exploitative romantic and sexual relationships.[2]

In addition to being drawn to an audience with whom I wished to communicate and a literary tradition that I hoped to speak back to and update, I felt compelled to contend with emotional and political storylines that felt present and yet unfinished just below the surface of my second academic book, a multiracial history of the largest extant plantation in the Cherokee

Tiya Miles, *Gardens of Memory: Ghosts, Grounds, and the Archives*. In: *Historical Fiction Now.*
Edited by Mark Eaton and Bruce Holsinger, Oxford University Press. © Tiya Miles (2023).
DOI: 10.1093/oso/9780198877035.003.0007

Nation of present-day Georgia.[3] I was propelled by these divergent desires to write Black feminist genre fiction for women readers and to retell a historical account of slavery and race in the Native American South in a form that would allow me to craft a more emotionally satisfying and hopeful ending than the textbook histories of racial slavery and forced removal allow.[4]

In the story that became *The Cherokee Rose*, the three main characters are Jennifer "Jinx" Micco, a Creek-Cherokee tribal historian and graduate student from Muskogee, Oklahoma; Cheyenne Cotterell, a wealthy African American interior designer and BAP "Black American Princess," from Atlanta, Georgia; and Ruth Mayes, the daughter of a Black mother and white father who writes for a "shelter" magazine in Minneapolis, Minnesota. Each is pulled out of her restless everyday life by spiritual forces unknown to her and compelled to travel to the same place: a nineteenth-century plantation home in the foothills of the Blueridge Mountains on land that once belonged to Cherokee slaveholders. The person who has called them there, the ghost of a young Afro-Creek woman who has access to both West African Indigenous and southern American Indigenous spiritual knowledges, needs their historical engagement as well as their personal growth in order to stop a sacrilege upon the land. On the hallowed ground of that plantation where so many had lived, loved, and died, the travelers find that an old garden holds secrets of the past that, once uncovered, show them not only what they share with one another across their many differences, but also what they have in common with the African American, Native American, and Euro-American women who once fought for freedom on those same grounds. After facing one another and the travails of history by way of emotional time travel set in motion through a diary discovered in the slave quarters, the women of the contemporary story emerge strengthened and connected, ready to face their futures and protect the place and people that they have come to love.

These characters, and the journey into the past that they would embark on together, took many years to coalesce in my thinking. The germ of an idea sprouted before I had any notion of what expressive form it would take. I was a graduate student researching my dissertation on slavery in the nineteenth-century Cherokee Nation in the late 1990s when the first image for the novel that would eventually become *The Cherokee Rose* appeared unbidden and free-floating. I had, for this research, visited historic plantation sites, which is surely what had begun the shaping of this picture in my unconscious mind. One day, perhaps while daydreaming when I should have been reading my secondary sources, I saw a young woman in my mind's eye. She was walking through a field of flowers toward a spacious, deteriorating plantation house, oblivious to the pageantry of nature around her because of an unseen weight of past pain that narrowed her sensory and emotional range. The image came and went in a flash. It was merely a snapshot of a woman alone, slowly moving uphill through a field of beauty that she could not recognize due to historical trauma.

The specific personal and communal history that I would eventually wrap around that woman, who turned out to be Ruth, the daughter of an abused and murdered mother, and her peers, was inspired by primary research and the vivid image of an enslaved woman that I first read about in the archives and then imagined on plantation grounds over a decade later while researching my second history on slavery in the Cherokee Nation. Some of the richest first-hand accounts on this topic were the letters and diaries penned by Christian missionaries from the Moravian Church who had traveled to Cherokee country in what is now Georgia to start a school and mission on the land of a wealthy Cherokee slaveholder named James Vann. In the small basement reading room of the Moravian Archives Southern Province in Old Salem, North Carolina, I had immersed myself in translations of the old German missionary script, reading about Vann, his family members, his missionary associates, and the enslaved people owned by both Cherokees and the Moravian Church. A woman named Pleasant stood out to me in these records. Pleasant was an enslaved mother of a young mixed-race boy, Michael, brought by the missionaries from North Carolina to the Cherokee Nation. The missionaries criticized Pleasant for cursing at them when they gave her orders and for carrying out her assigned tasks slowly and belligerently. Although the missionaries who sought to extract her labor saw Pleasant as a lazy, ungodly nuisance, I saw her as a person of remarkable inner fortitude. She exhibited intelligence, bravery, and creativity throughout her time in the Cherokee Nation by pushing back against her missionary-masters' wishes, seeking to protect her son from sale, forming bonds with other enslaved Blacks as well as Cherokees, and growing a garden that others in her community envied.

Pleasant had been enslaved on the Vann plantation, an estate that was known as Diamond Hill in the 1800s, and which, by the 1950s, was preserved, marked, and open to the public. I walked those grounds (the Chief Vann House State Historic Site, operated by the Georgia Department of Natural Resources) several times while working on my book about the family that had owned the estate and the people they had enslaved. It was during one of these visits in the sticky heat of July that the second seed of *The Cherokee Rose* sprouted.

I was walking among the trees by a live spring once considered sacred by Cherokees that had also inspired the name of the former Moravian Cherokee mission station on the grounds: Springplace. A generous senior colleague, Dr. Rowena McClinton, accompanied me. She was an expert on Moravian documents and a translator of the Springplace Mission diaries, who often sent me loose sheets of translated pages in the mail when she came across Pleasant's name.[5] I was discussing research with Rowena and feeling the soft, welcome breeze beside the waterway when I let my mind wander. I looked up at the trees, through the canopy of leaves filtering the day's languid light, and I imagined that I saw Pleasant there, sitting astride a sturdy branch and demanding my notice beyond distant academic interest. Glimpsing Pleasant by the spring that day, I felt moved by a sense of the untold stories of the more than 100 enslaved people who had lived on that land alongside her, and pushed to try to capture revelations about their lives that were perhaps unprovable, but nevertheless true to the human experience.

I do not say that I saw a ghost that late summer afternoon. I do say that I saw a figment—a figment of the historical record augmented by my imagination once it had been set free. Seeing Pleasant on that branch in her calico dress and headscarf unveiled for me a living sense of the past and a means of connecting to that past beyond the realm of my accustomed mode: academic history writing. Pleasant, the historical person held captive by missionaries, became the character Faith in The Cherokee Rose. The spectral woman in the tree transformed into Mary Ann, the spirit guide to Jinx, Ruth, and Cheyenne, who was modeled on a Creek historical figure whom I had uncovered in a Native American history research seminar taught by the Ojibwe historian Jean O'Brien.[6] I hoped that by writing the stories of women who lived in the past in a way that allowed for a deeper emotional connection than is often possible in historical writing, I could prepare the ground for a richer understanding of their struggles and strengths with women readers who enjoy climbing inside stories and who feel that the histories we inherit make us who we are today.

I knew for years that I should heed Pleasant's call, but knowing and doing are entirely different enterprises. I was an academic with three young children, classes to teach, articles to publish, and no time to spare for creative writing. Soon after my youngest child was born, I attended an annual conference of the Native American and Indigenous Studies Association in Minneapolis. One evening, I wandered into a fairytale-like bookstore in the Uptown neighborhood where the bookseller happened to be dressed like

Mother Goose. With my four-month-old son in the stroller beside me, I browsed the shelves and came across a book by Walter Mosley, my step-father's favorite crime novelist. *This Year You Write Your Novel* was the book's title. I bought it and tucked it inside my diaper bag. By the time that academic year of 2008–9 ended, I was ready to follow Mosley's prescription.

My family moved to Montana for the summer while my husband was engaged in wellness intervention research in a community partnership on the Blackfeet Reservation. During the days, I snatched time around car-ing for our five-year-old twin daughters and eight-month-old son to start the creative endeavor that Pleasant's visage had sparked years earlier. The project before me was daunting, but a single question guided my thinking, enabling me to cross the (arguably fluid) boundary between historical and fictional narrative construction. I had by then conducted extensive primary research on the Diamond Hill plantation. My book on the history of that place and its residents was in production at the University of North Carolina Press. I knew that the owner of that plantation, the legendary Chief James Vann, had been murdered under mysterious circumstances. His unknown assailant had never been apprehended, but historians believed that the per-petrator was his compatriot-turned-enemy. Knowing what I did of the lives of enslaved women, as well as Cherokee women, on Diamond Hill, I thought that in a world of my own creation, a fictional world, an alternate scenario was entirely plausible. Who killed James Vann? This became the mystery, the question around which I might weave a story. And my answer would be that the women of the Vann plantation, acting in an alliance built of love and necessity, had taken this abusive man's life in collective self-defense. I needed, then, to craft a story that realized that version of events, made it believable, and showed its relevance to the lives of women in our contem-porary society, women whom I knew and loved, like my family, friends, and the readers in a mystery book club that I had briefly joined during a parental leave after our twins were born.

I felt a devotion to this story that pushed me through the difficult moments when time was scarce, children were noisy, and faith in my ability to complete the thing wavered. But writing fiction, after fifteen years of writ-ing academic history, proved the most challenging part of this enterprise. I had been trained to accurately render the past as best as I could reconstruct it, to offer my analyses backed by evidence fairly and rationally interpreted. Over the course of my professional career, I had labored to build narratives that I could reasonably and responsibly support through primary and sec-ondary sourcing. Now that I was trying to write fiction set in both the past and present in a real place where historical lives had unfolded in ways I had already documented, I had a tough time letting go of the "known" past. In my initial efforts I adhered so closely to historical dates and events that I gave myself no room to develop a new plot. I had to resist a gravitational pull to write in footnotes (and settled for an Author's Note that explains the background for the story).[7] Finally, I found my way out of a data-bound tunnel when I reread the evocative, detail-rich diary of missionary Anna Rosina Gambold. Although I had read pages of her diary many times before when mining them for historical information, now I read decades of her daily journal straight through while sitting outside in the sunshine. Her observations were so sharp, her turns of phrase so captivating, that I became absorbed by her world. Anna Rosina Gambold, herself a writer of diaries, letters, and botanical papers with a literary quality, opened the door to fiction writing for me. I began anew by free-writing new entries of her diary in my best estimation of her voice. At first these diary pages adhered to the originals, duplicating the missionary's recorded dates, locations, and words. But before I realized a shift had occurred, the entries that I was writing in the voice of a character modeled on Anna Rosina took on a life of their own.

The historical Pleasant had inspired me to write this story about the Vann plantation and its inhabitants. The historical Anna Rosina had guided me into the heart of that story's pages. Shaping the lives of the wholly manufactured contemporary characters: Jinx, Ruth, Cheyenne, Adam, and Sally, was an extremely challenging second phase of the creative process. I struggled with making these characters real as people, with giving them things to do and words to say that were not mere re-enactments and recitations of the historical information that I sought to share with readers. In the end, with the feedback of editors and fiction writing workshop leaders who helped the manuscript along, I was able to enliven these characters, although I realize that my skills in dialogue and plotting are far from mature. By the time I finished the final draft of *The Cherokee Rose* more than five years after stumbling across *This Year You Write Your Novel*, I wanted to travel back in time to 2009 and visit my characters at their restored and repurposed historic site. The fiction had worked on me. I nearly believed that they lived on the former Vann estate, making new relationships and histories.

While I was completing an early draft of the novel and, coincidentally, started spending time in Detroit for research on a different project, I learned about the practice of tending memory gardens. I picked up on this idea while hearing gardeners in the city talk about planting gardens in memory of loved ones who had moved as the city's population began its steep decline. A friend might care for the old garden of someone who had moved away and left a vacant yard behind. A relative might transplant flowers from a departed loved one's garden into her own, or a daughter might replicate the shape and colors of her mother's previous plantings. Even if a loved one was long gone—having relocated to a new city, or even a place farther away, like heaven or the deep, star-dusted universe—a plant would bloom in that person's cherished memory. A plant would be the reminder of that loved one's life and stories. This beautiful notion of the memory garden became an essential element in the novel as I revised.[8] I finally completed and published the book in 2015, my willingness to let the story go and to take the ensuing professional risk having been encouraged by the life-changing gift of the MacArthur Prize.

Now, I like to think of myself as the keeper of a memory garden, too, in the form of new seeds in the soil and new pages on the past. As a first novel, and as a suspension bridge between my dutiful work as a historian and my fever dreams as a fiction writer, *The Cherokee Rose* contains many flaws.[9] Still, I hope that by sharing in the experiences of these characters and finding inspiration there, readers can bend their own lives toward care, remembrance, and justice, and like the flowers in the rose garden: grow.

7

Pilgrim's Progress

Researching *The Secret Chord*

Geraldine Brooks

I'm an Australian: I'm supposed to know about sheep. I can define jumbuck, dag, and blue belly. I know what a ringer is. I own a working kelpie from a station outside Orange. My childhood home had a print of Tom Roberts' painting *The Golden Fleece*. If I close my eyes, I can still see it: the light falling like a benediction on the bent back of the shearer, his muscled arm hooped across the sheep as his other hand vanished into the froth of falling fleece.

But Aussie merinos are one thing. The skinny, flighty sheep of the Samarian desert are, I'm learning, something else again. I've come to Israel with my 10-year-old son, who is acting as my research assistant for a novel I'm writing about King David. I've often brought my kids along on research trips like this one. Riding ponies across the Mongolian grasslands or lost in the alleyways of Venice, their unjaded eyes often notice things I've missed, while their expansive imaginations make unexpected leaps and connections. David would have been about 10 when we first encounter him in the Bible as a shepherd boy in these hills, and I'm curious to see how my son handles himself as the afternoon lengthens.

This novel, *The Secret Chord*, will be my fifth work of historical fiction and, as in all my books, I believe that the world I create will only be transporting for readers if it rests on the scaffolding of thorough research. But how do you research the life of a man who shimmers between history and myth in the Second Iron Age, 3,000 years ago? Archives, letters, journals, court documents—the usual staples of my craft—aren't available in this case. Outside the Bible, there is no written record of David. All I have are the few thousand words of his story scattered through the various books of Samuel, Chronicles, Kings, Psalms—the collected Hebrew writings that Jews call the Tanakh and Christians know as the Old Testament.

Geraldine Brooks, *Pilgrim's Progress: Researching* The Secret Chord. In: *Historical Fiction Now.* Edited by Mark Eaton and Bruce Holsinger, Oxford University Press. © News Pty Limited (2023). DOI: 10.1093/oso/9780198877035.003.0008

At the outset, I've realized that to look beyond those sparse, ancient, often cryptic words, I will have to do my research differently. I will have to go to the places associated with David and, as far as possible, try to do the kinds of things he is described as having done. Well, not the adultery and murder, perhaps, but the more quotidian things, such as herding sheep, riding a donkey or a mule, and cooking over a charcoal fire in a goat-hair tent.

So we've come to the Shefala, the undulating foothills that divide Israel's coastal plain from the sudden, swift rise of its craggy interior. When David united the Hebrew tribes around 950 BCE, this region was the setting for constant skirmishing between small Jewish farming communities and their better-armed adversaries, the Philistines, sophisticated city dwellers from the coastal plain. It's easy to imagine fighting taking place in these hills. For one thing, there's a military shooting range just across the valley, and the crackle of Uzi fire is a reminder that this land is still being fought over.

In a field hazed with the shoots of barley and oat grasses, my son and I stand confounded by a tawny flock of sheep and goats whose members stubbornly resist our efforts to segregate them by species. In the 1960s, Israel's then leader, David Ben-Gurion, granted more than 240 hectares for this reserve with the idea of recreating an entirely biblical landscape—a facsimile of the land of "milk and honey" that Joshua found when he led the wandering Hebrews across the Jordan river. But centuries of overgrazing had worn the land down to its rocky ribcage, so topsoil had to be trucked in to support the biblical species such as grapes, figs, pomegranates, olives, and dates that now flourish here.

Our mission is to herd a flock as David would have done, and maybe get some insight into how that experience shaped his personality. A lot of biblical leaders start off as shepherds. Abraham is minding his flocks when God singles him out to found a great nation. Moses is after a lost lamb when he sees the burning bush and is commanded to lead the Hebrew slaves out of Egypt. Jacob has to earn the right to marry his chosen bride by years of shepherding. David's childhood as a herder honed his sling skills as he kept the flock safe from the lions that once roamed here.

But our flock isn't ... flocking. They're heading off in several directions. I find myself wishing for the assistance of my kelpie. It's my son who finally has the insight that allows us to make some progress. He notices that goats, fleet and sure-footed, scatter to seek safety when you put pressure on them. But the sheep, which are slower, cluster together in a dense group with their heads on top of each other to protect their vulnerable necks. Understanding this enables him to, well, separate the sheep from the goats. The leadership lesson: know the nature of those you are trying to direct. Use their inherent qualities to best advantage. I reach for my notebook. When the time comes, I will place a young David in this kind of landscape and allow him to arrive at a similar insight.

Later, we sit on the herb-scented hillside and read Psalm 51, in which David implores God to forgive his adultery with Bathsheba and the murder of her husband Uriah. As we read the words "purge me with hyssop," we rub the fragrant leaves between our fingers. Hyssop is an undemanding plant that grows in sparse soil with little water, yet yields a big flavor and has numerous healing properties. In David's time, it was known as the symbol for humility—a quality he lacked once he had risen to power, united the tribes, and crushed his enemies.

A day later, we're driving over the beautiful Kidron mountains as the afternoon sun sets fire to the russet, cream, and ochre striations of chalk, flint, and dolomite. As we descend the switchback road to Ein Gedi, the Dead Sea shimmers in an opalescent haze. This landscape, and the way the light falls upon it, also will find its way into the pages of my novel.

We've jumped ahead in David's biography. He's a young man when he's here in Ein Gedi. He's won his famous battle with Goliath and become King Shaul's son-in-law and his most successful warrior. But in the first of many reversals that mark the story of David's life, he falls dramatically from grace. Shaul feels threatened by David's growing popularity among the citizenry and by his intimate relationship with Yonatan, Shaul's son and heir. David becomes a wanted man, running for his life, hiding in these hills and caves as the king pursues him, as the Bible relates, "even unto the most craggy rocks, which are accessible only to wild goats."

Wild goats, 10-year-olds. As Shaul pursued David, I'm trailing after my son, who is much fleeter and fitter than I am. As he races ahead of me up the dusty slopes, I can identify with the aging Shaul, never quite catching up with the renegade who always manages to elude him.

That night we travel to a Bedouin settlement to rest under goat-hair tents as David would have done when he went off to his many battles. We eat a dish that has remained unchanged since David's era: bread dipped in olive oil and za'atar—a thyme-like herb. We also try some ancient transportation methods—camels and donkeys—though later research discloses there were no camels in the Israel of David's period. And much as I might be tempted to mount my fictional David on a fine horse, accuracy forbids it. Horses were rare, and used to pull chariots.

Our final destination is associated with David's greatest years, the height of his power. After Shaul's death in battle on Mount Gilboa, David rises quickly to the throne. He seeks a capital city that will unite the tribes, and chooses Yebus, a fortified city that has never been conquered. David succeeds where others have failed, and renames Yebus "Ir David"—the City of David—a name many still use.

We visit a controversial archeological dig that has uncovered buildings dating from the Davidian period, including one whose size, decorations, and location suggest it may well have been associated with a leader of David's stature. But the dig runs under a Palestinian neighborhood and the residents are angry and suspicious of the tunneling beneath their homes. They watch, stony-faced, as our group lines up to tour the dig site. I want to see what kind of building might have been fit for a king in 900-and-something BCE. The Bible says David built a palace from dressed stone and cedar from the forests of Lebanon, but I'm skeptical: what could they possibly have meant by "palace" in the Second Iron Age? Turns out they meant ... palace.

The ruins suggest real opulence, with finely carved stonework and beautiful terraces that would have afforded magnificent views. I'm glad to be able to put David into rooms such as these, to imagine him as a recognizable king rather than a simple tribal leader.

Of course, getting the setting right is less than half the battle. It's the necessary but far from sufficient condition for the writing of compelling historical fiction. As my son and I head home, what looms before me is the greater, much more difficult task: to understand the emotional life of this man who experienced every emotion there is, luminous joy and bitter grief, the gains and losses of fame and infamy, the man who raised monstrous sons who raped, murdered, and rebelled against him, but who also fathered Solomon, a successor whose name would live as a byword for wisdom and good governance.

I can't travel to these insights; I can't buy a ticket. All I can do is dive deep into the experience of being human, holding fast to this lifeline: that our deepest emotions—love, hate, passion, fear, bereavement, exhilaration—are the constants of our common existence. I feel, as he felt, even though three millennia stand between us.

8

The Afronaut Archives

Reports from a Future Zambia

Namwali Serpell

"Most Westerners don't even know whereabouts in Africa we are." So said Edward Mukuka Nkoloso at a press conference announcing that he had founded Zambia's National Academy of Science, Space Research and Philosophy. It was 1964, and the British protectorate of Northern Rhodesia had just become an independent African nation. "Imagine the prestige value this would earn for Zambia," Nkoloso boasted. But over half a century later, most Westerners still don't know much about Zambia. Even fewer people, Western or otherwise, know about Nkoloso.

I'm a Zambian writer with an interest in science fiction and a bent toward absurdism; when I first found out about the Zambian space program, it was like discovering a whole new moon to roam. But as I dug through arcane Internet references and dusty archival documents, I learned that this moon had a dark side. Before Nkoloso had made his debut as a benign, possibly batty space enthusiast, he had been jailed, and likely tortured, for fighting to free his country from colonial rule.

I first heard of the Zambian space program in 2012, when my friend sent me a link to a video called "Afronauts," a trailer for an exhibit by the Spanish photographer Cristina de Middel. It began with title cards that explained, "In 1964, in the middle of the space race, Zambia started a space program that aimed to put the first African on the moon. The director of this unofficial program was Edward Makuka [*sic*]." This led me to a Wikipedia page for "Edward Makuka Nkoloso" [*sic*], and then to a YouTube clip from a show called *5 Terrible Predictions* about "the wacky world of Zambian astronauts." It showed grainy black-and-white footage from the 1960s of the man himself, fitted out in cape and helmet.

Nkoloso had apparently been training his space cadets by swinging them from long ropes, rolling them down hills in empty oil barrels, and bobbing them in streams to simulate water landings. His one female cadet,

Namwali Serpell, *The Afronaut Archives: Reports from a Future Zambia*. In: *Historical Fiction Now*. Edited by Mark Eaton and Bruce Holsinger, Oxford University Press. © Namwali Serpell (2023). DOI: 10.1093/oso/9780198877035.003.0009

Matha Mwamba, was raising twelve cats. Why? To be released upon landing on Mars, to make sure it was habitable. At the close of an interview with
Nkoloso, the British reporter turned to the camera and said: "To most Zam-
bians, these people are just a bunch of crackpots and from what I've seen
today, I'm inclined to agree."

When I read Nkoloso's own op-ed about the program, however, the out-
landishness of his project seemed to border on irony, even satire: "We
have been studying Mars from our telescopes at our headquarters and are
now certain Mars is populated by primitive natives ... a missionary will be
launched in our first rocket. But I have warned the missionary he must not
force Christianity to the people if they do not want it."

I was hooked. I began to hunt for information about this remarkable man.
But my research via the UC Berkeley library turned up only scattered refer-
ences to Nkoloso. There were some scholarly articles about colonial history;
Dominion Status for Central Africa?, a 1958 pamphlet published by Kenneth
Kaunda, who went on to become Zambia's first president; a 1988 inter-
view with Nkoloso in a travel rag called *Z Magazine*; a 2003 BBC program,
African Space; and a 2013 episode of a South African show called *Faces of
Africa*. From these resources, I pieced together a cursory biography.

Born in the north of the country, Nkoloso had been training to become a
priest at a seminary when he was drafted to fight overseas for the British during World War II. Upon his return, he started a school, headed a Veterans'
Association, served as a local councilman, became a traveling salesman for
pharmaceuticals, joined a political party, got arrested, and then, unaccount-
ably, started a space program. This sketch of his life had some incoherent
and inassimilable details, however, which tantalized the fiction writer in me.
For instance, how did Nkoloso's space program relate to his earlier efforts to
resist British rule?

Two anecdotes in particular grabbed me by the lapels. In 1956, Nkoloso
had stormed into a British District Commissioner's Office in the Northern
Province to protest the desecration of African corpses, which were being dug
up and relocated to make room for new white settlers. And almost a decade
later, just before Zambia gained independence from the British, Nkoloso and
his comrades had bribed a mortuary attendant in Lusaka to give them the
corpse of a white woman. They smeared goat's blood on it and transported
it to the whites-only Ridgeway Hotel. They turned out the lights in the bar
and threw the corpse on the floor. "This is the body of [Prime Minister Roy]
Welensky's wife," Nkoloso shouted. "We've just killed her. If you don't get
out of our country we will kill you too."

This was the same man with stars in his eyes? *This* was the "amiable lunatic" to whom journalists condescended as they roundly mocked his National Academy of Science, Space Research and Philosophy? I had dived into what seemed like a silly space opera only to find the corpses of colonial history there. The recurrence of this darkness—the darkness of death—prompted me to voyage into the heart of darkness to learn more.

***

Except that the heart of darkness, for me, is just home. On my next trip to Lusaka to visit my family, I made my way to the National Archives of Zambia. The Archives are not physically connected to a library, but rather housed in a 1970s-flavored concrete building quite close to the grand Anglican Cathedral, where my parents were married in the 1970s and where I went to Sunday School in the 1980s. In a small office, at a counter manned by diligent, impressively insouciant clerks, I filled out the first of many paper forms and paid the fee to register (discounted for me as a Zambian citizen). In passing, I asked the clerk about Nkoloso. Were there any files about his life or his space program? She raised an eyebrow. "Oh-*oh*? You're looking for Ba Nkoloso?" She smiled wryly and pointed around the corner. "We have a picture of him just there."

I strolled out into the lobby, where I found some peeling photocopies of black-and-white photos from the independence movement on the walls. A few displayed women—some bare-breasted—were holding signs: "TELL BRITAIN THE DAYS OF MISRULE ARE NUMBERED." "WE WANT SELF-GOVERNMENT." "NO ROOM FOR WHITE SETTLERS. U.N.I.P. SAYS KAUNDA KNOWS DEMOCRACY." In one picture, protestors carried a coffin on their shoulders, its side graffitied with the name "Roy Welensky": a mock burial of the prime minister whom Nkoloso had threatened at the Ridgeway with the borrowed white corpse of his "wife." Another picture showed President Kenneth Kaunda—or KK, as we call him—in front of a crowd. With him stood a man wearing an oversized army uniform, wielding a kind of paddle. Nkoloso! The caption identified him as a "late freedom fighter" and "firm supporter of Dr. Kaunda and UNIP." I remembered an article that said Nkoloso had been a kind of mascot for the United National Independence Party (UNIP). Here, he looked like what we now call a hype man—someone who rallies the crowd and introduces the main act. Nothing about outer space though.

I strolled back into the front office of the Archives. "Yes, but ... Isn't there anything else?" Heads shook slowly, shoulders shrugged languidly.

I requested one folder to which a historian had referred in an article, and searched for more leads in the xeroxed notebooks that serve as the Archive's catalogue of materials. I pressed my pen hard into the forms to make sure my call number requests showed up on the copies—there was an inky, slinky sheet between the two, a technology rarely seen these days beyond the occasional waiter's notepad or cab receipt. I sat at a large table in an over-air-conditioned, under-WiFi-ed reading room. I waited.

The folders—three at a time—that the clerk placed on the table in front me smelled of dust and the husks of dead insects. At first, there was nothing. Particularly disappointing was the thin folder for the "Lusaka Astronautical Society," which I had hoped might be an early version of the Zambian space program. The Society, "to promote the development of astronautics by the study of rocket engineering, space medicine and legislation, astronomy, navigation, astrionics, and other associated sciences," had apparently received government certification, but was cancelled in 1966 "due to no members." All the names on those documents sounded European—no Afronauts were these. I sent the folders back and filled out some more requests. This went on for a few chilly, rustling hours.

Finally, the folder on the Ndola Urban Council yielded some nuggets. Here was Nkoloso's name in the list of attendees at meetings with the British Colonial District Commissioner. Here were notes from the meetings, not direct transcriptions but with enough detail of syntax and diction to evoke a sense of a fiery young man standing up, raising objections, making requests, and, unlike his fellow council men, holding forth at length on the political bases of his arguments. At one point, Nkoloso predicted that the black and white races were destined to "become dialectic in the struggle for survival, to assimilate each other or co-existence will be at an end." Dialectic! *This* was the man they'd called "Zambia's village idiot"? There were no photocopiers so I typed notes on my laptop, manically transcribing until the archives closed for the day.

The next time I was home, on a whim, I asked for a folder provocatively titled "Luwingu Disturbance 1957"—Luwingu was the part of the country where Nkoloso had grown up. A box arrived rather than a folder. I opened it, itchy nose asneer. Then I sat up: "In a recent letter to His Excellency the Governor, Miss Audrey Richards wrote with reference to the death of Paulino Nseko, aunt of Makuka [*sic*] Nkoloso, following this woman's arrest after the Luena disturbances in the Luwingu District." Nkoloso's aunt? Death following arrest?

I went through the box, slowly piecing the story together. Caught up in arrests of miners on strike in the Copperbelt, Nkoloso had been sent back to his "home district" under house arrest. There, he urged locals to boycott the European store in town and to refuse to work as carriers, food servers, and census-takers for the British. He spoke publicly against the colonial government, the color bar (the African version of Jim Crow), and even the local chief, who, as Nkoloso put it, had "sold the country to the Europeans." These different factions—the freedom fighter and his people, the local chief, and the colonial officers—clashed dramatically in Luwingu, resulting in a warrant for Nkoloso's arrest, his escape into the bush, and his eventual capture at a mission school. He and his family and followers were arrested and jailed—and allegedly tortured in the process.

I pored over dozens of reports between colonial administrators, letters between members of Kaunda's independence party (then known as the African National Congress), and handwritten notes by Nkoloso himself from prison. He had even written to the Queen of England to seek legal aid under the Prisoners' Poor Society law. The authorities described him at one point as "a well-educated but unbalanced man," who was "imposing fear and gangster rule upon an otherwise peaceful and contented rural population." In the UNIP archives, housed in a dusty building on the other side of town, I found an onlooker's account of Nkoloso's arrest. It's handwritten, in blue ink, in far less fluent English than Nkoloso's, with delightful malapropisms, like "cloud" for the "crowd" that had surrounded and protected him. ("The cloud came and pushed him." "A cloud remained neutral.")

This report had clearly been doctored—edited in places, in a different handwriting and in black ink. The lines about the torture Nkoloso may have endured as a crusader for Zambian independence are crossed out, edited to concede only that the officers began "taking off his hair." There's a comment scrawled in the margins: "This was untrue but was said by the chiefs—This report covers the balance of the trouble as advanced from both sides." It was a perfect symbol of the Afronaut Archives as a whole: a hodgepodge of ink, a cacophony of claims, and in the words of its unknown annotator, a balance of trouble.

I confess, I caught a case of archive fever. But maybe just for *these* archives. The thing is, the documents about Nkoloso are especially conducive to the wonders of discovery for three reasons. Zambia is still understudied, especially our rich political and cultural history. So, there are many treasures to be unearthed in the archives. While the catalogues are hard to navigate, our archives are impressively complete—one legacy of British colonialism is that we are a people deeply committed to paperwork. There is a great deal of information but it hasn't yet been organized in a leading way. The documents are simply ordered chronologically—newest to oldest—which makes for an exciting backward investigation from ends to origins. And of course, Nkoloso is an incredible subject. He lived many lives—even more than Matha Mwamba's cats—and there are surprises around every corner.

***

You might think that writers conduct research in order and in earnest—that they gather materials, do interviews, read books, take notes. And only afterward is there a moment of integration where they put it all together and write the story or essay that incorporates all of those bits and bobs. My process is a lot less straightforward. For me, research is an ongoing process that both interrupts and feeds the writing. And the files and folders of research on my laptop look more like a jumbled drawer—with screenshots from Facebook groups, historical society bulletin boards, peer-reviewed articles, newspaper clippings, notes from interviews—than an organized file cabinet. Personal record-keeping, the archive, and collective memory all have important roles to play in preserving the details of life. Though I write in many different genres, including nonfiction journalism and speculative fiction, I'm always in pursuit of persuading the reader of what's possible. My historical research is a way to create a textural reality that undergirds the flights of fancy and philosophy in my writing.

I wrote a nonfiction piece about the Zambian space program for the *New Yorker*, which drew from the archives and from contemporaneous newspaper articles, as well as from my interviews with those who knew Nkoloso in his day, including his son and former president Kaunda. Even as I was writing that essay, I was already fictionalizing parts of Nkoloso's life and Matha Mwamba's life for my novel, *The Old Drift* (Hogarth, 2019). This led to a fortuitous coincidence between the research processes for the novel and for the essay. For both works of writing, I transcribed every document about Nkoloso that I found by typing it out on my laptop; I constructed a timeline of the events of his arrest, torture, and detainment; I extracted quotations that pertained to specific topics or that felt the most telling of his voice; and I thought long and hard about how to use the form and frame in each work to echo and re-enact the curiosity and wonder that Nkoloso's program continues to inspire.

The respective processes of research for the essay and for the novel diverged in three respects: verifying information, incorporating details, and constructing ambiguity about Nkoloso's program. The fact-checking that I went through for the *New Yorker* and my own efforts to confirm specific historical details were very different from the exploratory, haphazard process that I embarked on for the novel. Writing the article, there was due diligence involved: I had to set up contexts, like the political circumstances within which Nkoloso was working, in order to conjure a particular kind of persuasiveness. With the novel, much of the fact-checking happened retrospectively and came from readers, editors, my father. I'm deeply indebted to my Dutch translator, who had masses of questions, many of which Google couldn't answer, and who found misspellings of Zambian words that I had transcribed over from the erroneous history books. There are about 100 changes between the first and second editions of the novel.

The way that I incorporated these specific and (hopefully) accurate details into *The Old Drift* also entailed a different process from piecing together an argument for the essay. The essay—like this one—told the story of my discovery of Nkoloso and presented details as I uncovered them. In the novel, I chose to dramatize two moments in his life that felt the richest in detail and the most striking in action: his arrest at the mission school, and the recording of the footage of him training his cadets. I imposed my authorial prerogative to surround and infuse these scenes with intriguing quotations and facts from other sources, as well as entirely fictional scenes from Matha Mwamba's perspective: neither scene is an exact transcription of what happened. I also wrote a first-person interlude—which I later cut, along with three others in the respective voices of historical personages—that used language from Nkoloso's letters and interviews over the years, nearly all of which could be categorized as "complaints." This helped me figure out his verbal tics and beliefs so I could create sentences that he might have uttered.

For each genre, I chose a different structure to convey what I see as an intractable ambiguity about Nkoloso: was he mad? Or a genius? Was he serious? Or a prankster? Was the space program a con? Or a political movement in disguise? In the essay, I chose to present my evidence from various sources confirming each of these theories, and then, rather than deciding the issue, I analyzed what it might mean to view Nkoloso through a double lens. In the novel, I did something similar at greater length: I presented him from the point of view of Matha Mwamba, a true believer in the political revolution behind the program, but offered the points of view of others who genuinely believed in Nkoloso's mission to go to the moon. In one scene, I dramatized the uncertainty about Nkoloso's real purpose as the two sides of a lovers' quarrel.

In both pieces of writing, I tried to bring to life something a Zambian artist once said to me about our country: "We don't have a yes and a no. We have two yeses, and one of them means no." This epitomizes why Nkoloso has become the presiding spirit over my writing about Zambia. He had great historical and political significance. He also had great cultural and artistic significance. And he combined it with a Zambian sensibility that embraces the unknown in a subtle, ironic humor. His story feels like a precursor to all the speculative richness, complexity, and joy of Afrofuturism, a term that wasn't coined until thirty years after his space program.

I'm now expanding my essay about him into a full-length biography and a digital archive, which use his story as a way to explore civil disobedience and political pranks; Pan-Africanism and Marxism; gender and racial politics; science and technology; the intersection of protest and religion; and new theories of black subjectivity, culture, and art. Whether he was a kook, a crook, or an oracle, there are still so many facets of this remarkable man's life that I want the world to experience, so many quotations from his letters and interviews that call out to be heard. These documents are from the past, yet they feel like reports from a future Zambia.

9

Historical Fiction and the Fine
Art of Error

Bruce Holsinger

Nothing hurts a novelist more than a scathing review, and no scathing review hurts a historical novelist more than one expressed in the idiom of error. Anachronisms of style or technology, a misdating of a specific historical event, the flubbing of biographical details: verifiable errors in historical fiction can be profoundly undermining to a novelistic genre that prides itself on devotion to documentary veracity and conventional notions of archival rigor. While contemporary writers in the genre might live in fear of being called out by readers intent on tracking down anachronisms and howlers, the historical fiction of earlier eras was no less fraught with the anxiety of error. Consider an anonymous note evoking the historical fiction of the nineteenth-century writer Alfred de Vigny's *Cinq-Mars*, published in Balzac's *Le Feuilleton des journaux politiques* in 1830. Commenting on the novel's numerous historical fallacies—placing a named courtier in Chaumont when it was known he was in the Bastille at the time, introducing a mad spate of dancing in Richelieu's tent for the sole purpose of creating a sense of poetry—the reviewer faults Vigny above all for his betrayal of Truth (with a capital T):

> Finally, he had twisted the story like an old cloth that a sculptor uses to drape a young statue; he had seen some poetic scenes, and he had thrown them in the face of Truth, to convince us that artists live on lies, and that it is much less a question of putting the true in the false than the false in the truth.[1]

The reviewer's sculptural simile suggests a refined understanding of the relationship between fiction and falsification. Vigny's errors are artful, and deliberately so, creating their own twisted spectacle of a covered statue even as they mask the fresh face of *Verité*. If the author is successful in convincing

Bruce Holsinger, *Historical Fiction and the Fine Art of Error*. In: *Historical Fiction Now*. Edited by Mark Eaton and Bruce Holsinger, Oxford University Press. © Bruce Holsinger (2023). DOI: 10.1093/oso/9780198877035.003.0010 us that "artists live on lies," we the readers will suffer the fate of falsity, allowing the spells cast by the author's deceitful prose to mask the truth of the past. In another notice, a *Feuilleton* reviewer (perhaps the same anonymous critic) avows that one of Vigny's characters "resembles reality as the jeweled flowers of Fossin resemble the flowers of the fields."[2] Here, with reference to the famous jeweler Fossin, the reviewer implies that failed mimesis is an affordance of bad art, contaminated by deliberate artifice and pale imitation.

This chapter concerns the problem of error in historical fiction: error as a source of frustration but also beauty, pleasure, provocation, and marvelous invention. How are writers of fiction—people who fabricate for a living, and do it all the time, and try to sell their creative deceptions to readers and reviewers every day—equipped to think critically and creatively about the relationship between fiction and falsification or outright error? And how is the novelistic relation to these categories distinct from the critical or academic approach to error and its cousins? Criticism and fiction writing represent two distinct creative processes, of course, each with its own ways of knowing, and each with its own modes of making and unmaking the literary object. When it comes to historical fiction, critics and fiction writers have had distinctive but ultimately complementary relationships with the subject of error. As anyone who publishes historical fiction these days will tell you, readers in the genre delight in error every bit as much as they appreciate accuracy, an affinity they share with academic historians. In the nineteenth and twentieth centuries, one of the greatest insults a reviewer could hurl against a work of nonfiction historical scholarship was the sobriquet "historical fiction": as in, this book more closely resembles a work of historical fiction than a responsible work of historical scholarship, a discipline ideally free of the falsifications that characterize its fictional counterpart. In this respect, the culture of historical fiction participated in the same fetishization of error and its correction that Seth Lerer finds in the history of literary criticism: "the professionalization of literary study took shape through ... encounters with the erroneous: more specifically, through detailed engagements with the classical inheritance of rhetoric and philology."[3] The "academic's search for institutional and intellectual belonging" leads upward through a wild forest of error to the clear skies of fact-checked sublimity.[4]

The world of fiction writing is characterized by a somewhat different approach to error and fact, a sensibility more attuned to public shaming than professional failure, and in promoting a seamless relationship between aesthetics and rigor. But talk to enough writers in the genre and read enough self-reflective letters by past authors on its constraints and you will begin to see how the discourse of error and fact creates at times an ascetic culture of self-regulation, even self-censorship. The imperative to "get it right" functions as an archival superego that needles our souls with the fear of error as we knit together the facts and alternative facts that define the essence of our craft.

Let me offer a specific example that comes from my own experience as a writer of historical fiction with an academic background. The incident occurred years ago when my first novel was in production. At one point in the submission draft my protagonist, the medieval English poet John Gower, rides across the Thames in a barge with King Richard II, an incident based on a historical moment recounted in one of Gower's works.[5] During their conversation on the barge, Gower (again, in my early draft) twice addresses King Richard as "Your Majesty." It's the only conversation with the king represented in the novel, and I never thought twice about using that phrase. I had been studying and teaching the literature of the Ricardian era for a quarter century, and it never occurred to me that there would be anything wrong with using that phrase as a form of address to King Richard.

But when the manuscript went into production, I got a note from a copyeditor alerting me that "Your Majesty" when applied to the king before the sixteenth century was "a rather glaring error"—an anachronism that I should avoid at all costs. No, it's not, I thought, and simply scribbled a STET in the margin. The issue bubbled up to the level of an editor, who contacted me to let me know she trusted the copyeditor, who had convinced her that the phrase would need to go. We went back and forth a few more times until finally I was asked to consult a book called *Medieval Underpants and Other Blunders: A Writer's (& Editor's) Guide to Keeping Historical Fiction Free of Common Anachronisms, Errors, & Myths*, by Susanne Alleyn, a writer and critic who has published a number of novels set during the eighteenth century. Strongly advised to follow Alleyn's helpful guidance on the matter, I started reading *Medieval Underpants and Other Blunders*, beginning with the book's prologue: "this is not a book on how to write historical fiction," Alleyn writes. "There are many good books out there ... that do an excellent job of that. It is a book on how NOT to write historical fiction ... this guide is intended to point out, remind you about, and help you keep your historical fiction free of, not only the big honking howlers, but also the many, many lesser gaffes and howlers that keep turning up again and again in all kinds of Historical Fiction written by authors who should know better."[6] *Medieval Underpants* is currently in its third edition and from what I gather has become a widely respected resource for writers in the genre of historical fiction as a basic how-not-to-do book.

As I soon learned, the most pertinent section of the book for my purposes was a section called "Regarding Royalty," which addresses the historical point in question with an admirable precision:

> Regarding royalty
>
> Any movie or book in which somebody addresses an English king before 1534 as "Your Majesty" is probably getting it wrong, and before 1400 is definitely getting it wrong ... The facts: Henry VIII was the first English king to be officially styled "Majesty," after the 1534 Act of Supremacy that declared Henry supreme head of the Church in England and equal in earthly status to an emperor ... if your novel is set before 1400, always stick with "Sire" or "Your Grace" when someone is talking to the king.[7]

Well geez, I thought. I guess I lose.

But Alleyn's confidence here didn't sit right with me, and there was also something about the subject itself that was itching at my brain—I just couldn't give up yet. I probably could have found what I needed on Google Books, but I had a particular source in mind that I wanted to check, so I went to my university library, and ten minutes later had in hand two well-respected biographies of Richard II and another book on the political rhetoric of his reign. After a few minutes of paging around, I found a letter of petition to Richard from the House of Commons in 1391:

> To the most excellent and most renowned and most excellent prince, and most gracious lord, our lord the king, we your humble lieges the commons of your realm of England, that it should please *your highness and royal majesty* ... to grant the petitions that follow.[8]

There are dozens more extant examples of "your majesty" as a form of address for King Richard, in Middle English, Anglo-Norman French (as here), and Latin; the phrase appears in letters, in headings to petitions, in chronicles of Richard's reign written by historians who were alive in those decades, and any number of other sources. Beginning in the mid-1380s, Richard began to adopt the honorific "Your Majesty" as a way of invoking what Nigel Saul has called the "theocratic character" of royal authority: a "new vocabulary of address" to emphasize the king's status as *semideus* or a godlike, all-powerful ruler.[9] For a novel set right during these years, "Your

Majesty" was not only correct but perhaps essential to getting across the increasingly despotic ambience of Richard's reign.

Imagine my delight when I confirmed my suspicions. Not only was Susanne Alleyn wrong, she was spectacularly wrong—because it was in those very years just before 1400 when the king of England was actively working to get himself addressed as "Your Majesty." It thrilled me to discover how error-filled her own book had proved, and to mansplain my own correctness over the phone to my editor, with a little righteous shiver at the cycle of pleasure and error at work in this process. Think about it: my copy-editor discovers a putative error and calls me on it by referring me to a book devoted to correcting common errors in historical fiction; I in turn defend my putative error by drawing on my well-honed skills in primary academic research to correct a clear error in this supposedly error-*correcting* book on "medieval underpants and other blunders."

The sad ending to this story is that I wimped out. It was my first novel, after all, and I was reminded that a little bit of knowledge is a dangerous thing. If strong conventional wisdom dictates that "Your Majesty" doesn't belong in a book set in the fourteenth century, then you as author have to ask yourself, Is the retention of the phrase important enough to risk the uninformed ire of readers and reviewers, especially (shiver) English ones? Probably not, and the exchange between Gower and the king didn't rely on that particular form of address to get its point across. So I set it aside, tweaked a few sentences, and let the matter rest.

One of the reasons the episode has stayed with me is that it spoke to both my creative and scholarly selves, to my avocation as a writer of historical fiction and my profession as a literary historian, as well as to that dynamic between the making or invention of literary objects on the one hand, and the difficult process of their unmaking or unmasking in the act and form of scholarship on the other. I use the term *invention* deliberately to get at the rhetorical dimensions of historical fiction. In the classical rhetorical tradition, invention was one of the five canons of rhetoric (along with arrangement, style, memory, and delivery) that ideally shaped the public life of political and legal discourse, defined very broadly to include forensic rhetoric, declamations in the Roman Senate, and, later during the medieval era, even the hortatory structure of religious sermons and the writing of epistles. As Cicero defined it, invention is "the conceiving of topics either true or probable, which may make one's cause appear probable."[10] Crucially, for Cicero and for other Roman rhetoricians, the discursive conditions of a fact or a truth are as much a part of how we argue as the facts themselves. Historical fiction provides an odd, jarring perspective on this dynamic given the oxymoronic nature of the form: it's both history (what actually happened) and fiction (made up). Writers in the genre are always dealing on some level with the problem of invention: where do you get the historical stuff, the archival matter, that you're going to write about in your novel, and how do you begin thinking about its relative claims to authority and persuasion?

My own historical novels feature characters like John of Gaunt, Kathryn Swynford, and Richard II, figures whose lives we can trace in some detail in the historical record; they are populated with medieval poets such as John Gower and Geoffrey Chaucer, intellectuals such as Ralph Strode (an Oxford philosopher who may also have served as common serjeant of London for a period in the 1380s), and commoners like John or Eleanor Rykener, a sex worker apprehended in Cheapside and interrogated at the Guildhall during the same period.[11] Some of the same poets and thinkers I've written about in my scholarship figure in my novels as human beings endowed with emotions, articulated desires, intimate relationships with family and friends; and the world in which I imagine and place them is similarly filled with material objects and built environments that give sensual depth to their reinvented lives, to such an extent that my academic and fiction writing converge in unexpected ways.

But this is not the kind of writing I was ever "trained" to do, and it's not the kind of writing that defines my everyday profession. I've spent most of my career as a literary critic and a teacher of literature *taking apart* stories: questioning their logic, sifting their false moves and unacknowledged ideologies, the cognitive and creative errors that allow me to catch them and their authors out. To go from this kind of critical practice to the writing of realist and plot-driven fiction is to embrace a mode of written expression and a form of thought that have been trained out of our critical souls. Members of my generation of literature Ph.D. students were trained in what critics like to call the hermeneutics of suspicion. We were taught to be skeptical of any claims to narrative coherence, let alone the self-knowing narrative perspectives demanded by the form and style of the realist novel—a skepticism that cuts across numerous disciplines and schools of thought. The problem of suspicion is especially acute for me given that my historical novels are historical thrillers: on some level they're detective fiction, and as Rita Felski puts it, "*like the detective, the critical reader is intent on tracking down a guilty party.* Suspicion sets in motion a search for agents who can be held to account for acts of wrongdoing ... Why is it that critics are so quick off the mark to inter-rogate, unmask, expose, subvert, unravel, demystify, destabilize, take issue, and take umbrage?"[12]

Yet recreating the culture of medieval England has forced me precisely to suspend suspicion and skepticism in order to imagine a world I have always studied and taught from a critical distance, albeit with much affection for the literary objects in front of me. The writing of historical fiction places the author in the position very much like where the English philosopher R. G. Collingwood once placed the historian. "The history of thought, and there-fore all history," Collingwood wrote, "is the reenactment of past thought in the historian's own mind."[13] A writer of historical fiction, which demands the re-enactment of thoughts, feelings, and actions grounded in the conjured and manipulated points of view of specific historical personages, is bound to the conventions of a genre founded on subjectivity and storytelling in a very traditional, small-c conservative sense. When you write it you find yourself suddenly embracing the intentional fallacy; you become an unreconstructed humanist, imagining and making these characters as if they are your friends, indeed as if they are *you*. To me these people, this fiction-built world, are as real as it gets.

But then like anyone writing fiction I step back and see that it's all a fab-rication, or at least most of it is. Because one of your tasks as a historical novelist is to deceive to your audience—and deceive, repeatedly and con-vincingly, the very readers invested in the accuracy and verifiability of your re-creation of a particular moment in history. If you choose to write histor-ical fiction, you will constantly be treading those fine lines between the true and the accurate, the verifiable and the plausible.

Consider that founding proposition at the origin of nearly every histori-cal novel: that singular moment of intuition and invention, when an author asks the simple question, What if, at a certain point in the past ...? These moments go something like this: We know that the medieval poets Geoffrey Chaucer and John Gower were longtime friends and read one another's work in draft form, yet that both had significant misgivings about the manuscript culture in which they wrote. So, what if these two writers became involved in the search for a perilous manuscript of shadowy origin with potentially dire consequences for the realm? That's the premise of my first novel, *A Burnable Book*. Another one: we know that the Underground Railroad was a network of safe houses and back roads conveying thousands of slaves to freedom in the North. But what if "railroad" weren't a metaphor, and the phrase instead referred to an actual subterranean network of tracks and trains? The premise of *The Underground Railroad* by Colson Whitehead. A third: We know that the French coastal town of Saint-Malo was nearly destroyed by American and British forces late in 1944. But what if the blind daughter of a Parisian watchmaker and a gadget-obsessed German orphan met in the town's ashes in a moment of profound sorrow and glimmering hope? *All the Light We Cannot See*, by Anthony Doerr. And just one final example: we know that two men living in a midwestern college town were arrested and prosecuted and eventually convicted for trying to send weapons and money to agents of a hostile foreign entity. But what if those two men had instead attacked the citizens of this town, Bowling Green, Ohio, in a brutal massacre of its American inhabitants?

This was the premise behind Kellyanne Conway's uncompleted work of historical fiction, the massacre at Bowling Green, based on a fabricated incident she trotted out in an interview on MSNBC in 2017, early in the Trump administration: "It's brand new information to people," Conway avowed, "that President Obama had a six-month ban on the Iraqi refugee program after two Iraqis came here to this country, were radicalized, and they were the masterminds behind the Bowling Green Massacre." While Conway claimed a one-time misspeak, she had made a nearly identical claim several days earlier in an interview with *Cosmopolitan*; as she put it in that exchange, "two Iraqi nationals came to this country, joined ISIS, traveled back to the Middle East to get trained and refine their terrorism skills and came back here and were the masterminds behind the Bowling Green massacre ... taking innocent soldiers' lives away."[14]

I am enlisting the Bowling Green Massacre here not to be flip or glib, but to make a point about the imaginative mechanism that allowed Conway's erroneous invention to take on the life that it did. The thought process that leads Conway from a set of raw data to an invented historical incident casts in miniature the process that guides a historical novelist: a set of historical givens (in this case two Iraqi citizens were in fact arrested, tried, and imprisoned for conspiracy to aid and abet al-Qaeda in Iraq) spun into an elaborate and embellished narrative that seeks to recast a past moment through a set of alternative facts that were greeted appropriately with memorial markers, appeals to sentiment and patriotism, and other tongue-in-cheek acts of homage to Conway's faux history.

All politicians are liars, of course, though not all lies are created equal, and not all political lies are signs of malice or ill intent—so argues the intellectual historian Martin Jay in *The Virtues of Mendacity: On Lying in Politics*, which investigates the power and the importance of political lying, a tradition of deliberate, tactical untruth that goes back to the beginning of politics in the Western tradition. Jay identifies an uneasy distinction between fictionality and lying, a distinction never as clear cut as some thinkers and writers want it to be. As he argues, *intentional* fiction in forms like the novel is rescued from the charge of mendacity or deliberate error by a recognizable aesthetic framework: we all know we're reading fiction, so there's no expectation of verifiable truth on the reader's part. But this kind of logic doesn't exactly work for historical fiction, which virtually never reveals those moments that demand the reader's suspension of disbelief about the historical record, which it manipulates and falsifies mercilessly.

Other critics have similarly opposed fact and fiction as alternative ways of accessing some version of truth. Here is Donna Haraway in an influential discussion of the subject:

> Fiction's kinship to facts is close, but they are not identical twins. Facts are opposed to opinion, to prejudice, but not to fiction. Both fiction and fact are rooted in an epistemology that appeals to experience. However, there is an important difference; the word *fiction* is an active form, referring to a present act of fashioning, while *fact* is a descendant of a past participle, a word form which masks the generative deed or performance. A fact seems done and unchangeable, fit only to be recorded; fiction seems always inventive, open to other possibilities, other fashionings of life. But in this opening lies the threat of merely feigning, of not telling the true form of things.[15]

Haraway posits fact and fiction alike as processes contributing in their different ways to the forms of truth, though Latinists will note the pleasing error in her etymological distinction. Both terms are nouns built on past participles of verbs: "fiction" is derived from *fingo, fingere, finxi, fictum*, which gives us the Latin noun *fictio fictiones*; while "fact" derives from *facio, facere, feci, factum*, to make or craft. Both words, then, connote something made, or something made up: an object, that is, of invention.

Does this mean that any "fact" is just as fictional as fiction itself, or that fiction is necessarily a form of falsehood or even purposeful error as much as it aspires to telling difficult truths? As Nietzsche writes in *The Will to Power*:

> In opposition to Positivism, which halts at phenomena and says: "There are only facts and nothing more," I would say: No, facts is precisely what is lacking, all that exists consists of *interpretations*. We cannot establish any fact "in itself": it may even be nonsense to desire to do such a thing.

"Everything is *subjective*," ye say: but that in itself is *interpretation*. The "subject" is nothing given, but something superimposed by fancy, something introduced behind.—Is it necessary to set an interpreter behind the interpretation already to hand? Even that would be fantasy, hypothesis.[16]

Modern and contemporary theory is populated with many such notes of skepticism about the fixity or non-givenness of facts. Thus Judith Butler, invoking Monique Wittig, avows that "language is a set of acts, repeated over time, that produce reality-effects that are eventually misperceived as 'facts.'"[17] Such observations feed a common anxiety that there may be a finer line between scare-quoted facts and alternative facts than we want to admit. No coincidence that a debating expert on a *Vox* piece about Conway attributed her loose relationship with facts to "an almost 'postmodern' ability to recreate reality."[18] Now, the strawman charge of moral and empirical relativism has underpinned assaults on theoretical discourse for a long time, from conservatives and progressives alike; it's been a staple of polemic on the humanities since at least the 1980s, the Sokal Hoax, and the so-called theory wars.[19] I'm not suggesting for a minute that we abandon these schools of critical thought for a bland, less suspicious substitute. But perhaps we might leaven our lavishly theorized dough of scare-quoted facts with a healthy measure of fiction, which teaches us that there are other, equally inventive ways of accounting for alternative facts in our increasingly post-critical age.

Some of the most revealing of these fictional modes emerge within the rhetorical tradition itself: the canons of invention, arrangement, and style underpinning the idioms of common law and other legal traditions of the Common Era. The phrase "alternative facts," it turns out, has a long and proud genealogy in anglophone legal tradition, both civil and criminal, dating back to the middle of the nineteenth century—not coincidentally, I think, the heyday of the historical novel. "The main allegation in the new pleading," a Supreme Court of New York practice report from 1860 puts it, "is put in a form which cannot be verified, or rather which renders the allegation itself true, because it is that of a dilemma, and is wholly independent of either knowledge or information of either [of] the alternative facts assumed by it."[20] The phrase appears as well in a South African Supreme Court case from 1920 concerning a claim against a life insurance company:

A plaintiff may, of course, insert in his declaration an alternative claim which will take effect in the event of his not proving all the facts alleged, but only some of them; or he may allege additional or alternative facts which are not inconsistent with one another and on which he founds an alternative claim. But he cannot allege inconsistent facts or facts which are mutually contradictory.[21]

In this case the clear implication is that alternative facts must be consistent with other, previously offered facts, or at least that these alternative facts subsequently presented must not contradict those subtending the original claim. An alternative fact, then, is not a contradiction, it's just a different way of advancing the same claim—an element within a given case that goes to a distinctive, perhaps more compelling story.

An equally illuminating example comes from *The Complete Litigator*, a book about reality, perception, and persuasion in the culture of litigation. Here the authors promote alternative facts as instrumental to successful argument:

> Every expert's testimony is based on a certain set of facts processed in a particular way. You need to identify the facts upon which the expert bases his or her theory and shift alternative facts into the equation. Then, uncover contradictory facts with the help of your own expert, who also relies on a particular set of facts. Similarly, test the opposing expert's method by illustrating other methods that would produce a contrary result. Confront the opposing expert with the alternative facts, and ask that expert to consider his theory when the facts are changed.[22]

The phrase "alternative facts" appears here twice, both times to denote a certain array of new information shifted into an argumentative equation.

The key underlying concept here, of course, is plausibility—or to go back to Cicero, the appearance of probity or truth. In law the courtroom setting provides an acid test of plausibility; plausibility is similarly the acid test of historical fiction, as its earliest readers were anxiously aware. Indeed, this discomfort with "facts" as intermingled with "fiction" riled many critics of the genre in the first decades of the historical novel. A similar discomfort informs a commentary on *Cicely, or the Rose of Raby*, a 1795 "historic novel," as its title page called it, by Agnes Musgrave. The review appeared in the *Critical Review* the year following the novel's publication:

> It has been frequently and justly observed, that the mixture of truth which renders a historical novel interesting, makes it also deceptive. It is certain that the facts which are interwoven in the tissue of fiction have a tendency

to bewilder the youthful mind;—yet it is a question requiring some casu-
istry to solve, whether the writer who, by deviating into the regions of fancy,
awakens and calls into exercise the more exalted energies of the human
mind,—does not really benefit his species more than the plain narrator
of those sordid and disgusting facts which so frequently stain the page of
history. We do not mean to be the apologist of falsehood: but the title of
Novel or Romance, though affixed to the term Historical, ought in reality
to deceive no one.[23]

Striking here is the attribution of bewilderment and deception to the facts
and truths enlisted in historical fiction, as opposed to those unmannered
facts we find in the domain of history proper. Note the gendering of this
opposition: fancy and fact, sordid and romantic, exaltation and disgust:
while the historical novel interweaves its facts into the tissue of fiction in
the manner of a domestic textile, the "page of history" is stained by the "sordid and disgusting facts" presented in the voice of a "plain" narrator. Only
sophism can resolve the question of historical fiction's relative "truthiness":
indicative of the era's ambivalence toward the emerging genre. Consider
another famous review of an early historical novel, this one of Sir Walter
Scott's *Waverley*, a foundational text of the genre:

We confess that we have, speaking generally, a great objection to what may
be called historical romance, in which real and fictitious personages, and
actual and fabulous events are mixed together to the utter confusion of the
reader, and the unsettling of all accurate recollections of past transactions;
and we cannot but wish that the ingenious and intelligent author of Waverley had rather employed himself in recording *historically* the character and
transactions of his countrymen *Sixty Years since*, than in writing a work,
which, though it may be, in its facts, almost true, and in its delineations
perfectly accurate, will yet, in sixty years *hence*, be regarded, or rather,
probably, *disregarded*, as a mere romance, and the gratuitous invention of
a facetious fancy.[24]

The juxtaposition of the "almost true" and the "perfectly accurate" reflects a
near obsession with the status of the fact that comes out even in the subtitles
of early historical novels, as in the case of Maria Edgeworth's *Castle Rackrent:
An Hibernian Tale taken from Facts, and the Manners of the Irish Squires,
before the year 1782*, published in 1801.

So how does this fiction of plausibility work in practice and on the page? One could cite innumerable examples illustrating the strange alchemy of fact and fiction in the historical novel, or what we might call the deceptive arts of research. In *Midnight's Children*, Salman Rushdie interweaves passages lifted straight from academic history to inflect the political register of his characters' consciousness, counterpoising the sober historical prose of Stanley Wolpert's *A New History of India* (Oxford University Press, 1977) against the emotive tone of a birth during the Partition.[25] Pat Barker's *Regeneration* begins with a word-for-word transcription of Siegfried Sassoon's notorious "Finished With the War; A Soldier's Declaration," which Barker uses to stage the initial exchange between two characters over Sassoon's psychological state.[26] In each case these novels put before us a set of archival "facts," derived from a specific written document or historiographical source, even while subjecting the archive to critique and transforming it in uncanny ways through invention and even apparent error.[27]

I conclude with a more extended example, which comes from Hilary Mantel's *Bring Up the Bodies*. Written in a present-tense, third-person point of view from the perspective of Thomas Cromwell, the novel treats the events leading up to the imprisonment of Anne Boleyn in the Tower of London in 1536 and her subsequent execution. For one of the novel's culminating scenes, Mantel drew on the text of a letter written by William Kingston, the Constable of the Tower of London, on May 19, the day of Anne Boleyn's execution. The original letter, addressed to Cromwell, relates an exchange Kingston had with Boleyn during her final hours, and it seems intended to let Cromwell know the queen's state of mind as she awaits her death:

> This morning she sent for me, that I might be with her at such time as she received the good Lord to the intent I should hear her speaking as touching her innocence always to be clear. And in the writing of this she sent for me, and at my coming she said. Mr. Kingston I hear I shall not die afore noon, and I am very sorry therefore, for I thought to be dead by this time and past my pain. I told her it should be no pain, it was so little. And then she said, I heard say the executor was very good, and I have a little neck. And then put her hands about it, laughing heartily. I have seen many men and also women executed, and that they have been in great sorrow, and to my knowledge this lady has much joy in death.[28]

The letter portrays an extraordinary moment in the story of Anne Boleyn's life and death, always evoked by biographers as a sign of her pathos, her strength, perhaps her madness in her final hours. A prisoner about to be executed, putting her hands around her throat, even making a joke about the delicacy of her neck, suggesting that it shouldn't give the executioner much trouble.

Yet this whole account derives from a letter from Kingston to Cromwell, who had to be elsewhere when Anne spoke these notorious words. How do we know this? Because the Constable of the Tower was sending letters to him every day reporting from the Tower on Anne's circumstances and state of mind—and one of these letters is this one, containing the sole in-the-moment attestation of Anne's gallows humor about her little neck. While Cromwell is recorded as present during Anne's execution, the historical record doesn't tell us whether he visited her in the Tower during the period of her confinement, and almost certainly not on her last morning; and even if he had, he almost certainly wouldn't have heard these words from her mouth as Kingston had reported them.[29]

Almost certainly. But consider what Mantel does with this bit of Tudor archival facticity. Unlike the events narrated in Kingston's historical letter—written, again, on the very day of the execution with all its emotional immediacy—the novelized scene takes place several days earlier, when Cromwell himself visits Boleyn in her imprisonment. The passage comes at a moment of extraordinary tension, when Cromwell hesitates, full of doubt about the wisdom of the king's actions, knowing he may still possess the power to get Anne's sentence commuted and prevent her death—and for an instant it looks like he actually considers it:

It is a long moment. He feels himself on the edge of something unwelcome: superfluous knowledge, useless information. He turns, hesitates, and reaches out, tentative ...

But then she raises her hands and clasps them at her breast, in the gesture Lady Rochford had showed him. Ah, Queen Esther, he thinks. She is not innocent; she can only feign innocence. His hand drops to his side. He turns away. He knows her for a woman without remorse. He believes she would commit any sin or crime. He believes she is her father's daughter, that never since childhood has she taken any action, coaxed or coerced, that might damage her own interests. But in one gesture, she has damaged them now.

She has seen his face change. She steps back, puts her hand around her throat: like a strangler she closes them around her own flesh. "I have only a little neck," she says. "It will be the work of a moment."

Kingston hurries out to meet him; he wants to talk. "She keeps doing that. Her hands around her neck. And laughing." His honest gaoler's face is dismayed. "I cannot see that it is any occasion for laughter."[30]

The presence of Cromwell heightens the terrifying immediacy of Anne's words, of course, and you can sympathize with a novelist's desire to go with this particular alternative fact: how could Mantel's viewpoint character *not* be present to hear Anne's most famous and notorious pronouncement? How could such a ghoulish sentiment *not* be spoken in the narrative present of the novel? And the only way this can happen is if Cromwell is there, which he almost certainly wasn't.

The key sentence here, the sentence that allows the novel to get away with this seeming outrage against the archive, is "She keeps doing that." Those are Kingston's words to Cromwell upon leaving Anne's rooms in the Tower, and they leave the impression that Anne has expressed this same sentiment before, and perhaps will do so again—perhaps, indeed, on the very day of her death, so that Kingston can write about the exchange to Cromwell, as in fact he will do, and did do, on May 19, 1536.

She keeps doing that: One of the reasons Mantel was able to get away with this astonishing bit of trickery is the mechanism of the distantly plausible this sentence exploits (let's call it the writerly subjunctive, and any novelist knows it well: *Mmm, I guess it COULD have happened that way ...*). The sentence tells you everything you need to know about how historical fiction should approach the archive, honoring the historical contract it draws with the reader even while looking constantly for escape clauses, skirting along the boundaries of the feasible and the erroneous. The myriad inventions of historical fiction carry with them a critical capacity inherent to the genre at its best. *She keeps doing that*: Maybe this is one of the reasons Kellyanne Conway is no Hillary Mantel. It's not just that she was lying about the Bowling Green Massacre, feeding us alternative facts that turn out not to be true or accurate; more devastatingly, it's that her fictions aren't plausible. Because historical fiction models or should model a certain creative and critical humility with respect to the bare facts of history, which are never unmediated or uncontestable, of course, yet demand some ethical recognition or accounting for within the built world limned in fiction. If the genre's capacities for suspicion are always more implicit and differently inventive than in the domain of criticism, this should not keep us from recognizing the vitality of historical fiction as a powerful lens on the thrilling contingency of error even in its most peculiar and provocative guise.

PART III

GENRES

10

Historical Fiction, World-Building, and the Short Story

Gavin Jones

On the evening of November 26, 1933, a crowd gathered outside the Santa Clara County Jail in San Jose, California. It wanted blood. Inside were two local men, Thomas Harold Thurmond, an unemployed house painter, and John Maurice Holmes, a Union Oil salesman, who were being held awaiting trial for the kidnapping and murder of another San Jose resident, the 22-year-old Brooke Hart. Hart was son of a famous San Jose family, and heir to a fortune founded in Hart's Department Store, an institution in downtown San Jose, and a symbol of the family's civic prominence in the successful and growing city. By all accounts, Hart was a likeable and popular young man. He was kidnapped on November 9, 1933 on leaving the store, after which the family received a number of ransom notes and calls. Thurmond and Holmes were arrested for the kidnapping in mid-November, after the police traced Thurmond's ransom call to the Harts, at which point Thurmond made a confused confession, naming Holmes as his accomplice (Holmes initially refuted the accusation and claimed innocence, supported by strong alibis). Media interest in the crime was intense, with transcripts of the confessions, full of gory details, appearing on the front pages of the major newspapers. Amid a national backlash against a slew of kidnappings in the 1930s, newspapers called for the severest punishment for the accused. When the disfigured corpse of Hart was discovered by two duck hunters on November 26, public calls erupted for the lynching of the accused men, fueled by rumors of an insanity plea. Rounded up from the bars, urged on by local media, and with the tacit approval of California governor James Rolph, Jr., a mob stormed the jail, broke down the door with a length of pipe, assaulted the sheriff and deputy sheriff, and dragged Thurmond and Holmes—the former unconscious by this time, the latter resisting all the way—to adjacent

Gavin Jones, *Historical Fiction, World-Building, and the Short Story.* In: *Historical Fiction Now.*
Edited by Mark Eaton and Bruce Holsinger, Oxford University Press. © Gavin Jones (2023).
DOI: 10.1093/oso/9780198877035.003.0011

St. James Park, where the two battered, partly naked men were hung from trees before a crowd that may have been as large as 15,000 onlookers, making it about the size of the larger "lynch carnivals" of the 1930s (see Fig. 10.1).[1]

Fig. 10.1 San Jose, California: November 27, 1933. The body of John Holmes, alleged kidnapper and slayer of Brooke Hart, shown after a mob which dragged him from the county jail had completed its work. © Underwood Archives/age fotostock.

John Steinbeck would turn these historical events into fiction in his short story "The Vigilante," written in 1934—when the events were still fairly fresh—first published in *Esquire* magazine (as "The Lonesome Vigilante") in 1936, and eventually included as the eighth story of *The Long Valley* (1938), Steinbeck's major collection of short stories published a year before *The Grapes of Wrath* (1939). Steinbeck was no stranger to turning historical events into fiction. Steinbeck's novel *In Dubious Battle* (1936) used incidents that Steinbeck gathered from a strike of cotton pickers near Fresno, California. *The Grapes of Wrath* was based generally on the plight of Oklahoman migrants fleeing the Dust Bowl, and more specifically, a major episode in the novel drew directly from what Steinbeck called "great gobs" of information that he gleaned from his friend Tom Collins's documentary reports of conditions in the Weedpatch migrant labor camp near Bakersfield, California.[2] Perhaps one of the reasons why *Grapes* had such a social impact, leading to the formation of government committees to investigate the labor conditions it represented, was the immediacy of its relationship to historical events. As Steinbeck commented to his agent, Elizabeth Otis, concerning an earlier draft of *Grapes*: "I'm trying to write history while it is happening and I don't want to be wrong."[3] Another reason why the novel gained factual weight was its very status *as* a novel. Written quickly, in approximately 100 days, *Grapes* was also written slowly as Steinbeck attempted to paint a detailed picture for the reader. "Must take time in the description, detail, looks, clothes, gestures," he wrote in the journal he kept while writing the novel. He worked to pile on details slowly until "the whole throbbing thing emerges."[4] A reason why *Grapes* stands as historical fiction ("I have never believed that *The Grapes of Wrath* was exaggerated," commented Eleanor Roosevelt)[5] is its employment of world-building techniques inherent in the novel as a genre.

As Yi-Ping Ong has argued from an existential perspective, novels tend to assume a totality and autonomy, a completeness of readerly experience that is related to the free, inward subject of liberalism and to the novel's ability to make knowable (and hence to sanction) the larger classes and institutions of which it is part.[6] Novels are primed to fictionalize historical experience in part because of their capacities of length and accumulated detail—Ong points to the Victorian novel's rendering of very large, completely described spaces, lending them an effect of "clotted thingness"[7]—that allow for the reader's immersion in specific situations and close identification with the lives of characters. But what of the short story? How does it, as a genre, bring history and fiction together? Or rather, what *kind* of history do we receive within the spatial and temporal limitations of the short story? Do we simply get "less" history, a miniature version, or is it inherently history of a different type? My chapter suggests some answers to these questions by looking in detail at the close and fraught relationship between Steinbeck's "The Vigilante" and the historical record, particularly regarding the questions of race with which Steinbeck grappled in his story.

Steinbeck undoubtedly knew the details of the Hart kidnapping and the Thurmond–Holmes lynching that took place in the hometown of Steinbeck's wife, Carol Henning. The story of the crime and lynching was all over the newspapers, both locally and nationally, not least because of the political circus that followed the lynching when Governor Rolph applauded the actions of the mob and was roundly condemned by President Franklin Roosevelt and former President Herbert Hoover. There are numerous parallels between Steinbeck's story and what we know of the events of the evening from various newspaper accounts. The locations are similar, the park (the scene of the lynching) being directly opposite the jail; the hang trees are elms in both factual and fictional accounts. The details of the extraction of the victims from the jail are very similar too: in both instances the jail door is battered down by the mob, which at first mistakenly identifies the wrong prisoner, finally knocking the victim (Thurmond in the real events) unconscious in the cell before dragging him out. Steinbeck's use of the term "driving line" to describe the rushing mob suggests a direct borrowing from records of the actual event, in which sporting cries of "We want a touchdown" and "Hold that line!" marked the holiday-like atmosphere.[8] The breaking of streetlights, the stripping of the victim (Holmes in the real events), and the attempts to burn the victim's body are common to both fictional and historical versions, as is the subsequent obsession with obtaining souvenirs of the horrific proceedings.[9] In Steinbeck's version, however, there are not two victims of the lynching, only one. And he is not white, as were Thurmond and Holmes. The victim of the lynching, in Steinbeck's story, is a single, African American man.

But he wasn't always black. At the beginning of the Long Valley ledger—the manuscript of this and a number of other stories—Steinbeck lists "The Vigilante" as the final story completed in Summer 1934, giving it a culminating role in a series of stories that comprise the bulk of *The Long Valley*.[10] In this accounting, "The Vigilante" follows the stories "Flight" and "Johnny Bear," but in the manuscript ledger "Flight" is actually followed by an earlier, incomplete draft of "The Vigilante," or rather a quite different story based on similar events and ideas, an unpublished story called "Case

History." "Flight"—the third story of *The Long Valley*—ends with the death of Pepé Torres, a young Mexican American who murders a man (presumably a white man, or at least, as Pepé recounts the events to his mother, someone who "said names to me I could not allow") in a bar fight. He is subsequently pursued by nameless vigilante assassins into the mountains, where Pepé is gradually reduced to an animal in his desperate attempt to escape. When Pepé is finally shot by his pursuers (in the history of lynching in the West, those identified as Latin American or Mexican comprised the largest group of victims, followed closely by whites),[11] the language of a more conventional lynching shimmers behind the description: his "body jarred back ... Pepé swung forward and toppled."[12] Immediately following the end of "Flight" in the manuscript ledger, divided by an elaborate hashtag, comes Steinbeck's realization of his next lynching story:

> New work. One story which occurred to me last night is so delicate and difficult that I don't feel justified in taking regular work time to it. If I do it, it will be at night on my own time. This is not a time for experiments on company time. There is too much work to get out. This monday afternoon must be given to working out this weeks [*sic*] story and perhaps beginning it. New pen now. Gold colored one. It probably isn't gold. The back of it writes nice and fine though. Running all day today and is fine. Caught a whole can full of snails. The bottom of my stomach is dropping out with accumulated loneliness—not loneliness that might be mended with company either. I think Carol is the same way. There's a haunted quality in her eyes. I'm not good company to her. I can't help her loneliness and she can't help mine. Perhaps this is a good thing. It may presume some kind of integrity. Maybe it is exactly that kind of hunger that keeps us struggling on. I must get on to work. I'm wasting time now. Only work cures the gnawing. Maybe the work of last week wasn't good but the doing of it was good. I'll shave. That will make me feel better.
>
> —John Ramsey—hated the war and misses it. Came home to the quiet, the lack of design for the war was a huge design. Wanders lost on his farm looking for a phalanx to join and finds none. Is nervous and very lost. Finally finds the movement in a lynching. War shock not so much war as the ceasing of war drive. Hunger for the group. Change of drive. What does it matter. The mob is not a wasteful thing but an efficient thing.[13]

This personal aside is typical of Steinbeck's process of composition. Steinbeck's writing was often a kind of dialogue, either with himself as in this

case, or with specific individuals to whom he would attempt to explain concepts and to overcome the loneliness of writing. Always so concerned with
the tools of his trade and with his rate of production, Steinbeck turns to the
task of work as an answer to his existential crisis. But work is not the right
word for this new story, an experiment that is not only difficult but *delicate*:
deeply intimate and personal. He shaves to prepare himself to tackle a question that can only be whispered to oneself in the dead of night. What does it
feel like to participate in a lynching?

At least in obvious details, the protagonist of "Case History," John Ramsey, is quite different from Mike, the central character in "The Vigilante,"
although the name *Ramsey* does predict Mike's role as the front end of
a human battering ram that knocks down the jailhouse door. Ramsey is
explicitly a shell-shocked veteran of the Great War, which places the setting
of the story back in the late 1910s or early 1920s. The story seems retrospective in terms of its place in literary history too. We might think of John
Ramsey as an echo of Harold Krebs in Ernest Hemingway's "Soldier's Home"
(1925), a classic story of trauma in which everything Krebs has experienced
in the war is necessarily absent, displaced onto a need for order found in
Krebs's fascination with the patterns on women's dresses or with the rules
of a softball game.[14] Hemingway's story works by implication and omission,
but Steinbeck's draft reads more like the details are still being worked out by
the writer himself. The plot is a clumsy effort to place Ramsey in a position
to explain Steinbeck's theories of collective action to the reader. Ramsey's
shellshock gradually develops, he goes to the hospital to treat his nervous-
ness, and then temporarily leaves his wife to live alone in a cabin on a nearby
hill where he can read and think. Steinbeck seems eager to take Ramsey to
a place where he can discuss matters at length, in an extension of the dia-
logic mode in which Steinbeck often contemplated the relationship between
the individual and the group.[15] After Ramsey's friend Will McKay—the editor of the local newspaper—sees Ramsey participating in the lynching of
an accused child murderer, all Ramsey wants to do is talk. What follows is
a long dialogue, the bulk of the story, in which Ramsey tries to convince
McKay of Steinbeck's holistic theory of the phalanx: "Man is an unit in a
greater creature which I call the phalanx. The phalanx has pains, desires,
hungers and strivings as different from those of unit man as unit man is
from unit cells. The nature of the phalanx is not the sum of the natures of
the men who compose it, but a new individual, having emotions and ends of
its own."[16]

Steinbeck abandoned this unfinished draft for good reason. The long-winded explanation of the power of groupthink may lead to Ramsey's self-awareness and partial cure, but to the reader it seems a long way from the details of the lynching that sparked such public interest. Not that "Case History" isn't based to some degree on the events in San Jose. We encounter several details shared with the newspaper accounts, some of which are carried over to "The Vigilante." The streetlights are smashed to throw the town into darkness; the jailhouse door is broken down with a ram; the victim is perhaps dead before being hanged; the crowd attempt to burn his feet with lighted newspapers.[17] In "Case History," the lynching victim's race is not specified. Presumably he is white in Steinbeck's mind at this point, although this early draft is not without its racial signifiers. Ramsey is typed as white: blond. The initial sense of urgency at Ramsey's nervous collapse emerges when he is "found dead drunk in a negro house of prostitution." We learn too, from Ramsey's explanation to his journalist friend, that the mob tore off the victim's genitals, in a "symbolic action which has full emphasis only in the phalanx mind." "The units wouldn't have thought of that but the phalanx nearly always thinks of it. It happens at nearly all lynchings," reports Ramsey, though such activity would more typically be reserved for African Americans accused of "crimes" against white women. (From what we know of the Holmes and Thurmond lynching, neither victim was castrated.) "Case History" leans further toward "The Vigilante" in the links it makes between lynching and sexuality, and in the importance of the spectacle of the lynching. The moment when the journalist McKay realizes that his friend is at the center of a lynch mob becomes a moment of photographic exposure: "At that moment a flashlight flare went out. The blue lighted picture remained before Will's eyes. Helping to swing the railroad tie against the door he had seen John Ramsey, blond hair flying, eyes wild."[18]

The second draft of "The Vigilante" is also in the Long Valley ledger. It is exactly three handwritten pages (the final words, "I feel," are made to fit by snaking vertically up the side of the page), about half the length of "Case History." The story is followed by one of Steinbeck's process notes in which he describes how another draft story, "The Cow," died of "something or other and was replaced by the little bit of a story called The Vigilante. That story even with the second draft only took two days."[19] The manuscript of "The Vigilante" in the Long Valley ledger is very like the final published version. It remains uncertain whether Steinbeck considers "Case History" to be the first draft of "The Vigilante," or whether another draft existed prior to the second version in the ledger, but the point is still good: the story flashes in his mind, occupying him wholly in an intense process of composition that is also an aftermath or revision of an initial attempt. Whereas "Case History" is set in Steinbeck's birthplace of Salinas, "The Vigilante" moves explicitly to San Jose. The manuscript version identifies specific streets (their names only slightly changed),[20] while the published version gets the time of the lynching almost exactly right.[21] Which is to say that "The Vigilante" moves closer to history (in terms of location, scene, the details of the lynching process), even as it steps farther away by changing the race of the lynching victim in a switch that complicates an important detail. The victim in the story is the solitary and exceptional "nigger," as the other characters call him, though the story still contains a key detail in the original, historical events: the fear felt by the jail's other prisoners that their identity might be mistaken for that of Holmes or Thurmond, fellow whites (a fear surely redoubled because the mob was looking for two men, not one). We might say that the racial identity of the lynched character in Steinbeck's "The Vigilante" is produced *against* history, or at least in tension with the known and feasible details of the event.

One reason for this change of race, perhaps, was that Steinbeck wanted to disguise the location and divert attention from San Jose's "Night of Shame."[22] But then why lean so heavily on historical detail at all—indeed, why make the second version of the story adhere to the historical record much more closely than the first? Why not set the story in the American South (some critics mistakenly believed the story was set there) rather than having it part of Steinbeck Country, the central California region at the heart of Steinbeck's geographical imagination? After all, "Saint Katy the Virgin," another story in *The Long Valley*, is set in medieval France. But instead we have a story focalized through a participant in a historical event who cannot quite remember it aright, a figure living in "a dream-like weariness, a grey comfortable weariness."[23] Mike's crisis of memory ties into broader problems that haunt the history of lynching in the United States, just as the change of race underscores lynching as a national not a Western outrage, one that targeted African Americans disproportionately, and became a bloody cauldron of racist motivations that continued to receive national attention in the 1930s. The way that Mike tries to remember the lynching is significant regarding that history. Lynching was, in part, a crime of spectacle. Its horrendous violence was viewed by thousands at the time, including the photographers who memorialized events in lynching postcards that received wide distribution then, and continue to draw crowds to exhibitions today.[24] When Mike looks back at the events of the San Jose lynching, the description evokes the specific medium in which such events were remembered:

> Mike filled his eyes with the scene. He felt that he was dull. He wasn't see-ing enough of it. Here was a thing he would want to remember later so he could tell about it, but the dull tiredness seemed to cut the sharpness off the picture. His brain told him this was a terrible and important affair, but his eyes and his feelings didn't agree. It was just ordinary. Half an hour before, when he had been howling with the mob and fighting for a chance to help pull on the rope, then his chest had been so full that he had found he was crying. But now everything was dead, everything unreal: the dark mob was made up of stiff lay-figures. In the flamelight the faces were as expression-less as wood. Mike felt the stiffness, the unreality in himself too. He turned away at last and walked out of the park.[25]

Mike's moment of bewilderment and estrangement becomes an attempt to achieve photographic clarity: he wants a sharp picture as a memento of his experience. The split that he feels, between his thoughts and his eyes, some-what corresponds to a typical lynching photograph in which the evidence of horrendous crime, usually in the upper half of the image, is juxtaposed with the disturbing "ordinariness" of the scene below, as in Lawrence Beitler's famous photograph of the lynching of Thomas Shipp and Abram Smith in Marion, Indiana, in which a crowd of white men and women mingle in flir-tatious happiness and curiosity in the foreground (Fig. 10.1 has a similar dynamic). Scholars of lynching imagery have described how photography was incorporated into the lynching itself, as the photograph came to medi-ate the experience both for viewers and, indeed, for some of the victims.[26] Images of lynching in general tend to make us aware of the taking of the pho-tograph itself as an act of memorialization even as they confront us with the uncanny presence of violent racism in American life. As Dora Apel observes, the spectacle of lynching embodied "the relationship of power to helpless-ness, citizen to outsider, privilege to oppression, jubilation to degradation, subjecthood to objecthood, community to outcast, pride to humiliation."[27] But in Steinbeck's version, feelings are more muted and confused, as if Mike himself is in disturbing ways also a victim of these events.

Steinbeck would undoubtedly have seen photographs of the San Jose lynching, in the numerous newspaper accounts that followed. The photo-graphic record of the San Jose lynching is quite unusual in depicting the

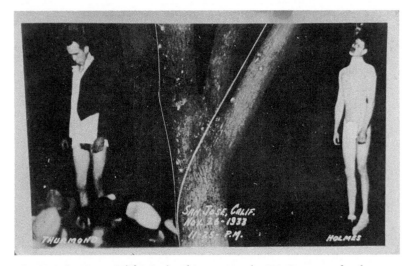

Fig. 10.2 San Jose, California, lynching postcard, 1933. Brosamer family private collection, used with permission.

various stages of the lynching, from the breaking down of the jailhouse door to the hanged bodies of Thurmond and Holmes.[28] The photographs, in other words, form a narrative, and indeed specific images help us to understand key aspects of Steinbeck's story. (As suggested by the be-hatted crowd in Fig. 10.1, another curious point about the San Jose lynching is that it occurred in a prosperous middle-class community, a point that Steinbeck emphasizes in his story.)[29] Steinbeck may even have seen souvenir postcards of the lynching, one of which spliced two photographs together to suggest that Thurmond and Holmes were hanged side by side (Fig. 10.2), just as Steinbeck splices an African American character into the historical record. This image would also have emphasized a quality that Steinbeck clearly drew from the lynching: its sign of the combined power of mob action. In another photograph (Fig. 10.3), we see a group of approximately a dozen men working together with the long pipe to break down the main jailhouse door. Concerted action—what Steinbeck called the phalanx—is produced from a disparate chaos of the crowd, the signs of its previous assembly strewn as garbage in the foreground.

Fig. 10.3 is an image of implied process, of individuals becoming a collective group with a primordial power and motive direction beyond the official laws of the state—a power greater than the sum of its parts. The breakdown of social norms and values relates to the amoral, biological quality of the

Fig. 10.3 San Jose, California: November 27, 1933. The lynch mob using thirty-foot-long pieces of pipe to break down the iron doors of the county jail. © Underwood Archives/age fotostock.

phalanx that Ramsey theorizes in "Case History." And as Mike's bewilderment implies, this mob action, because it is defined by a transitory moment of emergence, cannot quite be remembered or spoken into being.[30] We can understand the photograph's relation to history in a similar way. Fig. 10.3 is documentary "evidence" of a social formation and mob action. But it is also severed from historical narrative, freezing this moment in time. The flash going off in the lower left of the image, lighting the scene of action, implies how photographers are another kind of phalanx, complicit with the action of the mob (the artist Ken Gonzales-Day, in his book about lynching in the West, observes among this garbage an unbroken flashbulb in what he describes as "one of the earliest uses of a flashbulb in the history of lynching").[31] But then the image is also inadequate or belated to what it sees precisely because of its awareness of the technology of seeing. An uncropped version of this photograph that appeared on the front page of the San Francisco *Chronicle* reveals in lower left the full figure of the photographer taking the photograph, making the image one of image-making itself.

A study in focalization, the story's point of view is accordingly drawn to moments of self-conscious looking—the blue streetlight that illuminates the scene, the neon sign BEER that Mike follows into the bar, a patrolling police-man's flash that lights store windows—as if the narrator's own sight is stained by what was witnessed, or as if the story is cognizant of what Jacqueline Goldsby argues about lynching photography more generally: it makes vision itself "legible as a cultural operation."[32] But the story presents not a looking at but a looking *back*, an *afterimage* following a flash, in which photochemical activity continues in the retina. This phenomenon clearly interested Stein-beck for he would return to it at the climax of *The Pearl* (1947), when a fleeing Kino is able to sneak up on his trackers in part because a struck match "left a picture on Kino's eyes," one with an indexical quality that enables him to see how the men are positioned.[33] Mike is likewise trapped in a condition of melancholy belatedness in which he is recoiling from a flash, attempting to get back to that moment of becoming still burning in his eyes. We expe-rience something similar in another moment when Mike looks back at the scene of the lynching:

> In the center of the mob someone had lighted a twisted newspaper and was holding it up. Mike could see how the flame curled about the feet of the grey naked body hanging from the elm tree. It seemed curious to him that negroes turn a bluish grey when they are dead. The burning newspaper lighted the heads of the up-looking men, silent men and fixed; they did not move their eyes from the hanged man.[34]

This moment looks back in ways other than Mike's retrospective glance. It looks back implicitly to earlier lynchings that were illuminated by flares rather than by the car headlights or the photo-flashes of the modern-day lynching. Metafictionally, it looks back to Steinbeck's source texts, the local newspapers in which he must have read the details and seen the photographs of the lynching. In its rather literal reference to details from these news-paper accounts—especially the attempts to burn Thurmond—the moment suggests the parallels between the details of the San Jose lynching of white victims and the more violent lynchings of African Americans, as does the stripping away of clothes. Here the San Jose lynching is something of an exception to the general rule noted by scholars of lynching: that black and white victims were treated very differently.[35] (The NAACP leadership was aware of the Thurmond and Holmes lynching, responding to Governor Rolph's endorsement of the crime by organizing a Writers League Against

Lynching, which petitioned Congress to pass an anti-lynching bill in the mid-1930s.)[36] But ironically, this moment suggesting parity between the races is the moment when Steinbeck changes the racial identity of the victim from white to black, indicated here by the dubious racial "fact" concerning skin-color change. The "bluish-grey" of the dead African American victim reflects the "blue street light" that first illuminates the scene, as if the racial change has been produced *by* the flash of electric light, just as the flash of composition in which Steinbeck changes the victim's racial identity makes this such a problematic short story. In her history of flash photography, Kate Flint writes that flash could ironically lighten the skin of its black victims in a "bleaching glare" that carried, through the context of lynching, "additional, especially charged overtones of violence, exposure, and white racial hatred." The flash here, though, changes white to black, hence literalizing a process that Flint observes more generally in flash photography's slicing of moments out of darkness: "the moment before the picture was taken and the moment afterwards are radically different in terms of lighting, shadow and visibility from the one that the flash lit up for us."[37] The flash here is a moment of compositional realization—that the victim, for the story to work, must be black not white—which splits apart "Case History" and "The Vigilante."

If the story is one of looking back for Mike then it is one of re-vision for Steinbeck. He rewrites the earlier version, adhering so closely to the historical record while departing vastly from it. Race, the difference between black and white, is thus produced before our eyes. To Mike, the lynching is important as a spectacle: it is a "thing" that must be "[done] right," especially regarding the stripping and the hanging of the victim. Part of this logic of "doing it right," on Steinbeck's part at least, is altering the racial identity of the lynched victim to tap the filthy stream of racist motivation that made lynchings so sickeningly compelling to many white participants and observers. A central sign of this spectacle is the piece of torn blue denim that Mike helps rip from the pants of the victim. (Souvenirs, bits of cloth from clothing, parts of the hang tree, even in some cases parts of the victim himself, were common in lynchings, and the San Jose lynching was no exception. In Lawrence Beitler's photograph of the Marion lynching, two young women hold pieces of cloth, presumably souvenirs from the pants of the victim, perhaps charged with erotic power.)[38] After some haggling, Mike sells half of the cloth to the barman for a couple of dollars so that the barman can display it with a printed card. "The fellas that come in will like to look at it," he says.[39] A souvenir, Susan Stewart argues, maintains its power because it is a *partial* trace of a previous authentic experience, one that does not simply record the event but rather allows the possessor to describe experience through the "invention of narrative." Quoting Hegel, Stewart describes the original, authentic experience as "the bacchanalian revel, where not a member is sober," the escaped materiality of which is recaptured through the viewed object. Having a metonymic relation to the original scene even as it divides past from present, the souvenir "will not function without the supplementary narrative discourse that both attaches it to its origins and creates a myth with regard to those origins."[40] But in "The Vigilante," the patch of denim leads only to a partial narrative—Mike tells how he helps remove the victim's clothes—echoing how the characters in the story are unable to narrate their own experience. "It don't make you feel nothing," says Mike, other than to feel "cut off and tired, but kind of satisfied, too." In fact, Mike does what should be impossible regarding a souvenir, according to Stewart's argument at least: he sells it.[41]

Mike's division and sale of this small patch of textured experience equates him with Steinbeck the short story writer making literary material from a truncation and hacking of a historical event. (The relationship between "Case History" and "The Vigilante" is embodied in that patch of denim: the former story explains the sexual motivations that often underpinned lynchings, while the latter story implies it through this artifact and the thin threads of Mike's conversation with his wife at the end.) With characters unable to recall the nature of their experience, the story works through fragmentation and allusion; rather like Stewart's idea of the souvenir, it implies an attachment to historical origins while also creating a myth of those origins.[42] The story is itself the curiosity in its sustained description of bemused recoil, as if Mike is also recoiling from the flash: he cannot see in the same way again as he descends from an ecstatic metamorphosis to an isolated, human present, one of confusion and mourning for a lost fullness of group belonging. "The Vigilante" is a kind of souvenir in the way that it participates in a historical moment while revising it to resonate with the national horrors of a racialized—and racist—imaginary. This participation in the historical moment is perhaps why the story leaves us with more questions than answers, why it produces such a confused array of possible responses. Goldsby describes this confusion as a characteristic of reactions to lynching in general, the way that it leads to various theories as people seem at a loss to account for its presence in American life: for example, lynching was a peculiarity of the South; a fulfillment of Freudian sexual pathologies; a process of "making" whiteness and masculinity; a condition of the anxieties of emerging industrial modernity.[43] Accordingly, the point of the story is its refusal to explain. By changing the race of the victim from white to black, Steinbeck aligns his story with the art of protest in the decade of the Scottsboro Boys even as it removes subjectivity from the black victim of the lynching (whose guilt is never questioned) and refuses to see Mike and the other townsfolk as the agents of terror.

It is an easy critical gesture to excuse Steinbeck's work as confused on a number of political questions. In "The Vigilante," the silences concerning the racism at the heart of the mob's actions (Mike and the bartender may debate whether all African Americans are "fiends," but the motives of the mob are unambiguous: they were out for the blood of a "nigger fiend") create problems that are difficult to reconcile on the grounds of vagueness, uncertainty, or ambivalence.[44] The switch of the lynched victim from white to black distances "The Vigilante" from the historical record. But more significantly, it compromises the kind of theorization—the "species-sense," the interest in the biological nature of human group formation—that marks so much of Steinbeck's thought. The point here is that Steinbeck could have written a story about the power of the superorganism without changing the race of the victims of the San Jose lynching. In fact, the shared whiteness between mob and victim, the lack of racist motivation, would have made the point about group psychology stronger still. What makes "The Vigilante" "work" as a short story—its refusal to explain, the falling away of the explicit theorization that mars "Case History"—is the specter of racism in American life, a haunting reality that Steinbeck's imagination is, in this particular case, incapable of confronting.

In its treatment of race relations in the West, "The Vigilante" implies a retroactive viewpoint, one of bemused recoil. The effect depends on its curtailed status *as* a short story, its refusal to completely explain. If Steinbeck was impacted by photographs of the San Jose lynching in his construction of "The Vigilante," then his story implies a kind of historical vision that resonates with photographic seeing—a resonance that returns us finally to some of the peculiarities of the short story as a form of historical fiction. The parallel between the short story and the photograph is at least as old as Edgar Allan Poe, who offered one of the first theories of each medium. Both are temporally delimited, capable of "unity" of effect, productive of a special kind of attention, and responsive to forces within democratic culture.[45] Subsequent writers have thickened the links between photographs and short stories. Eudora Welty—photographer and short story writer both (and indeed another white writer who tells a lynching story from the lyncher's problematically unjudged point of view)[46]—saw both forms as snapshots, offering a "peripheral awareness" of their subject.[47] Noting how photographers and short story writers talk about art in similar ways, the Argentine author Julio Cortázar (whose story based on a photograph was subsequently adapted into Michelangelo Antonioni's 1966 movie *Blow-Up*) described photographs and short stories as working in parallel: "cutting off a fragment of reality, giving it certain limits, but in such a way that this segment acts like an explosion which fully opens a more ample reality, like a dynamic vision which spiritually transcends the space reached by the camera." If cinema is an "open order" like the novel, developing through a synthesis of multifaceted elements moving toward a climax, then photography and short stories work inversely, through a delimited image or event whereby readers move not horizontally, as in the novel, but vertically up and down in interpretive space.[48] Making us think directly of the treatment of vision in "The Vigilante," Nadine Gordimer similarly writes: "Short-story writers see by the light of the flash; theirs is the art of the only thing one can be sure of—the present moment." Its photographic capturing of isolated moments of consciousness rather than the cumulative arc of a life makes the short story—unlike the novel—correspond to the loneliness and isolation of the individual in modernity and to the break-up of the conditions of middle-class life.[49] Such loneliness and isolation, as we saw, haunted Steinbeck when he turned to the story of "The Vigilante."

    Unlike Ong's normalizing and totalistic understanding of the novel, which allows readers to fully enter its imaginary experiences and lends it the power of historical veracity, Steinbeck's "The Vigilante" works to unmake the coherence and authority of the classes and institutions it represents. The middle-class community at the heart of the story becomes strange, alienated (and alienating), fragmented, and ethically problematic. This unmaking of normalcy returns not to the story's purported totality as an artwork, its alignment with the forces of history, but to the incompleteness of what it represents. "The Vigilante" behaves like a photograph in its peripheral rather than its direct awareness of events. It suggests how, as a genre, the short story's relation to history is not, like the novel's, horizontally developmental and encompassing (even welcoming), but instead vertically layered and discomforting as Steinbeck takes historical events and embeds into them, at a deeper level, a counterfactual detail that the story is unable to account for. The story thus shares many of the qualities and contradictions that Susan Sontag, Roland Barthes, and others have detected in the photographic image. Like Barthes' idea of the "mad" photograph that works through a revulsive movement of time, "The Vigilante" confronts "the wakening of intractable reality."[50] Mike remembers and reports the physical details of his experience, many of which are true to the historical record, yet he still cannot see enough, he still cannot recall the feelings motivating his participation in the lynching. The brevity, suddenness, and incompleteness of "The Vigilante"—its photographic "short-story-ness"—embodies loneliness and disconnection, a splitting apart of society into individual fragmented experiences.[51] The experiences it represents are not totalistic but curtailed, not developmental but revulsive, not world-building but defamiliarizing and difficult. Like Sontag's idea of the photograph, Steinbeck's story is not a statement about the world so much as a piece of it.[52] It is a "raw record," a participation, even an intervention in history.[53] Behaving like a lynching photograph itself, the story gains a photographic authenticity but it lacks ethical responsibility toward what it captures. Its tone of bewildered recoil recognizes but fails to judge the shocking presence of racist violence in American life.

11

War in a Woman's Voice

Maaza Mengiste

I own a picture of a young Ethiopian girl whom I have started to call Hirut (Fig. 11.1). She is in her teens, and her hair is pulled away from her face and hangs down her back in thick braids. She wears a long Ethiopian dress and even in the aged, black-and-white photo, it is easy to see that the dress is worn and stained. In the photo, Hirut has turned from the camera. I imagine that she is looking down at the ground, doing her best to focus her attention on something besides the intrusive photographer who is beside her, getting ready to shoot. I have given her a rifle that is the last gift from a dying father, and her fate will be tied to a promise she made to never let it out of her possession. There is a war coming in Ethiopia and she has been told that she must work with the other women to prepare supplies for the men who will fight. It is 1935 and Hirut is orphaned and she has never gone further than 5 kilometers from her home. When they say: We must defend our country, Hirut wonders to herself: How big is a country? And she will continue to ask this question as Benito Mussolini invades Ethiopia and she is pushed— by decisions wholly her own and not entirely of her making—closer and closer to the front lines until she is holding a rifle and pulling the trigger and wishing all her enemies dead. This is the premise of my novel, *The Shadow King*.

Just how much can a picture tell us? Photos of Ethiopian girls and women were used to entice Italian men into joining Mussolini's army. The soldiers were promised a quick war and an African adventure. They marched into Ethiopia singing songs of what they would do to Ethiopian women. Many packed their cameras along, eager to document this great journey that was surely the farthest that most had ever been from home. I have been collecting their photographs for well over a decade, poring over images—of quotidian military life, of deliberate brutalities, of friendships and camaraderie—to find what they may have never intended anyone to see. I have sat for hours at a time staring at the faces of Ethiopians—men, women, children—who were forced to live with the occupying force. I have tried to read what hovers just

Maaza Mengiste, *War in a Woman's Voice*. In: *Historical Fiction Now*. Edited by Mark Eaton and Bruce Holsinger, Oxford University Press. © Maaza Mengiste (2023). DOI: 10.1093/oso/9780198877035.003.0012

Fig. 11.1 Hirut (photograph from the author)

out of view. That overly stiff posture of an elderly man next to a relaxed and smiling Italian soldier might hint at deep fear and discomfort. That bruised mouth on a prisoner pointed to ill-treatment, regardless of the casual arm around that prisoner's shoulder. Those rows of girls, staring bare-chested and blank-eyed into the camera, might be saying more with their remote gazes than any shout for help could convey. That woman in her long dress staring into the camera with defiance might know more about what lurks in the hills behind the photographer's shoulder than he does.

I was aware, even as I looked at these photos, that they were made by men to shape and reshape their memories. In photographing Ethiopian civilians and prisoners: men and women, boys and girls, these Italian men were reimagining themselves. Like those familiar photographs that colonialists sent back from the territories they claimed needed "civilizing," every picture became a narrative that he was creating about himself, about war. What, then, could I really glean from these images? What survived after sifting through the crafted narrative held within each photographer's frame? In *The Unwomanly Face of War*, Svetlana Alexievich states that, "Everything we know about war, we know with 'a man's voice.' We are all captives of 'men's' notions and 'men's' sense of war. 'Men's' words. Women are silent," she contends. I was not sure that women were silent, but I did know that they were not heard. What would it mean to tell a war story with a woman's voice, with her sense of war, with her notions of what it means to be a soldier? I went back to the photographs in my collection and began to isolate those that specifically depicted women. I glanced away from the male photographer, drew the girls and women around me, and bent toward them to listen. What could they tell me about Hirut?

I built my story of Hirut and the Italo-Ethiopian war of 1935 in increments, folding archival research into my own readings of the photographs I was collecting. I set pictures with discernible locations onto a map of Ethiopia, pinning those that I could to dates and battles, recreating historical moments out of fragmented information in order to understand the intimate, personal details that I thought I could detect. What started to crystallize and sharpen in front of me was often breathtaking: a series of lives, once held immobile and silent between shutter and aperture, stepped out of the shadows of history and into brighter light. They lent me words. They pointed me in new directions. They pushed those photographers further away, full of indignation and fury, and beckoned me on toward uncharted terrain—toward *their* war. Following their lead, I began to write my book.

I had no idea when I sent my fictional Hirut to war that my great-grandmother, Getey, preceded her: flesh and bone, blood and pride, paving the path for my imagination. I did not realize, when crafting Hirut's story about losing possession of her father's gun, that my relative Getey had experienced something similar. My great-grandmother's story was a discovery made during a casual conversation with my mother, one of those moments when she stopped me as I was telling her about one of my photographs to say, "But don't you know about Getey, your great-grandmother? Don't you remember?"

What I remembered were all the stories that I had heard growing up, stories of men going to war: those proud, ferocious fighters who charged at a better-equipped, highly weaponized army with old rifles while barefooted and dressed in white. I imagined these men, so simple to spot, charging into valleys and flinging themselves at the invading foreigners, their throats grown hoarse from battle cries. My imagination tethered all the stories into an extended narrative, the images spinning in front of me then looping when I reached the limits of my comprehension. In this war, men stumbled but did not fall. Men gasped but did not die. Those white-clad men ran toward bullets and tanks, heroic and Homeric, myths brought to life. I would shut my eyes and see it all unfold: a thousand furious Achilleses shaking off that deadly cut and rising onto undamaged feet again and again. I remembered the war like this, told in what Alexievich calls "a man's voice," regardless of who did the telling.

My great-grandmother, Getey, was a girl in 1935 when the Italian Fascists invaded Ethiopia. As war loomed, Emperor Haile Selassie ordered the eldest son from each family to enlist and bring their gun for war. There was no son in Getey's family who was of fighting age. She was the eldest, and not even she was considered an adult. In fact, she was in an arranged marriage but too young to live with her adult husband. In order to fulfill the emperor's orders, her father asked her husband to represent the family, and he gave the man his rifle. This act must have felt like a final betrayal to her. (Eventually, she would leave this arranged marriage and a husband she did not like.) She rebelled and told her father she would enlist in the war and represent her family. She was, after all, the eldest. When her father refused, she took her case to court and sued him. And she won. When the judges announced their verdict, she raised the rifle above her head and sang *shilela*—one of the songs that warriors sing just before battle, when they meld their fearlessness and fighting prowess into melody and rhythm. Then she took the gun and went to join the front lines.

I knew Getey as an old woman, essentially bed-ridden but alert. I have no solid memory of what she looked like: to my child's eye, she was simply old, a petite woman with skin molded almost entirely out of gentle wrinkles. The day I went to visit her, not long before she died, I spent most of my time with other relatives who had gathered in the home she shared with her daughter. I had my camera but I did not take any pictures of her. She was in bed, tucked into a corner of the house, isolated from the talk and revelry happening in the other room. Though stories about her stubbornness and spiritedness had seeped into the descriptions I heard of her, I knew nothing back then of her experiences during the war. She had been relegated to the position of a respected elder, someone gazed upon through the thick haze of time, discernible but essentially unseen.

After learning Getey's story, what I had suspected from my examination of news articles and photographs such as Fig. 11.2 solidified into tangible

Fig. 11.2 Photograph of armed women soldiers (author's personal collection)

knowledge that came from my own family and coursed through my blood. Women were not only the caretakers in the war against Italy and the Fascists, they were also soldiers. Even though it was difficult to find these stories, the more I researched, the more women I found tucked inside the lines of history. A photo here, a headline there, a short article over there. The process was often slow and frustrating, but it was undeniably exhilarating. "We were there," I found myself thinking. "We were there and here is proof," and I imagined Getey stepping in front of me, rifle raised, a song in her throat, and pushing me forward. Because: how many more were there, waiting to be spoken into being?

Myth: That war will make a man out of you. That aggression—and anger—is the territory of men. That in conflict, the sisters of Helen will wait breathlessly inside the gates of Troy for victory or defeat to decide their fates. That when we speak of war, we speak of tested resolve and broken spirits and wounded bodies and imagine them as masculine figures clad in uniform: filmic images drifting past our imagination, buoyed by stories and textbooks and literature. Yet there is Getey; look at her slinging that rifle over her shoulder, saying goodbye to her younger brothers and father, and marching to the front lines.

Fact: Women enter into struggle, whether political or personal, well aware of the bodies in which they exist. We recognize our strengths even as we are reminded of the ways we can be made vulnerable. We know that the other battlefield on which another kind of war is fought is the one bordered by our own skin. No uniform or alliance can completely erase the threat of sexual assault and exploitation that wants to make us both trophy and contested territory.

Imagine Hirut on the top of a hill, rifle ready, prepared to ambush the enemy. Along the way to this war, she is forced to contend with sexual aggression and then rape by one of her own compatriots. The smoky terrain of the front lines has expanded to engulf Hirut herself: her body an object to be gained or lost. She is both a woman and a country: living flesh and battleground. And when people tell her, "Don't fight him, Hirut, remember you are fighting to keep your country free," she asks herself, "But am I not my own country? What does freedom mean when a woman—when a girl—cannot feel safe in her own skin?" This, too, is what war means: to shift the battlefield away from the hills and onto your own body, to defend your own flesh with the ferocity of the cruelest soldier, against that one who wants to make himself into a man at your expense.

Helen of Troy, gazing across the bloody battlefield of the Trojan War, cannot imagine herself independent from the men who wage war in her name. When that great Trojan warrior, Hector, approaches her, she looks at him and understands that she is as much bound to the battle unfolding beyond the gates as any soldier. She laments the decisions of the gods, of Zeus, who have turned her body, her self, into a catalyst for conflict. "Hereafter we shall be made into things of song for the men of the future," she tells Hector in Homer's *The Iliad*. She can never extricate herself from the war. She will never have an identity beyond that of prized possession and stolen treasure, something to be reshaped and reconfigured, and then sung by men well into the future. She may not have known that while she mourned her fate, Pentheselea, that mighty Amazon warrior, would soon stand bravely in front of Achilles and wage battle with such unrelenting ferocity that Achilles would mourn while killing her, sensing a fighting spirit like his own, perhaps.

While developing Hirut's narrative, I read the stories of female soldiers from across the centuries. From Artemisia of Caria in 480 BCE to the women in the army of the Kingdom of Dahomey in early eighteenth-century Benin, to the more recent Yazidi women's army that fought against the Islamic State of Iraq and Syria (ISIS), I have come to realize that the history of women in war has often been contested because the bodies of women have also been battlefields on which distorted ideas of manhood were made. If war makes a man out of you, then what does it mean to fight beside—or lose to—a female soldier? For centuries, women have been providing their own answers to this. But history—that shape-shifting collection of memories and data replete with gaps—would want us to believe that every female soldier plucked out of oblivion and brought to light is the first and only one. But that has never been true, and it is not true now.

12

Alternate-History Novels and Other Counterfactual Fictions

Mark Eaton

Alternate-history novels have long been a popular subgenre of historical fiction. These novels are based on so-called counterfactuals, thought experiments proceeding from speculative questions, such as what if the South had won the Civil War, for example, or what if Germany had not been defeated in World War II? The gambit of alternate-history novels is to imagine how certain events might have turned out differently than they did. These speculative fictions are often horrifying insofar as they imagine worst-case scenarios, and surely for that very reason, they can be highly entertaining. By forcing us to reconsider what we thought we knew about the past, however, they can also be illuminating. For what's at stake in alternate-history novels are not merely counterfactual thought experiments, of course. The very idea of invoking other possible historical worlds presupposes a materialist, though importantly not deterministic view of history. Counterfactual fictions raise questions about human agency and responsibility in history. In turn, by invoking the possibility of alternative pasts, they inevitably raise questions about the present: How would the world we live in today be different if history had unfolded in this way, or some other way?

Alternate-history novels are a relatively recent invention in literary history. In her book *Telling It Like It Wasn't: The Counterfactual Imagination in History and Fiction* (2018), literary critic Catherine Gallagher claims that they only emerged as a subgenre in the twentieth century. In the nineteenth century, historians began to write what Gallagher terms "alternate histories," which is to say long, continuous narratives that depart from the historical record, but such works tend to feature "dramatis personae [drawn] exclusively from the actual historical record."[1] The inclusion of fictional characters in an alternate-history narrative marks the advent of a new genre. To be sure, there had been earlier time-travel novels in which fictional

Mark Eaton, *Alternate-History Novels and Other Counterfactual Fictions*. In: *Historical Fiction Now*.
Edited by Mark Eaton and Bruce Holsinger, Oxford University Press. © Mark Eaton (2023).
DOI: 10.1093/oso/9780198877035.003.0013

characters are transported back into the past to change the course of history, such as Mark Twain's *A Connecticut Yankee in King Arthur's Court* (1889). But the first true alternate-history novel was Frank Williams's *Hallie Marshall: A True Daughter of the South* (1899), a now largely forgotten work that first introduced fictional characters in an alternate-history narrative. Like Williams's novel, Ward Moore's *Bring the Jubilee* (1953) imagines a world in which the South won the Civil War and combines backward time travel with alternate-history narration. Unlike *Hallie Marshall*, *Bring the Jubilee* was immensely popular and proved to be hugely influential on subsequent writers. "*Bring the Jubilee* was the first of some thirty novels published in the last half of the twentieth century to construct imaginary Americas," writes Gallagher, "where the changes in our history lead to significantly different interracial arrangements."[2] Invented at the turn of the century and then revived in the postwar period, alternate-history novels brought counterfactual narration into historical fiction, thereby creating a new subgenre that proliferated in the late twentieth century.

By the first decades of the twenty-first century, writers such as John Banville, Michael Chabon, Kazuo Ishiguro, and Philip Roth had elevated the alternate-history novel to the status of literary fiction, just as so many writers had been doing with so-called genre fiction—detective novels, fantasy, science fiction, and so on—thereby giving these genres greater cultural cachet. Even so, popular novels still dominate the genre at a time when alternate-history novels have become something of a literary growth industry. One measure of the genre's popularity is the fact that Stephen King wrote an alternate-history novel in which a fictional character travels back in time to prevent the assassination of John F. Kennedy. "I've never tried to write anything like this before," King remarked. "It was really strange at first, like breaking in a new pair of shoes."[3]

When Philip Roth brought his own considerable literary gifts to the genre, he produced one of his finest novels, *The Plot Against America* (2004). Nothing less than a masterpiece of counterfactual fiction, this is an alternate-history novel in which the aviator Charles A. Lindberg wins the 1940 U.S. presidential election over the incumbent, Franklin D. Roosevelt, and proceeds to impose his anti-Semitic ideas, taking the country in a decidedly fascist direction. In this chapter, *The Plot Against America* will serve as a case study for exploring what alternate-history novels can bring to our understanding of historical fiction more broadly. But first I will take us on a short detour to consider Philip K. Dick's *The Man in the High Castle* (1962), which helped establish alternate-history novels as an important subgenre of historical fiction in the first place. Then I will move on to a third, somewhat anomalous example of alternate-history fiction: Colson White-head's Pulitzer Prize-winning novel, *The Underground Railroad* (2016), in which the author deliberately risks anachronism in order to portray the U.S. antebellum period in ways that clearly depart from the historical record, bringing the atrocities of chattel slavery into relief. Whitehead represents instances of medical experimentation on African Americans that resemble the infamous Tuskegee syphilis study, for example, which were actually undertaken in the 1930s. Taking liberties with the historical record, White-head seems to want to convey greater continuity between the nearly 250-year practice of slavery and many subsequent forms of racial injustice.[4] Together, these three case studies will show how contemporary writers have used anachronisms to scramble the historical record or transpose actual events to different times and places.

When historical fiction writers do find it necessary to diverge from the actual facts of history, they typically try to finesse them as much as possible, so as not to call attention to the changes. They usually justify them by saying that they afford some heightened dramatic effect. In contrast, contemporary writers of alternate-history novels diverge from the facts deliberately and ostentatiously. In novels by Philip Dick, Philip Roth, and Colson White-head, as we will see, diverging from the historical record opens up new ways of thinking about or understanding the past. By imagining different outcomes to pivotal historical events such as elections and world wars, and by developing alternate histories on the basis of those different outcomes, alternate-history novels and other counterfactual fictions challenge both official accounts and popular memories about the past. Alternate-history novels are among the most intriguing subgenres of historical fiction, and any account of historical fiction now would be incomplete without them.

1. The Pacific States of America

Why do the outcomes of war constitute such an irresistible historical terrain for alternate-history novels? According to Paul K. Saint-Amour, a defining feature of alternate-history novels is "the loading of a pivotal moment or event with such consequence that it splits history into a *before*, which corresponds to real-world history, and an *after* that diverges from it."[5] This helps explain why alternate-history novels so often postulate a counterfactual outcome to war, because war, like political elections, provides ready-made pivotal moments that split time into a before and after. But there may be other reasons why war and political elections feature so prominently. In an article titled "War, Counterfactual History, and Alternate-History Novels," Gallagher asks why these novels so often conjecture that the United States "lost wars it quite decisively won."[6] If Ward Moore's *Bring the Jubilee* (1953) is one of countless novels in which the South won the Civil War, Philip Dick's *The Man in the High Castle* envisions a world in which Germany and Japan emerged victorious at the end of World War II. This counterfactual "what if" scenario would prove to be a highly generative one for many subsequent popular novels, such as Robert Harris's massive bestseller *Fatherland* (1992). But it was Dick's 1962 novel that got there first. Winner of a Hugo Award for Best Novel in 1963, Philip K. Dick's *The Man in the High Castle* brought considerable attention to the alternate-history novel genre at the height of the Cold War. If American writers seem to be particularly fixated on the Civil War and World War II, it may be because "their alternate worlds closely resemble some important aspects of current American reality," as Gallagher has observed.[7] Thus, *Bring the Jubilee* envisions a "nightmare version" of the post-bellum South that could easily be mistaken for the thoroughly seg-regated South of the early 1950s when the novel was written, while *The Man in the High Castle* similarly reflects the Cold War and the Civil Rights movement during the period in which it was written.[8]

The pivotal moment in this novel is an assassination attempt on the life of then-President-elect Franklin Delano Roosevelt, an event that in fact tran-spired on February 15, 1933, when an Italian-American anarchist, Giuseppe Zangara, shot and killed Chicago mayor Anton Cermak and four others in Miami, Florida during a speech by Roosevelt, less than a month before the latter was sworn in for the first of what would turn out to be an unprece-dented four terms as U.S. President. In real life, Roosevelt survived the attack. But what if the assassination attempt had been successful? *The Man in the High Castle* gives readers one possible answer to that question. Roo-sevelt's untimely death plunges the country even deeper into economic depression, averts the New Deal, and prevents the United States from enter-ing the war. Predictably, this helps the Axis powers defeat the considerably weakened Allied forces, setting the stage for an invasion of the United States.

Based on this counterfactual premise, *The Man in the High Castle* creates a compelling if somewhat implausible narrative of what might have followed in the aftermath of an Axis victory. The novel depicts a radically reconfig-ured postwar world, with the Pacific States of America ruled by Japanese officials from the occupied capitol of San Francisco, while Germany controls the Eastern United States (there is a neutral zone in the middle so-called flyover states). By 1962, when *The Man in the High Castle* is set, Germany has re-enslaved African Americans, drained the Mediterranean Sea to create farmland, and colonized Mars and Venus, thus adding Dick's trademark science-fiction element and making this novel eligible to win the 1963 Hugo Award.

The Man in the High Castle is perhaps most interesting for my purposes because it features another fictional alternate-history novel within it. Written by the reclusive writer Hawthorne Abendsen and banned in German-occupied territories, *The Grasshopper Lies Heavy* is a novel in which Roosevelt survives an assassination attempt and the Allies win the war: "The book is fiction. I mean, it's in novel form. Roosevelt isn't assassinated in Miami; he goes on and is reelected in 1936, so he's president until 1940, until during the war. ... Naturally, it's got a lot of fictional parts; I mean, it's got to be entertaining or people wouldn't read it."[9] Obviously, the plot of *The Grasshopper Lies Heavy* corresponds to what actually happened. While its contents are counterfactual to the characters within the novel, *The Grasshopper Lies Heavy* in effect de-familiarizes the actual outcome of World War II for readers of the novel *The Man in the High Castle*. This effect is heightened when readers of *The Grasshopper Lies Heavy* speculate about its alternate history. One character is skeptical about whether the New Deal could have been as effective as depicted. Another character wonders if the nuclear arms race of the postwar period is plausible. Still another character, the antiquities dealer Robert Childan, opines about what would have happened if Germany and Japan had lost the war: "If Germany and Japan had lost the war, the Jews would be running the world today."[10] This contrarian view about the scenario depicted in *The Grasshopper Lies Heavy*, which, again, is closer to the actual history, underscores an overt anti-Semitism that persists in the postwar period.

Unsurprisingly, the German consul in San Francisco, Hugo Reiss, also takes issue with the counterfactual scenario depicted in *The Grasshopper Lies Heavy*, yet he marvels at "the power of fiction, even cheap popular fiction, to evoke. No wonder it's banned within the Reich territory; I'd ban it myself."[11] What concerns him most about the novel is that the author portrays Hitler's death; nonetheless, he finds himself mesmerized by the book: "How could that be? Reiss asked himself. Is it just this man's writing ability? They know a million tricks, those novelists."[12]

The dramatic irony inheres in the fact that, unlike Reiss, we know that Hitler *did* die, and the actual postwar world is more or less what the novel describes. Contemplating the vertiginous scrambling up of history in this scene, readers, too, recognize the power that alternate-history novels have to make us reconsider the past, wondering how it might have turned out differently.

Another similarly uncanny moment in *The Man in the High Castle* occurs when the Japanese Trade Minister, Nobusuku Tagomi, is mysteriously transported into the real world of the novel's 1962 setting, which is to say the actual historical world, not the alternate-history one. Sitting on a park bench in San Francisco, Tagomi inspects a mysterious silver object, triangular in shape, that he has just bought from Robert Childan's antiquities shop, when suddenly some sort of alchemy transports him sideways into present-day reality, as it were: "God, what is that? He stopped, gaped at hideous misshapen thing on the skyline. Like nightmare of roller coaster suspended, blotting out view. Enormous construction of metal and cement in air."[13] Tagomi turns to a passer-by in a rumpled suit and asks him what it is. "That's the Embarcadero Freeway," the man replies. "A lot of people think it stinks up the view."[14] The Embarcadero Freeway opened in 1959 despite fierce opposition from residents who objected to ruined sightlines and traffic noise, a harbinger of the so-called "freeway wars" of the 1960s and 1970s.[15] This curious scene renders the newly constructed freeway as a sort of anachronism, even though it was very real at the time.

What happens next only reinforces the reader's sense of disorientation. Seeking "respite" from the "disturbance" of the freeway, Tagomi enters a "dingy lunch counter" on a street corner:

> Only whites within, all supping. Mr. Tagomi pushed open the wooden swinging doors. ... All stools taken by whites. Mr. Tagomi exclaimed. Several whites looked up. *But none departed their places. None yielded their stools to him. They merely resumed supping.*
>
> "I insist!" Mr. Tagomi said loudly to the first white; he shouted in the man's ear.
>
> The man put down his coffee mug and said, "Watch it, Tojo."[16]

To understand this scene, we must remember that Tagomi, as a member of the ruling Japanese party in Dick's counterfactual setting, would have expected deferential treatment from the white people in the lunch counter. The white man's warning, "Watch it, Tojo," is evidently meant to be a racial slur, but it refers of course to Tojo Hideki, a Japanese general who became Prime Minister of Japan and initiated the attack on Pearl Harbor. He was later executed for war crimes in 1948. One of the great ironies of *The Man in* the High Castle is that it was in fact U.S. forces that occupied Japan between 1945 and 1953, not the other way around, and of course the specter of Japanese internment camps during the war haunts Dick's fictional setting involving Japanese occupation of the Pacific States of America. But the lunch counter scene may also deliberately invoke the broader desegregation movement of the 1950s and 1960s that had been launched only two years earlier, in 1960, with sit-ins at an F. W. Woolworth's lunch counter in Greensboro, NC. "Where am I?" Mr. Tagomi wonders. "Out of my world, my time and space."[17] A disorientation borne of the fact that he has returned to a world of de-facto racial segregation in the early 1960s.

While alternate-history novels like *The Man in the High Castle* "flaunt the novelist's general prerogative of departing from the historical record," it is worth noting that they depart from the historical record to produce distinctly *worse* outcomes, as Saint-Amour points out.[18] This case study in particular portrays the United States being defeated in a war that it actually won, so the question remains, as Gallagher poses it: "Why in the postwar period did we begin imaginatively to snatch defeat from the jaws of victory?"[19] One answer might be that in the first two decades after the war, there was a palpable sense of relief, a feeling of "disaster averted."[20] The author may also be "motivated by a desire to prove that *it could* have happened in the US."[21] In Dick's alternate America, fascism has won the day; authoritarian states are the new normal. Another answer is that by 1962 when the novel was published, the most consequential outcome of World War II was not lasting peace, but a permanent Cold War and the alarming prospect of nuclear annihilation. Finally, it was also becoming abundantly clear that the prosperity generated by the postwar economic boom was certainly not shared by all, and the tensions around equality and opportunity were building. The country in 1962 was on the threshold of a volcanic eruption. Saint-Amour poignantly suggests that "by immersing us in a worse alternative from which we long to come home," alternate-history novels like *The Man in the High Castle* may paradoxically invoke aspirations for a better America, or what he calls "homesickness for a different present."[22]

2. The Plot Against America

Throughout his long career, Philip Roth has repeatedly blurred the lines between fact and fiction.[23] *The Plot Against America* is no exception. The aviator Charles A. Lindbergh decides to run for president and wins the

Republican nomination in the U.S. presidential election of 1940. Promising to keep the United States out of the war then escalating in Europe, Lindbergh runs a campaign based upon isolationism and populist nationalism against incumbent President Franklin Delano Roosevelt, who broke with political tradition to run for an unprecedented third term as president. To the astonishment of virtually everyone in the United States, Lindbergh wins the election in a landslide:

> The November election hadn't even been close. Lindbergh got fifty-seven percent of the popular vote and, in an electoral sweep, carried forty-six states. ... Though on the morning after the election disbelief prevailed, especially among the pollsters, by the day after that everybody seemed to understand everything, and the radio commentators and the news columnists made it sound as if Roosevelt's defeat had been preordained.[24]

Only weeks after winning the election, hence before the inauguration, Lindberg travels to Iceland to meet personally with Adolf Hitler and sign a non-aggression pact, the Iceland Understanding, followed by a similar agreement with Japan known as the Hawaii Understanding. Meanwhile, some journalists contend that Germany may have meddled in the election to help Lindberg win.[25]

What attracted Philip Roth to the alternate-history novel genre? According to the author's own account, he wanted to experiment with an alternate history that more or less dovetailed with his family's actual experience of wartime in the 1940s:

> My every imaginative effort was directed toward making the effect of that reality as strong as I could, and not so as to illuminate the present through the past but to illuminate the past through the past. I wanted my family to be up against it precisely as they would have been up against it had history turned out as I've skewed it in this book and they were overpowered by the forces I have arrayed against them. ... I've tried to portray them here as faithfully as I could—as though I were, in fact, writing nonfiction.[26]

It is as if he has ventured into a new genre, the alternate-history novel, only to treat it as memoir. Written in the first person, Roth represents an escalating national crisis from the point of view of an 8-year-old boy named Philip Roth. "I wanted nothing to do with history," young Philip tells us. "I wanted to be a boy on the smallest scale possible."[27] History evidently has other ideas. Americans are strangely in thrall to a president who denigrates the free press and systematically erodes civil liberties. In Roth's nightmare scenario, the "plot against America" is orchestrated not by foreign adversaries or extremists, but by a deranged demagogue inside the White House.[28]

In a postscript appended to the novel, the author offers a standard novelistic disclaimer: "*The Plot Against America* is a work of fiction."[29] Yet he also includes "A True Chronology of the Major Figures," a list of "Other Historical Figures in the Work," and "Some Documentation" of his archival sources, all of which are "intended as a reference for readers interested in tracking where historical fact ends and historical imagining begins."[30] The primary archival source is a speech titled "Who Are the War Agitators?" (1941), which Charles Lindberg gave at an America First Conference rally in Des Moines, Iowa. He condemns "the persecution of the Jewish race in Germany," yet he warns against allowing the "natural passions and prejudices of other peoples to lead our country to destruction," and "for reasons which are not American."[31] Lindberg employs an egregious political demonology here by implying that American Jews are not fully American, and distinguishing us versus them: "We cannot blame them for looking out for what they believe to be their own interests, but we must also look out for ours."[32] According to his biographer A. Scott Berg, Lindberg warned elsewhere that we must "guard ourselves against attack by foreign armies and dilution by foreign races," so as "to preserve that most priceless possession, our inheritance of European blood."[33] In the novel, Roth momentarily takes on the role of a historian by parsing the archival sources before reverting back to memoir mode at the end of the passage:

> When Lindbergh wrote proudly of 'our inheritance of European blood,' when he warned against 'dilution of foreign races' and 'the infiltration of inferior blood' (all phrases that turn up in diary entries from those years), he was recording personal convictions shared by a sizable portion of America First's rank-and-file membership as well as by a rabid constituency even more extensive than a Jew like my father, with his bitter hatred of anti-Semitism—or like my mother, with her deeply ingrained distrust of Christians—could ever imagine to be flourishing all across America.[34]

What are the circumstances that might have allowed a populist leader to galvanize the racist and pro-Nazi elements that were indeed present in America in the 1940s, "the ordinary Americans, tens of thousands of them, maybe millions of them," who shared Lindberg's repugnant views?[35] At another rally held at Madison Square Garden on February 20, 1939, an estimated 22,000 people gathered in support of a blatantly pro-Nazi group called the German-American Bund, which testified to the "strength and influence" of the "Nazi movement in the United States."[36]

Roth's fictional account of the 1939 German-American Bund rally is largely accurate—and dramatically riveting. To understand "how vital" the pro-Nazi movement in America was, the author provides "an intensified experience of counter-history" by recreating the rally itself.[37] Festooned with banners featuring slogans such as "Keep America Out of the Jewish War" and "Stop Jewish Domination of Christian Americans," Madison Square Garden is filled with "some twenty-five thousand people who had turned out to support President Lindberg's invitation to the German foreign minister and to denounce the Democrats for their renewed 'warmongering.'"[38] Whereas the actual German-American Bund was investigated by the FBI and its leaders brought up on criminal charges, President Lindberg brings an end to such efforts in the novel: "But under Lindbergh, government efforts at harassing or intimidating Bund members ceased and they were able to regain their strength. ... The deep fascist fellowship uniting the Bund was now masked by vociferous patriotic declamations on the peril of a worldwide Communist revolution."[39]

Another crucial hinge moment in *The Plot Against America* is when President Lindbergh disappears in an apparent plane crash, which sets in motion "dark days" in which Vice President Burton Wheeler takes over the White House, illegally detains the First Lady, and imposes martial law across the land. When beloved radio personality Walter Winchell is assassinated at a protest rally in Louisville, Kentucky, the Roth family decide they must leave the country for Canada: "we'd been overpowered by the forces arrayed against us and were about to flee and become foreigners. I wept all the way to school. Our incomparable American childhood was ended."[40] As if to confirm their worst fears, the government begins detaining prominent Jewish leaders "under suspicion of being 'among the ringleaders of the Jewish conspiratorial plot against America.'"[41] Meanwhile, the U.S. military shuts down all newspaper offices and radio stations in New York, and army tanks close off all bridges and tunnels into the city. Mayor Fiorello LaGuardia is one of the few politicians willing to speak out: "It can't happen here? My friends, it *is* happening here."[42] LaGuardia is promptly arrested. Alarmed by these developments, Philip reflects that a "political catastrophe of unimaginable proportions was transforming a free society into a police state."[43]

LaGuardia's offhand remark, "It can't happen here?" refers, of course, to the title of Sinclair Lewis's novel *It Can't Happen Here* (1935). Although not an alternate-history novel, Lewis's dystopian novel follows the rise of a similar populist political figure, Berzelius Windrip, who is elected president and, within a year of his inauguration, imposes martial law throughout the land. More egregious violations of civil liberties soon follow. Through the strong-arm tactics of his Gestapo-like police force, the Minute Men, President Windrip implements Plank Nine of his platform: arresting journalists who speak out against him, banning opposing political parties, and seizing private assets, especially from Jews. The narrator informs us that Jews "began to escape to Canada; just as once, by the 'underground railroad' the Negro slaves had escaped into that free Northern air."[44] The Secretary of Culture, Dr. Macgoblin, orders public book burnings reminiscent of those carried out in Germany in May 1933. And when riots break out in African American communities, Windrip's security forces respond with swift reprisals in a genocidal campaign of "massacres" aimed at "eliminating the Negroes."[45] In short, Americans are now living in a state of exception: "Every moment everyone felt fear, nameless and omnipresent."[46]

Lewis wrote *It Can't Happen Here* to sound the alarm that it could indeed happen here. The author's wife Dorothy Thompson was a prominent journalist who interviewed Hitler in 1931 as a foreign correspondent in Berlin. After a series of articles "warning Americans about the Nazi propaganda machine that masked the vicious persecution of Jews," she was expelled from Germany in 1934.[47] Interestingly, Thompson appears as a character in *The Plot Against America*. In the memorable scene at the 1939 Bund rally at Madison Square Garden, Thompson is ejected for exercising her "constitutional right to laugh at ridiculous statements in a public hall."[48]

The novel's "counterfactual detour" into alternate history eventually comes to an end.[49] Ann Lindbergh Morrow, the First Lady, is ironically the one who saves the day. She denounces Wheeler's "seditious administration" and then spearheads the effort to restore democratic norms, which "culminates two and a half weeks later, on Tuesday, November 3, 1942, in a sweep by the Democrats of the House and the Senate and the landslide victory of Franklin Delano Roosevelt for a third presidential term."[50] A month later, in December 1942, the Japanese launch a surprise attack on Pearl Harbor, and the novel returns to history, except the date is wrong by exactly one year, as if the counterfactual energies of his narrative had somehow spun out of authorial control.

3. The Ledger of Slavery

Colson Whitehead's novel *The Underground Railroad*, which won both a Pulitzer Prize and a National Book Award, is best understood not as an alternate-history novel, but as a work of historical fiction with deliberately anachronistic and counterfactual elements. Most prominently, Whitehead represents the Underground Railroad as an actual underground railroad. Similarly, he transposes historical events such as the Tuskegee syphilis experiments from the twentieth century to the antebellum period. Doing so de-familiarizes and re-contextualizes events, such that readers may find themselves second-guessing their knowledge of history. Were there any twelve-story buildings with elevators before the Civil War? Did any state legislature pass a law making it illegal for Black people to live there? These and other questions will surely puzzle readers of *The Underground Railroad*. As the author explains in an interview, "once I made the choice to make a literal underground railroad, you know, it freed me up to play with time a bit more. ... [I]t allowed me to bring in things that didn't happen in 1850—skyscrapers, aspects of the eugenics movement, forced sterilization and the Tuskegee syphilis experiment."[51] Of course, this does not mean that he leaves the facts of history behind. Instead, he alternates between mostly realistic depictions—the Randall plantation in Georgia, for example—and other, more imaginative leaps into speculative history. But what cultural work do these departures from the historical record do for Whitehead, exactly?

To answer that question, let's look more closely at the North Carolina chapter. Early in the chapter, the station agent Martin Wells tries to explain to Cora why the North Carolina legislature had passed a law banning all individuals of African descent from residing in the state:

> As with everything in the south, it started with cotton. The ruthless engine of cotton required its fuel of African bodies. Crisscrossing the ocean, ships brought bodies to work the land and to breed more bodies.
>
> The pistons of this engine moved without relent. More slaves led to more cotton, which led to more money to buy more land to farm more cotton. Even with the termination of the slave trade, in less than a generation the numbers were untenable.[52]

The sheer size of the Black population, in other words, brings with it the potential for a revolt.

"It was not difficult to imagine the sequence when the slave cast off his chains in pursuit of freedom—and retribution," the narrator tells us. "The whites were right to be afraid. One day the system would collapse in blood."[53] Whitehead dares to pose the counterfactual question: What if there was a large-scale slave revolt in the South, one more consequential than Nat Turner's 1831 rebellion? He then proceeds to imagine the sequence when the slave cast off his chains:

> The slaves walked the roads between towns with their scavenged weapons: hatchets and scythes, knives and bricks. Tipped by colored turncoats, the white enforcers organized elaborate ambushes, decimating the insurgents with gunfire and running them down on horseback, reinforced by the might of the United States Army. At the first alarms, civilian volunteers joined the patrollers to quell the disturbance, invading the quarters and putting freemen's homes to the torch. Suspects and bystanders crammed the jails. They strung up the guilty, and, in the interest of prevention, a robust portion of the innocent.[54]

The passage evokes a scenario that the South had long feared: a sort of race war inspired by the only successful slave revolt in the Americas, the Haiti revolution. Brutal reprisals soon follow, and the "revolts were squashed."[55]

The state legislature then decides that the only viable way to prevent further uprisings is to expel all slaves and former slaves from the state, embarking on a brutal campaign of what we might call Black removal: "The new race laws forbid colored men and women from setting foot on North Carolina soil. Freemen who refused to leave their land were run off or massacred."[56] North Carolina did not in fact experience a significant slave revolt, although Turner's rebellion in Southampton County, Virginia took place only 20 miles from the border with North Carolina. Nor did it ban all Black people from the state. Nonetheless, the chapter is meant to invoke similar exclusion laws enacted to prevent Black people from settling in Oregon, as Whitehead explains: "the North Carolina section seems like this fantastic, alternate universe ruled by white supremacy, but Oregon was founded on white-supremacist principles."[57] As with the Tuskegee syphilis experiment, the author is willing to forgo strict historical accuracy. By scrambling up times and places, he seems to want his readers to re-examine the legacy of slavery more closely.

Whitehead did a considerable amount of research in preparation for the novel. He read slave narratives by Frederick Douglass and Harriet Jacobs, as well as interviews with former slaves conducted by the Works Progress Administration in the 1930s. He read widely in recent scholarship on slavery and the Underground Railroad by Edward E. Baptist, Fergus Bordewich, and Eric Foner, among others. Historians have long recognized that capitalism and slavery were deeply intertwined, and recently scholars have demonstrated the truly global economic reach of the slave trade.[58] The specificity of Whitehead's fictional Randall plantation, especially the elder Mr. Randall's fortuitous decision to switch from tobacco to cotton, suggests that the author is familiar with at least some of this scholarship, as does the passage cited above in which Martin Wells attributes a growing demand for slaves to the global cotton industry. For another example, consider a passage in which the narrator describes the accounting practices used by slaveholders:

> List upon list crowded the ledger of slavery. The names gathered first on the African coasts in tens of thousands of manifests. The human cargo. The names of the dead were as important as the names of the living, as every loss from disease and suicide—and other mishaps labeled as such for accounting purposes—needed to be justified to employers. At the auction block they tallied the souls purchased at each auction, and on the plantations the overseers preserved the names of workers in rows of tight cursive. Every name an asset, breathing capital, profit made flesh.[59]

In contrast to slavery's blatant commodification of human flesh, Cora's own personal accounting system is more humane: "The peculiar institution made Cora into a maker of lists as well. In her inventory of loss people were not reduced to sums but multiplied by their kindnesses. People she had loved, people who had helped her."[60] Cora offers here a hard-won wisdom about what really matters, a sliver of hope in the midst of an otherwise unflinching portrayal of relentless violence.

By focusing on Cora's interiority and her lived experience of slavery, *The Underground Railroad* provides a window on the condition of social death and the systematic dehumanization of enslavement.[61] "We are grounded in the consciousness of the protagonist Cora as she takes us from place to place," writes literary critic Valerie Babb. "The technique provides readers with a sense of touring scenes from slavery as she draws back the curtain to reveal its ugly details."[62] After fleeing from the horrors of the Randall plantation in Georgia, Cora finds herself in the neighboring state of South Carolina, which ostensibly "has a much more enlightened attitude toward colored advancement than the rest of the South."[63] By all appearances, she is much better off than she had been on Randall, but soon enough, she learns that appearances can be deceiving. A young doctor from the North, Dr. Aloysius Stevens, explains to her that "South Carolina was in the midst of a large public health program" of sterilizing young Black women, often against their will, "in the name of population control."[64] He tells Cora that the procedure is still entirely voluntary for young women like herself, but she is understandably alarmed by this information.

It turns out that the hospital is conducting another experiment on African American men. Sam confides to Cora that he overheard a different doctor, Dr. Bertram, bragging about his work:

> His patients believed they were being treated for blood ailments. The tonics the hospital administered, however, were merely sugar water. In fact, ... [they] were participants in a study of the latent and tertiary stages of syphilis. ... The syphilis program was one of many studies and experiments under way at the colored wing of the hospital. ... Controlled sterilization, research into communicable diseases, the perfection of new surgical techniques on the socially unfit—was it any wonder the best medical talents in the country were flocking to South Carolina?[65]

Whitehead invokes the infamous Tuskegee syphilis experiment, a forty-year study conducted under the auspices of the U.S. Public Health service between 1932 and 1972. The author clearly risks undermining historical accuracy by transposing this experiment to the antebellum South, where it becomes a kind of puzzle for Cora to solve: "Cora had been figuring on Sam's news all day, holding it up to the light like a hideous bauble, tilting it so."[66] Like Tagomi's mysterious silver triangle in *The Man in the High Castle*, the metaphorical bauble of Sam's disturbing news serves to teleport Cora herself—and Colson Whitehead's readers—to another time and place.

The South Carolina episode seems to invoke not only the Tuskegee syphilis experiment, but also the forced sterilization and selective euthanasia conducted by the Nazis during World War II.[67] And nowhere is the connection more apparent than in the next section, North Carolina, when Cora finds herself in what she calls a "Museum of Terrible Wonders."[68] When the station agent, Martin Wells, shows her what North Carolinians euphemistically call The Freedom Trail, in which the "corpses hung from trees as rotting ornaments" for as far as the eye can see, Cora cannot help but wonder: "In what sort of hell had the train let her off?"[69] Martin and his taciturn wife Ethel hide Cora in their cramped attic for months on end, like Anne Frank hiding out in her secret apartment. Cora catches glimpses of the outside world through a "jagged hole" facing the street and the park opposite.[70] Peering through the hole, Cora witnesses a weekly festival on Friday nights featuring music, theatricals, and what she takes to be a "coon show" performed by two White men, "their faces blackened by burned cork."[71] And suddenly the truth dawns on her: "In North Carolina the negro race did not exist except at the ends of ropes."[72] No wonder the state of North Carolina begins to resemble Nazi Germany, or Nazi-occupied France, complete with its own inverted version of the French Resistance: "After a lull in white arrests, some towns increased the rewards for turning in collaborators."[73] In France, collaborators were the traitors who colluded with the Nazis, whereas here they are decent, "kindhearted citizens" like Martin who risk their own lives to hide fugitives "in their attics and cellars and coal bins."[74] The term "collaborator" here almost amounts to a deliberate malapropism, yet taken together these and other resonances with the Holocaust form a pattern that reminds us of the striking similarities between chattel slavery in the eighteenth and nineteenth centuries and genocide in the twentieth century.

As we have seen, the most common plot device of alternate-history novels is the hinge moment, which splits off from actual history and either prevents known events from happening or allows previously unimaginable events to occur. Cora's initial journey via the Underground Railroad into the counterfactual world of South Carolina might be considered a kind of hinge moment, and it does function much like time travel, as if "the underground railroad was laid in the direction of the bizarre," and she "had been conveyed into a chamber of horrors."[75] But even if, as I have argued, The Underground Railroad is less an alternate-history novel than simply a work of historical fiction with counterfactual set pieces and other fantastical elements, it clearly shares the iconoclastic, revisionist impulse behind the novels we have examined in this chapter. While rooted in slavery's archives, The Underground Railroad ventures into the surreal, which gives it the feel of speculative fiction. Here is Whitehead describing his own unique approach:

> I didn't see any particular value in doing a straight historical novel. The use of certain fantastical elements was just a different way to tell a story. If I stuck to the facts then I couldn't bring in the Holocaust, and the KKK, and eugenic experiments. I was able to achieve a different effect by altering history. Instead of sticking to what happened, it was being more concerned with what might have happened. ... Being able to play with time

and different historical episodes allows me to, hopefully, tell a different story of America than the one it tells itself.[76]

The enduring appeal of alternate-history novels surely has something to do with the impulse to reckon with past atrocities, to pass judgment on history. By revisiting the past and imagining the roads *not* taken, however, counterfactual fictions can potentially challenge us to aspire to a better future.

13

Last Camp

Téa Obreht

Quartzite is a tiny town in La Paz County, Arizona. It's one of those bright, gone-in-an-instant flashes along Interstate 10 that feels utterly roofless—all sun and open sky—and yet, somehow, simultaneously full of secrets. During winter months, a glut of gem shows draws streams of vacationing snowbirds to its main thoroughfare. Pride of place in its solitary graveyard belongs to a squat, brilliantly tiled pyramid, a mausoleum whose shape might strike blow-ins as odd, but not especially out of place. Pyramids, after all, belong in the desert. So do camels—and this particular pyramid happens to be topped with the rusty silhouette of one of those. To an unknowing visitor, the whole ensemble might look like just another piece of desert kitsch.

In truth, however, this unlikely monument is the "last camp" and final resting place of a man identified by the grave-marker as "Hi Jolly." Born Philip Tedro in 1828, he earned this delightful moniker upon his 1856 arrival in Texas, where "Hadji Ali," the name he had adopted after making the pilgrimage to Mecca, proved unpronounceable. His memorial plaque goes on to establish that he was "born somewhere in Syria" (to Greek and Syrian parents, themselves Ottoman subjects), and first set foot in this country, together with several compatriots and a small herd of dromedaries and Bactrian camels, as a member of the U.S. Camel Corps, a bizarre and all-but-forgotten experiment intended to test the feasibility of using camels as pack animals in the military's exploration of the Southwest.

It might surprise you to learn that, for a region with such a fixed mythos, the American West is bursting with such obscure oddities. The particulars of this one bowled me over a few years ago. I was struggling through the second draft of a new novel, feeling happier with the research—which involved visiting tiny regional museums all over Wyoming and South Dakota—than I was with the story, the bulk of which, I could already tell, was doomed. And then: an unexpected mercy. An episode of one of my favorite podcasts, *Stuff You Missed in History Class*—popular with nerds like myself, who like to make sense of the present from the past's weirdest minutiae—spun a

Téa Obreht, *Last Camp*. In: *Historical Fiction Now*. Edited by Mark Eaton and Bruce Holsinger, Oxford University Press. © Téa Obreht (2023). DOI: 10.1093/oso/9780198877035.003.0014 turn-of-the-century fireside yarn about two homesteading women who find themselves beset by an unidentifiable apparition on their Arizona ranch. What they see is impossible—unless, of course, you know about the Camel Corps. Which they did not. And, until that moment, neither did I.

Having dedicated so much time to researching the history of the West, I couldn't believe this information had eluded me for so long. A camel in the Southwest? *What a thing*, I thought. *How did it get there?*

I think it's fair to say I started writing *Inland* the moment I asked myself that question—though in truth I gave my previous book another half-hearted go for another month. All the while, *Inland*'s questions kept goading me. Who were the two women in the house? Were they sisters? Friends? How long had they been living there? What minutiae of their lives did this bizarre encounter disrupt?

It's a funny thing, the writer's obsession. You never know what's going to run away with your whole existence; and once something does, the only thing to do is follow the questions wherever they lead. Personally, I never do so expecting to arrive at any conclusions; one of writing's reigning pleasures is the inevitability that any glimmer of an answer will immediately spawn more and more unknowns. So there I found myself, abandoning a pretty much completed manuscript and setting off down the road toward the characters I wanted to learn about: Lurie, a Balkan immigrant and former outlaw who finds himself joining the Camel Corps; and Nora, a home-steading woman whose town is desiccating in more ways than one while she waits for her newspaperman husband to return with water; and, eventually, Hadji Ali.

Over the four years I wrote *Inland*, I often asked myself why a former Yugoslav who grew up in Cyprus and Egypt felt so irresistibly drawn to the West, on the page and in life. I think the answer lies with wanting to under-stand more about my adoptive country than the facile cowboy myths I was fed growing up; with wanting to understand more about my Bosniak grand-mother's womanhood than I knew; with feeling homesick for the beauty of the landscape and drawn to the communities at the periphery of legend; and, maybe above all, with the man buried under that strange pyramid, out where the arid vein of Highway 10 meets Highway 95, a place, like so many in America, that I bypassed countless times on my way to some more alluring destination, never suspecting how much it would one day mean to me.

It's like that, America. Its ghosts seem to haunt from both the past and the future. And though Hadji Ali is not the book's principal specter, he was nevertheless the thing that most haunted me: an Ottoman subject caught between his old empire and his new one, not quite belonging anywhere; the warden of creatures that were utterly pedestrian to him, but a source of end-less fascination to everyone who encountered them. Did he feel unexpected pride, caring for such controversial charges? We know he was a prideful man; once, many years after his time with the Corps, he supposedly crashed a camel-drawn cart through a party in protest of not having been invited; I have also found at least one instance of his visiting an Arizona newspaper office to remind everybody not to forget the Camel Corps—to no avail.

We don't know whether he was a decent man. We don't know whether he considered himself Greek or Turkish or Syrian or American. We don't know whether the sins of empire troubled him when he followed the army across Native lands. We don't know whether he considered himself a loving husband or father, though we do know his wife left him when he refused to give up wandering. Whatever else he may have been, I believe he was restless, caught between his old self and his new, belonging less and less to his own past as the years wore on, but somehow, inexplicably, never getting closer to home.

Hadji Ali lived in Tyson's Wells, not far from his resting place, until his death in 1902. His pyramid, I'm told, is the most visited place in Quartzite.

When last I went to see him, I stood for a long time beside my mother on the dirt road leading to his tomb. It was April. The golden hour in western Arizona—so full of light and shadow it defies description. In my haste to pack for this last-minute trip, I had forgotten to bring Hadji Ali an offering. I tried to affix some meaning to the broken pens and dried-out chapsticks strewn about the bottom of my purse. Maybe it wouldn't be so bad to tuck a MetroCard between the stones of his grave? Anything to not come all this way and leave nothing behind. Then, to my amazement, my roving fingers caught the edge of a magnifying glass—small, plastic, quite ordinary save for being one of several that, for some unspecified reason, my grandmother had been tucking into the folds of my wallets for as long as I could remember. I hadn't used any of those wallets for years. They were all back home in New York, wrapped in tissue paper, too precious to carry around and risk losing now that she was gone. How this magnifying glass found its way into that particular purse, on this particular trip, I'll never know. I am certain, how-ever, that when she plucked it out of some tchotchke jar at the Kalenić green market in Belgrade, or off some roadside stand along the Dalmatian coast, she could never have imagined it might end up here, of all places: thousands of miles away, in a blistering and unfamiliar desert, on the grave of a stranger who left this world thirty-four years before she entered it.

But that's exactly where it is.

PART IV

EPISTEMOLOGIES

14

Historical Impressionism and Signs of Life

The Blessing and Burden of Writing the Past

Jessie Burton

My historical sources, or what we might call "the past," exist in a present-day symbiosis with my fictional process. The past is as much a story for me as today is, equally subject to narrative bias, exclusion, and embellishment. Seeking to re-present the past is an impossible act, and not just because physics forbids it. The fact is, as soon as you start writing a story set in the past, in order to "get close" to that very same past, a paradoxical gap grows between the original material and the new presentation. Believing this, I suppose I've never come at my source material in a particularly respectful fashion. I've had a writer's hunger, and a reader's hunger too. Am I making a new past? Maybe; and one as equally unstable. I've been looking at the past to give me something. I've used it to get somewhere else—not somewhere higher, or better. Just somewhere different.

"History" has had an enormous imaginative hold on my decision to become a writer of fiction. There's nothing fixed, or solid, about the past, and sometimes, when I'm "finished" with my sources, I feel I have merely swapped one fiction for another. I've added in characters, divided it into chapters, given it a beginning, a middle, and an end. I have subsumed the inchoate shape of history into something manageable, and called it a novel. The past is a patchwork of stories I have unstitched and sewn back together to make another. I've never thought much before now about morality or accountability in my fiction—the writer's hunger again, overriding every-thing! A certain innocence and irreverence proved vital in sticking to my dream of writing and being published. Up until now, when called upon to make a testament as a user of history, I have resisted. But here we are. I'd like

Jessie Burton, *Historical Impressionism and Signs of Life: The Blessing and Burden of Writing the Past.*
In: *Historical Fiction Now.* Edited by Mark Eaton and Bruce Holsinger, Oxford University Press.
© Jessie Burton (2023). DOI: 10.1093/oso/9780198877035.003.0015

to talk about the kind of history I wanted to offer to the reader. I'd like to reflect on what good I think this genre can do.

***

Back in 2012, after I had drafted my first novel, *The Miniaturist*, for the seventeenth time, I felt it was ready to be looked at by literary agents. I was not met with much enthusiasm. One of the overriding comments I received was this: "Historical fiction is over." I didn't even know that what I'd written was historical fiction. I was also told it was a "quiet book." I didn't even know books had decibel levels. When eleven publishers were forced to go into auction to buy it some months later, and when in 2014 it was published and my life turned upside down, I learned my first vital lesson in publishing: nobody knows anything for sure. Also: that people still like books set in a place they know they cannot reach by any other way than through the act of reading. As a conduit for metaphysical tourism, an outlet for curiosity, a form of fictional reparation and a chance for empathy, an opportunity for stylistic flair and innovation, a means to escape, but also to go into the pages and find the familiar: fiction we call historical has never been more popular.

My first novel was set in the mercantile, hypocritical world of seventeenth-century Amsterdam, and my second, *The Muse*, published in 2016, took as its settings 1960s London and 1930s southern Spain before the outbreak of the Spanish civil war. Therefore, by dint of my authorial choices so far, both organic and deliberate, you would call me a historical fiction writer, or, as Hilary Mantel described it, someone who "works imaginatively with the past," a description I prefer.

However, I didn't intend to write within the genre of "historical fiction." *The Miniaturist* was set in the past almost as a matter of obligation, because the item around which the book revolves, a huge Dutch cabinet house, was built in 1686. I spotted it in the Rijksmuseum in Amsterdam, it enchanted me, and thus began a highly enjoyable but necessary involvement with the mores and habits of that city's past. In order to write my fiction, I needed to understand a society that might permit the construction of such an expensive and useless marvel in the wake of a century of Calvinism. *The Muse* was to be a study of Caribbean immigration to 1960s London, and the psychic scar of civil war on ordinary people. The main drive of *The Miniaturist* was the philosophy of feminine emancipation, both imaginative and literal, and *The Muse* became an examination of the cost of artistic creativity. The "past" had less to do with it in both cases.

The detailed, yet physically unreachable settings of seventeenth-century Amsterdam and 1936 Andalucía were inextricable from the process of writing the novels, but *transmitting* them was not my main intention when writing. Historical detail was the decorative wallpaper with which I furnished my two houses, but their aesthetic appeal turned into a primary marketing tool once they were sitting on bookshop shelves. The taxonomizing of the books under "historical" came after the books were written and taken off me. This is probably because it is a very human trait to categorize things, and publishing needs to make money, and bookshops need filing systems. I suppose given that life is such a chaos, we can at least attempt to impose some order on the creative interpretations of it that are offered up.

When I write, I try not to write about history. I try and write about people who lived in what we call "history." I take my cue from two books: *A Traveller in Time*, by Alison Uttley, a book I first read when I was 11, which enraptured me with its sights, smells, and sounds of Tudor Derbyshire. The second was published sixty years later: *Wolf Hall*, by Hilary Mantel, a novel whose stylistic innovation set itself apart from the genre and broke new ground for more to come, the seemingly effortless inhabitation of a long-dead statesman whose worlds and selves are so palpable to us that the readerly experience is akin to the raising of a literary Lazarus. For me, there is no self-consciousness or historification here, despite ample opportunity— it is the Tudors, after all. Instead, there is psychology, physicality, humor, poetry, the employ of fiction at its highest—and it is a difficult feat to pull off. Very few do it.

Speaking from my own limitations, I know I am not a writer in the market for telling you exactly how all life in a past society used to be. Yet it often feels as if I am expected to do so. If literary novelists fail to do that in state-of-the-nation, modern-set fiction, why am I expected to be able to do it of past societies? We are often seen as lesser writers, in the market for sub-literary "vignetting." But a book set in twenty-first-century New York is as full of vignettes as one set in seventeenth-century Amsterdam. It's all still fiction. Writing closer to the era of your actual birth does not make you a more accurate writer.

Writers who work with history are often deemed to have failed in conveying the amorphous, glorious quality also known as *life*. We cannot be existential or physically authentic, because our novels also include descriptions of taffeta curtains or barouche boxes, and the currency our characters spend is florins. Life isn't corsets and lieges anymore; perhaps I hadn't noticed? Incidentally, I think the same criticism is also levied at writers of science fiction and fantasy. But sure, Ian McEwan can remain "literary" and therefore "truthful" whilst using the voice of an embryo to narrate his novel. (Sorry, Ian.)

I chose the phrase "historical impressionism" because I think it's what I do. Impressionism is the nearest form of artistic style I can think of to describe how I turn the hard pallet of history into the more alluring bed of fiction. I take an impression, I take another, and another. From a distance, it *looks* like history, it *sounds* like history, but when you get up close to it, history has become a blur amidst the story, a subjective, beautiful mass of color that has no discernible shape within the dominant form of the novel's structure. The reader walks through the world I have created as she might through Monet's water lilies. She knows she's in a garden of blue and green tranquility, but she can't see the outline of every leaf.

I often call my work with history an impressionist act, because I am passing on a softened likeness of dead people, dead societies, dead beliefs, masks whose broken edges are mine to fill with fiction, and make deceptively wearable. It's the same as your own face, only … different. We love our art to be recognizable as much as we want it to be a curio, and I think that historical fiction scratches that itch.

***

There is nothing radical in the observation that novelists and historians share contrarian streaks, rebellious natures, a propensity to stand on the edge of society looking in, a mutual desire to present something old as something new, sometimes even as something *true*. Historians, historically speaking, have been as selective with the facts as novelists. First and foremost, with both disciplines comes interpretation; emphasis, not mimesis. In fact, I believe that anything else but subjectivity is impossible in both disciplines. The objects of our focus are dead; we are still alive. We use their alphabets to spell any words we please. Despite cross-referencing, deep research, and painstaking diligence, can we ever know the absolute truth? When it comes to interpreting history, all we have are various versions of the truth, and nearly all could be arguably true.

However, I think historical novelists can sometimes be *more* respectful to their sources than historians are, because they are afraid of the accusation of sub-intellectual understanding, of misinterpreting their research. Thus, psychological acuity can give way to fetishized historical detail; obsessive historical recreation outweighs lightness of touch and nuance. It's all "how it definitely used to be" instead of "how it arguably could have been"—so we are left with something safe or honorable, the product of pastiche. Novels become homages to history. Conversely, some historians—and I emphasize *some*—have always struck me as more arrogant than novelists, as if they themselves are not telling a story too, as if they think the act of putting facts into story form dulls their intellectual sheen.

History has to take second place to my desire to show off—that is, to write. And as Hilary Mantel has said: we are obliged to be accurate and fair, but we don't have to be neutral. However: I'm not saying that good historical fiction should have no accountability. That desire to entertain wouldn't be there if it weren't for the offerings of the past. And given that historical fiction seems to enter a reader's consciousness in a more emotional, entertaining, pervasive—some might say insidious—fashion, than "straight" books of history, which seek to inform in prescriptive, didactic ways that might be off-putting, as novelists we do have to be careful. There is a good question to be asked over the novelist's responsibility when cherry-picking the past. But I don't think we should go entirely the other way; to deny our power and fail to cherish our imaginations. Historical novelists have a chance, literally, to write some wrongs!

So how to do it best? Failing the miracle that one might be able to write like Hilary Mantel or Toni Morrison, I suppose for the rest of us the task is to get close to your source material, enough for it to have a liminal effect on your artistic skills, and to undergo a subsequent process of dissociation to make space for the imagination to enter in. Or another way of putting it: when I researched what became *The Miniaturist*, I was looking for signs of life.

The historical sources I used individually in both my novels had to coalesce and lose their dominance in the name of entertainment. All kinds of social historical detail were accrued; I wanted to know what women did with their menstrual cloths. How uncomfortable *were* they? What did they eat on Christmas Day, and at what time? Had the light gone by then, and how much did they value a beeswax candle over a tallow one? How did they grieve? Did they like children, or did they treat them like tiny adults? How prevalent was lobster as a meal?

I didn't want to know all this simply in order to *show* all this. I was looking more for the psychological knock-on effects such conditions would create; the drip-drip creation of emotional stalactites, clinging to the ceilings, obstacles in the fight to live. Three or four excellent reference books sufficed in my search, books for which I am eternally grateful. The questions I asked of them turned into a cornucopia of other information that helped me weave the social fabric of that novel. To this, I added some postcards of Vermeer's and De Hooch's work, Blu-tacked to my bedroom wall. A seventeenth-century recipe book, called *The Sensible Cook*, helped too: as did Google maps, because the old center of Amsterdam looked very much in 2010 as it did in 1686.

There was a lot I needed to discover, and historians had painstakingly paved the way for me. And then, in a perverse way, I tried to forget that path. I wanted to create a fictional universe, not a historical recreation. An impression. None of the facts and opinions I accrued could ever substitute the soul of the novel, although their accrual was essential, and they brought me closer to that shining light.

I wasn't a novelist at this point, let alone a historical one. I wasn't thinking about *responsibility*. I wasn't even conceiving of a novel—I was simply writing a story, a story I would like to read, whose fundamentals—Golden Age Amsterdam, a miniature house, the merchant world, the role of women, and the treatment of outsiders—interested me. I had no expectations that I was going to be published. I was temping as a personal assistant in the financial district in London in between acting jobs, writing chunks of the story to myself in the bodies of emails, and printing off versions of the manuscript when the hedge-funders were out at lunch. Sometimes, I wrote the story on my smartphone on the commuter train home. It was a very ad-hoc, clandestine existence, as patchwork as the way I was treating the history I was plundering.

When the story turned into a published book, and became very popular, people demanded that I tell them how to research their own historical novels, or asked me: How did I make it feel so *real*, such a synthesis of the past into their present-day imaginations? They told me they could smell Cornelia's pastries, or taste the blood in their own mouth as the master's dog was murdered. I didn't always know how to respond. The honest answer was: I read some books, I made some observations, I closed my eyes and imagined.

I'm not saying this to be facetious. I feel, at times, a fraud. A fraud, because I used history as a stepping stone to get somewhere else.

***

Here, I need briefly to consider some of the negative commentary my first book drew. Don't worry, this isn't going to be a self-pitying rant—the wounds have healed!—and I am genuinely interested in the sociological implications of the critical censure that *The Miniaturist* received, and how it affected the way I presented my second foray into reimagining the past.

Briefly, to explain the plot of *The Miniaturist*; Nella, a young, white woman, comes to Amsterdam to be married to a man twice her age. The household she pitches up in is a strange one. Her husband won't touch her, her new sister-in-law is twitchy and secretive, the society in which they operate is a sermonizing police state, sanctioned by the priests. The servants are not much more forthcoming. Quickly, Nella discovers that her husband prefers men, and that their manservant, Otto, a Black man emancipated from the plantations of Suriname, is in a sexual relationship with the sister.

I was reviewed well, but I also received some sneering reviews. I was accused, in various quarters, of ticking politically correct boxes, of playing self-righteous bingo. A Black man, a gay man, frustrated women chafing against their domestic ropes, who find an outlet in speaking their mind, the devil take the consequences? How very *modern*. How very *improbable*. I was accused in *The Observer* of projecting my own contemporary, feminist ideals onto my main characters.

(Admittedly, in a telephone interview with *The Guardian*, as I hunched by the loo on a train carriage as we rode in and out of signal, I was asked again to describe my book. I was bored of saying "historical," I was tired and cranky, and I didn't really know what to say. As the train roared northwards, I replied in desperation, "it's feminist Golden-Age fiction." That four-word descriptor has followed me round ever since.)

But! said the detractors—feminism wasn't *invented* yet! Nella would *never* think like this—never assume that she had the right to speak her mind, or take her husband's place at the trading table. She would never believe that she could be the architect of her own fortune. For them, it was a question of the veracity of history over pleasing psychology. (None of them were historians, I might add—and indeed, an actual historian, the late, and greatly revered, Lisa Jardine, expert of the Dutch Golden Age, read it and loved it. As you can see, the wounds have definitely healed ...)

Whilst Nella would never personally call herself a feminist, I can look at her and consider her a blueprint for one. Consider her upbringing—eldest sister of three, used to getting her own way, surviving an alcoholic father and desperate mother who presses her into a marriage of convenience. Consider her nature—bold, over-imaginative, sexually hungry—then place her in a claustrophobic (yet strangely enlightened) environment in multicultural Amsterdam—and watch her struggle to keep the windows of her mind ajar, whilst simultaneously opening some new ones.

I did not feel that anything in my plot was without the realm of possibility. It just hadn't been the dominant narrative of history. Widowed

Dutchwomen often took over their deceased husbands' businesses, women married later than their European counterparts, and once married, they carried on working alongside their husbands. Amsterdam gave me almost *carte blanche*, with its trading power, its proto-capitalist outlook, the base for the world's first corporation (the United Dutch East India Company), reactionary catnip for the Calvinist preachers who saw it as a den of vice and luxury, being also one of the only places in Europe where forbidden books were easily accessible. Black people were being employed as musicians and manservants; objects of fetish and status, yes; but what went on behind closed doors? Women could hold hands with their partners on the street. A French diarist saw this, was scandalized, and wrote it down for me to find, centuries later. Women were perhaps becoming itchy to do more than rock a cradle and stay at home—and public society, run by men, didn't like it. How do I know this? I don't for sure, but we can surmise from the slew of homilies and panicky poems about keeping women indoors and pregnant, which spread like a rash in Holland around the time my novel is set, that there was some form of existential rebellion fomenting. If everything had been peaceful, perhaps those poems wouldn't have been required.

My process was an act of combining hard fact, educated guesses, and creative thinking. Reading some of these commentaries, it struck me that some people felt that that blackness and gayness and women's political and personal frustrations had been invented sometime around 1950. Some people don't believe there were gay people alive before then. Of course, some people don't think they exist even now. There seems to be the belief that Black men and women, Asian men and women, indeed, people who *weren't white*— even existed in the Western world outside the narrative of slavery. They have not been taught at school, as I was not taught at school, that the world was so interconnected already by this point, thanks mainly to the transatlantic slave trade and Western presence in the East.

But then—you only need to look at who was rich and who was literate, who could secure the narrative power to shape history. Who had the money to write the books of that history, to make voyages and pass comment? Who could create legacies from thin air, and pass them down from son to son to son to son, until enough generations had sufficient prejudice and misguided knowledge, bolstered by economic power, that it was almost inevitable that such legacies seemed set in stone? Who was the innocent and who was the savage? The narrative is stubborn. Even now, it sometimes feels irreversible.

This issue, for me, really feeds into the question of what the past should look like in my historical fiction. As a child, there were oceans of facts I never swam in. I'm not alone. We have drowned in our own whiteness in the Western world, which is ironic, considering that white people, historically speaking, oversaw most of the drowning. I also grew up believing that all women, regardless of their skin color, had the same experiences in patriarchal societies. Patently, this could not be more untrue. My education in history was a game of Anglicized, whitewashed Chinese whispers, the truth turned into a strange and simplified slogan.

***

I'd been challenged on the accuracy of my presentation of "history" in my first novel. And because I wanted the version of "history" in my novels to be taken seriously, I ended up adding a bibliography at the end of my second novel. The first novel—arguably *more* historically detailed and distant in terms of time period—was blissfully free of solemn proofs of intellectual credibility, working entirely as an unapologetic piece of fiction. I don't regret that bibliography in the second novel, but it raises some questions. Did I put that bibliography there to prove to my detractors that I had indeed perused the primary sources, that the more outlandish happenings in my book were entirely plausible? Was I trying to reassure my readers that I was capable of taking them on an authentic journey? Possibly. I know I also wanted readers to have easy access to some of the more interesting books I'd read in order to understand the Caribbean's stormy relationship with England, and to have some good films to watch and poetry to read if they fancied it. I hoped the book stood strongly enough as a novel in its own right for me also to show my researcher's hand.

Whatever it was, it was a self-conscious act that ties in to one of the single most important aspects of historical fiction being published today. We could call it representation. We could call it "seeing yourself." We could frame it as the question: *Whose past do we want to tell?* And furthermore, *who is telling it?*

Happily, my readers agreed with me. I had some very enjoyable experiences with readers writing in, glad to see a person of color in a historical novel who wasn't a slave. Or for writing a queer character, whose sexuality was not the dominant aspect of their presence in the novel. I didn't do this to win politically correct bingo, or a woke-cookie. I did it because, as I said earlier, it was how I understood "the past." Those people have always existed; it's just they didn't have the pencil and paper as easy to hand, in order to commit themselves and their experiences to posterity.

The past is not so distant to me. We have not come so far. Racism, homophobia, misogyny, and the demonization of the poor are not new things, although historically, they have operated under far more diffuse, or silent names. I'm not fantastical with my history: I am actually quite rational. And I am not alone in my excitement that, as historical novelists, we can attempt to tell these "new-old" stories, working as we do within such a popular, evergreen genre.

An exciting novel which achieves this, and one of the most radical historical novels I have ever encountered, is *The Book of Night Women* by Marlon James. It's probably the most violent novel I've read, and one of the best. Written in a patois that as an English-language native you quickly acclimatize to, the depiction of the daily degradation and survivalism on a British sugar plantation in Jamaica at the turn of the eighteenth century is more of a political *tour-de-force* than any text book on slavery I've ever read, never mind its imaginative power. Reading it, I realized that bar a mention in Jane Austen's *Mansfield Park* of Sir Thomas Bertram's interests in Antigua, or Jean Rhys's *Wide Sargasso Sea*, her Caribbean-set response to Charlotte Brontë's *Jane Eyre*, my literary diet had barely contained any negative depictions of European colonialism and power as a direct result of slave labor. I called *The Book of Night Women* radical, but it is also rational in its intention and execution.

In her brilliant debut novel, *Homegoing* (2016), a story which traverses the seventeenth-century Gold Coast slave trade, the antebellum plantations of the South, 1960s Ghana, and the crack-riddled streets of 1970s New York, among other locales, Yaa Gyasi has shown us what new historical fiction can do. It feels as if Gyasi, a Ghanaian-American woman, has walked up to a cumbersome telescope and swung it round, and here we are, faced with constellations that have always been there, but whose patterns we have yet to teach ourselves.

But again, hers is no history lesson. Hers is an offering of entertainment. Gyasi is a *novelist* first, not an historian. Here, however, is what I take as the most objective passage in the novel, where, as a writer of this story, as a woman, as a Black woman, and as a possessor of more than one nationality, Yaa Gyasi's own credo comes to the fore:

"History is Storytelling," Yaw repeated. ... "We must rely on the words of others. We believe the one who has the power. He is the one who gets to write the story. So when you study history, you must always ask yourself, Whose story am I missing? Whose voice was suppressed so that this voice could come forth? Once you have figured that out, you must find that story too. From there, you begin to get a clearer, yet still imperfect, picture."

I can't say it better than that. And I like the fact that Gyasi admits that it remains an *imperfect* picture. Yes, we must make a balance, we must tell the stories that for too long have remained untold—but we must also admit that we work within the walls of fiction. However permeable its membranes feel, it is still a fiction.

My guess is, the same consciousness applies for history, too.

***

Writing historical fiction is both a blessing and a burden. The burden is not the matter of "getting it right," but rather, the challenge to do the research diligently, so that the past, or history, becomes immanent in the reader's experience, so assimilated into the art that it feels effectively invisible. Another burden is accepting other people's disappointment that you didn't write the past the way they wanted.

The blessings, however, are greater. Writers of historical fiction are not trying to change the psychological spectrum of the past. We're trying to augment it, using a crowbar to prize open some pretty rusty brackets. In this way, we act as historians. But for me, the way we act as artists is more exciting. The narrative virtuosity and revelatory beauty of the prose of *Wolf Hall* dropped a line of stones into a forest where all of us who work imaginatively with the past now wander. And consider *Lincoln in the Bardo* by George Saunders; a novel that plays on historicism and sources, ambitious within the genre for focusing on the mysterious time after death, but nevertheless rooted in an historical fiction tradition that deals with the dead as familiar.

"History" in these novels, unless it is ironically signposted, as with *Lincoln in the Bardo*, succeeds because it is invisible, hidden either by a seductive voice (as with *Wolf Hall* or *Night Women*), or by setting and import (as with *Homegoing*). The best historical novels are the irreverent ones, the confident ones, the ones that trust their reader, the ones led by character and language rather than information. The skill of these writers makes sure we never forget they are artists, first and foremost.

As readers of historical fiction, we are taken on an escape route at the same time as being plunged into the psychological realities of being human, the legacies of the past echoing into our present. The double bind of historical fiction thus indulges us in a truly unreachable fantasy, at the same time as it exposes us to all-too-palpable realities. As a writer of such fiction, I find that a blessing indeed.

15

Novelties

A Historian's Field Notes from Fiction

Jane Kamensky

Here in the twilight of the Enlightenment, academic historians have fallen in love with how little we can know. Over the last fifty years, people, events, even places in the past have grown more obscure to many of us. Compare a work of history written in 1960 to one published in 2010, and you might wonder whether the mists of time have somehow thickened.

Can aspects of the novelist's imagination help us to cut through the fog? Several years ago, the historian Jill Lepore and I published a novel we wrote together. Set in Boston in 1764, *Blindspot* started out as a lark, a gift for a friend. It grew into a project that felt important, even urgent, to us as scholars: a different way of knowing and telling the past. What follows are nine lessons learned in that effort to conjure a known and knowable world: a Then as real as Now, in our minds and on our pages.

1. Face It

Most historians suffer from prosopagnosia: face blindness. My coauthor and I had written a goodly number of pages when it dawned on us that we had yet to tell our readers what our two first-person narrators looked like. In a novel that is, in large measure, about seeing, such description seemed a matter of duty. Our readers, not to mention our narrators themselves, needed to know how tall Fanny and Jamie stood, the color of their hair, the cut of their proverbial jibs.

How tough could such an accounting be? This was fiction, after all; we answered only to our characters. But confronted with this delectable task, we promptly choked. Their eyes, how they twinkled; their dimples, how merry: it seemed we had naught but rank cliché at our fingertips.

Jane Kamensky, *Novelties: A Historian's Field Notes from Fiction*. In: *Historical Fiction Now*.
Edited by Mark Eaton and Bruce Holsinger, Oxford University Press. © 2011 The Historical Society (2023).
DOI: 10.1093/oso/9780198877035.003.0016

How do you take stock of a human face? Every time you walk into a bus, a bar, or a classroom, you take people's mettle visually, instantly, almost without thinking. But the sheer narrative terror of that moment made me realize that, as historians, we seldom confront the embodied nature of past individuals. We're capable of writing the history of the self, or the history of the body, or even the history of sexuality, without crafting characters capable of staring back at us, as a good portrait does.

Writers of fiction give their characters faces and yea, even bodies, in a variety of ways. Consider this description, so thorough and meticulous that it bends in spots toward inventory:

> Thomas Cromwell is now a little over forty years old. He is a man of strong build, not tall. Various expressions are available to his face, and one is readable: an expression of stifled amusement. His hair is dark, heavy and waving, and his small eyes, which are of very strong sight, light up in conversation: so the Spanish ambassador will tell us, quite soon. It is said he knows by heart the entire New Testament in Latin, and so as a servant of the cardinal is apt—ready with a text if abbots flounder. ... [H]e is at home in courtroom or waterfront, bishop's palace or inn yard. He can draft a contract, train a falcon, draw a map, stop a street fight, furnish a house and fix a jury. He will quote you a nice point in the old authors, from Plato to Plautus and back again. He knows new poetry, and can say it in Italian. He works all hours, first up and last to bed. He makes money and he spends it. He will take a bet on anything.[1]

Cromwell, of course, is a character from history and from fiction, in this case Hilary Mantel's magnificent novel, *Wolf Hall.* Her description begins with a physical body, and a face, courtesy of Hans Holbein's 1533 portrait. But then she peers through the eyes to the soul, as if she knows the guy, and her reader should, too.

Can historians do anything quite so wonderful? We don't know the inner life of our subjects the way a novelist can know her characters. After all, a writer of fiction invents the soul whose windows the eyes become. Mantel's Cromwell isn't, can't, and shouldn't be history's Cromwell. Thomas Cromwell merely lived; Mantel's Cromwell soars. Yet almost every line in her description can be fully sourced: to the portrait, to Cromwell's letters, to contemporaneous descriptions of the man. At bottom, Mantel's path to knowing Cromwell isn't all that different from a scholar's. The magic comes in the author's moral confidence in what she's got—and then, of course, in the telling. Biographers, who live a long time with their subjects, offer readers hard-won, hard-working encapsulations of character all the time. Historians, trained to concentrate on the background at the expense of the figure in the portrait, do so less often than we might.

Of course, those who study remoter pasts and less celebrated people rarely even know what their subjects looked like. Yet no matter how obscure the actors, they had eyes and mouths, expressions and gestures that quickened the pulse of loved ones and triggered the loathing of enemies. Even when we cannot see the people we write about—perhaps especially then—we'd do well to remember that they weren't made of paper, and didn't pass their fleeting lives in acid-free boxes within temperature-controlled archives. They lived behind faces and within bodies, in heat and in cold, pleasure and pain, experiencing the present from the inside out. Their present became our past, and we're stuck working from the outside in, from the page to the person. That's no excuse for confusing the journey with the destination.

2. Taste It

The challenge of "facing" our subjects represents the merest tip of a vast and complex phenomenological iceberg. As a sometime novelist, I spent a lot of time presumptuously tasting, hearing, smelling, seeing, and feeling on my characters' behalf. Since *Blindspot* is set in the sweltering summer of 1764, that wasn't always pleasant.

The novelist is not alone here. In the last two decades, the "history of the senses," pioneered by scholars including Michael Baxandall and John Berger (sight), Alain Corbin (smell), and Richard Rath and Mark Smith (sound), among others, has become a flourishing subfield.[2] I admire this work a great deal. But for all its sophistication, the history of the senses is as remote from sensorily rich history as the history of the body is from embodied history.

Because they create rather than discover a world, writers of fiction constantly index and mobilize the senses. Think of Proust's madeleine, surely the most famous cookie in literature, whose lime-scented crumbs set off a four-page-long reverie that begins in Swann's aunt's kitchen and spreads to encompass "the whole of Combray, and its surroundings, taking their proper shapes and growing solid ... town and gardens alike, from my cup of tea."[3]

In nonfiction writing it can be no coincidence that some of the best sensory-laden storytelling comes from authors not burdened by Ph.D.s. Consider two examples, each describing the day-to-day operations of the print trades in the eighteenth century. The first comes from a superb work of academic history, Jeffrey L. Pasley's *The Tyranny of Printers*:

> Though printing had its cerebral and prestigious aspects, it was still a dirty, smelly, physically demanding job. One of the first chores that would be delegated to a young apprentice printer was preparing the sheepskin balls used to ink the type. The skins were soaked in urine, stamped on daily for added softness, and finally wrung out by hand. The work got harder from there, and only a little more pleasant. Supplies of ink were often scarce in America, so printers frequently had to make it on site, by boiling lampblack (soot) in varnish (linseed oil and rosin). If the printing-office staff survived the noxious fumes and fire hazards of making ink, their persons and equipment nevertheless spent much of the workday covered in the stuff.[4]

This is lucid, economical writing, pointed toward a set of important questions about the role of printers in the emergent public sphere of the early United States.

Now compare Pasley's to this description, by the journalist Adam Hochschild, of James Phillips's London print shop, hard by the Bank of England, where a crucial meeting of Granville Sharp's antislavery society took place in May 1787:

> Type would be sitting in slanted wooden trays with compartments for the different letters; the compositors who lined it up into rows, letter by letter, would be working, as the day ended, by the light of tallow candles whose smoke, over the decades, would blacken the ceiling. ... Around the sides of the room, stacks of dried sheets, the latest antislavery book or Quaker tract, would await folding and binding. And finally, the most distinctive thing about an eighteenth-century print shop was its smell. To ink the type as it sat on the bed of the press, printers used a wool-stuffed leather pad with a wooden handle. Because of its high ammonia content, the most convenient solvent to rinse off the ink residue that built up on these pads was printers' urine. The pads were soaked in buckets of this, then strewn on the slightly sloping floor, where printers stepped on them as they worked, to wring them out and let the liquid drain away.[5]

Though the two passages rely on some of the same sources, Hochschild's version owes as much to Dickens as to Pasley. It is specific and transporting rather than generic and distancing. Key differences reside in the sensory details: one paragraph, three senses. Sight: the blackened ceilings, the smoking tallow candles. Touch: compositors' fingers flying over cast-iron type, the heft and texture of the wooden-handled pads, the disequilibrium of standing on that sloping floor. And, of course, smell: the close shop on a warm spring night reeking of piss as well as Enlightenment ideals.

These sensory details give Hochschild's scene volume. But they do more than that. The sight, feel, and smell of the shop impart a frisson of opposites—these are "unlikely surroundings," as Hochschild puts it, for a key moment in the transformation of humanitarian thought. Then, quickly, we're on to the substance of that meeting, an intellectual history drawn from tract literature. Sensory does not mean sensational.

3. Place It

Historians have long argued for the importance of place. Francis Parkman's timeworn dictum, go there, marries well with the material-culture scholar's more recent mantra, events take place. Great nonfiction writing honors both commandments.

In the writing of *Blindspot*, I would like to believe that our historians' commitment to place served us well. We "went there," Parkman-style, tramping through the tangled streets of Boston's North End, and setting up camp in an early eighteenth-century house museum, whose cramped staircases and tiny rooms with walls out of plumb became home to the characters in the novel. We couldn't possibly have understood our characters—not just their sensory lives, but the proxemics of the eighteenth-century port town—had we not done that kind of homework.

But the place-based writing lesson I'm referring to here is slightly different, something closer to what the young Bill Bradley once told John McPhee: "When you have played basketball for a while, you don't need to look at the basket. ... You develop a sense of where you are."[6] Fiction requires an author to possess a constant sense of where the characters are—where, that is, besides on the page.

If a scene started on the road to the Boston Neck, and then the action went someplace else, we had to know the route, whether it took us via Washington Street or via flashback. We got a copy of John Bonner's 1764 map and "walked" it constantly. If a conversation began in the parlor but ended in the painting room, we needed to get the speakers upstairs. But having a sense of where you are doesn't require you to describe it in painful detail. It's a question of trust. To feel secure in your hands, the reader needs to know that you know exactly where the action in your pages is taking place, even (or especially?) if that action unfolds in other pages.

Knowing where you are concerns not just place, but position. First-person narration is particularly unforgiving in this regard: if the narrator doesn't see it, think it, read it, or overhear it, neither she nor the reader can know it. But even a first-person narrator takes in the world at more than one focal length. Some narrative junctures demand close-ups; others, crowd shots. Since we were writing a novel of eighteenth-century art, we thought about shifts in scale and depth of field in those terms. Some scenes needed the intimacy of a portrait by Joshua Reynolds, while others called for the teeming distance of a Hogarth engraving. As eighteenth-century theorists of the picturesque pointed out, the eye likes variety. So, too, the mind's eye.

4. Smile Every Now and Again

Here in the late age of "human nature," we are loath to universalize. But I'm going to risk it. Everybody laughs, even under Stalin or the Taliban. In sickness and health, famine and feast, war and peace, the emotional lives of human beings are multidimensional and complex. We have highs and lows, often both at once. History deserves a broader emotional range than the tight-lipped expressionless stare of a newscaster.[7]

One of *Blindspot*'s narrators couldn't manage to laugh at her plight, even when it was funny; the other had little but laughter—sometimes misplaced—with which to meet the world's travails. The chiaroscuro of his lightness and her darkness created one kind of emotional variegation. Another came from history itself. At one key juncture in the novel, two characters cross into what an eighteenth-century writer would have called the bower of bliss, only to discover upon waking a handbill detailing draconian new restrictions visited upon the town's slave population. With the full freedom of fiction at our disposal, we wrestled with this unseemly juxtaposition. We thought about moving up the publication of the handbill, or postponing it, anything to give our lovers the chance to bask in a rosy glow a while longer. For a fleeting moment, we considered softening the laws, so our characters didn't have to face anything quite so dark as ... history. And then we decided to allow the emotional contradiction of pleasure and pain in the past, just as we do in the present, every time we laugh at a funeral, or weep amid plenty.

5. Turn Off the Metronome

Thinking in time is the historian's master skill; years are the vertebrae of our disciplinary spine. Mathematically speaking, each year is always and ever the same, a 365 and ¼-day whirl through the seasons and round the sun.

Yet we experience time's relentless march differentially. August sprints; February crawls. When my children were toddlers, the days felt like years; the years, like days. Life romps and rushes, outwaits and outpaces us.

Novels revel in the unevenness of human time. Fiction allows some moments to be languorous, others hectic. Each can be enchanting. A slow-moving stream of time invites reverie. Nicholson Baker's haunting and strange first novel, *The Mezzanine*, a sort of Ulysses in miniature, begins, "At almost one o'clock I entered the lobby of the building where I worked and turned toward the escalators," and ends, 135 pages later, "[a]t the very end of the ride" up the moving staircase to the floor above.[8]

In mystery, by contrast, time habitually flies. The calculus of the page-turner is all first derivative; speed increases at an increasing rate. "I fear that events begin to outpace my pen," confesses *Blindspot*'s compulsively candid yet unreliable male narrator—more than once.[9]

Plot time—for all its contrivance—in some ways approximates real time, at least as physics understands it. *Pace* Stephen Hawking: time bends. History too often trudges: left foot, right foot, cradle to grave. We would serve our readers better by moving, on occasion, by way of leaps and bounds, or baby steps, just as life does.[10]

6. Play It Forward

Though life's pace—past and present—is uneven, time's arrow moves in one direction. The shattered cup doesn't pick itself up from the floor. We know this in our bones (or, Hawking says, we deceive ourselves into believing it). Yet historians too rarely cultivate a fully operational sense of our subjects' present, and, consequently, of the irreducible contingency of their future. Staring into the past, we flatten the horizon; it's all so then to us. Trained to value distance, we favor the retrospective half of Kierkegaard's famous maxim: "Life ... can only be understood backwards." Writing a novel—a novel in the realist mode, at any rate—shifts attention to the other half of the aphorism: "But it must be lived forwards."[11]

Historians understand *Blindspot's* temporal location—the waning months of 1764—as a passage in a deepening imperial crisis that, we know, would not resolve soon or peaceably. But *Blindspot's* narrators don't understand their lives that way at all, any more than their neighbors John Hancock and Samuel Adams could have done. Our invented Stewart Jameson sees that summer and fall as a passage in the building of his competence and the deepening of his humanity. The rocky fortunes of Boston in the wake of the French and Indian War matter a great deal to him, but the squawks of townsfolk against the Sugar and Currency Acts (passed that year) and the Stamp Tax (already anticipated) amount to little more than background noise. Around our other narrator, the 20-year-old Fanny Easton, the circle of the present contracts still further, by dint of her age and gender and poverty. Geopolitical time means little to her. Neither character knows even remotely how the story will end—and that's just their story (as we defined it), never mind The American Story. Even when they sensed that they lived in Historic Times, past actors—real ones, I mean—were no less mired in the noise of the now than we are.

7. Work It

One of my all-time favorite books is Richard Scarry's *What Do People Do All Day?* Published in 1968, when I was 5 years old, it's still a steady seller. Like all of Scarry's work, its brilliance lies in the visual clutter of everyday life. Every page is crammed with a tangle of characters and tools and tasks showing the dense web of exchange connecting Farmer Alfalfa, Blacksmith Fox, Grocer Cat, Stitches the Tailor, and even Mommy. Lowly Worm pops up unexpectedly and always with great brio. Scarry's young reader, just past small-object fascination, barely knows where to look. (It's like Hogarth that way, with the satire dialed down a notch.)

In Scarry's busy, busy world, "Everyone is a worker."[12] Certainly the illustrator foregrounded work because the choice gave him wonderful things to draw. But he also seems to sense what many artists—including writers—know rather better than most labor historians. Work fascinates. Work matters. Work makes us human. Scarry and Vermeer, Steinbeck and Dickens, Alice Munro and Edward P. Jones: great artists wring profound beauty and epic significance from the ordinary labors that consume most of the waking hours of most people, in every past and every present.

An example: Philip Roth's *American Pastoral* is a sprawling novel about many things, ranging from love and loss in the household of Seymour Irving "Swede" Levov, the "household Apollo of the Weequahic Jews," to the seismic shifts that shook the urban United States in the 1960s. Throughout Roth's pyrotechnic changes of key and register, Newark Maid, the glove business that Levov inherited from his father, sounds a basso ostinato. Despite its name, Newark Maid manufactures on the margins of the American empire, in Puerto Rico. Why? Because Newark, once "the city where they manufactured everything," has lately become "the car-theft capital of the world." The work and the workers and most of the customers are gone, and the people left behind "don't know a fourchette from a thumb," Levov complains. "What's a fourchette?" our narrator asks. The Swede explains:

> The part of the glove between the fingers. Those small oblong pieces between the fingers, they're die-cut along with the thumbs—those are the fourchettes. Today you've got a lot of underqualified people, probably don't know half what I knew when I was five. ... A guy buying deerskin, which can run up to maybe three dollars and fifty cents a foot for a garment grade, he's buying this fine garment-grade deerskin to cut a little palm patch to go on a pair of ski gloves. I talked to him just the other day. A novelty part, runs about five inches by one inch, and he pays three fifty a foot where he could have paid a dollar fifty a foot and come out a long, long way ahead. You multiply this over a large order, you're talking a hundred-thousand-dollar mistake.[13]

The historian, who tends to traffic in abstractions, might rewrite this passage to highlight important themes: white flight, deindustrialization, globalization. Operating far above the ground upon which steel-toed boots trudge or the worn linoleum upon which rubber-soled white nurses' shoes squeak, we bypass the doing of work and the making of things. We want our readers to think about capitalism and democracy.

The novelist wants you to ponder those things, too. But first, he wants you to smell the glove.

8. Feel Your Way

History is work, too: the work of scavenging tattered remnants of the past. After writing *Blindspot*, that labor felt different. Which is to say, it felt, full stop. Having imagined an early American life from the inside out, I found myself allowing Intuition to accompany me into the archives. Sometimes Empathy pulled up a chair in the reading room, forcing Detachment and Skepticism to scoot over a mite.

Thus hemmed in on every side of a long wooden table in the attic library of the Royal Academy of Arts, which sits just far enough off Piccadilly to mute the street noise of central London, I recently read Sir Joshua Reynolds's sitter books, twenty-six duodecimo volumes spanning the decades from 1757 to 1790. Among those who study eighteenth-century culture, they're a well-known source. Curators use them to document the provenance and prices of the grand-manner portraits that took Sir Joshua to the very pinnacle of the European art scene. Cultural historians have used the volumes to map Reynolds's social circle, which included Samuel Johnson, Hester Thrale, David Garrick, Joseph Banks, and others of equal glitter and distinction.

I read the Reynolds sitter books in the course of researching a new project on American artists in Georgian London. *Blindspot* was done, but I couldn't quite shake the consciousness of our characters, Jamie and Fanny, who had struggled to make a living of art in Boston in 1764. Reynolds—His Majesty's Principal Painter in Ordinary, the founder and longtime president of the Royal Academy—wasn't struggling. The sitter books document the whirl of polite society: audiences with the greater gentry, afternoons in coffeehouses, evenings at the opera. Reynolds's self-portraits likewise fashion the artist as a visionary genius, all eyes and mind, clean hands.

But Reynolds's sitter books are the household accounts of a preindustrial artisan. Every year, he painted like a house afire in May and June. In December, his appointments petered out just after noon. Why? Because, as I learned in the two o'clock dusk of that London winter, the light began to fail. The great Reynolds, like everyone else of his place and time, was a slave to the harsh diurnal realities of northern Europe. Lords and ladies beseeched his services; King George and Queen Charlotte sat for him in 1779; Reynolds commanded the muses from great heights. But the sitter books show something quite different: a working man whose social elevation might be compared, at many junctures, to the status of a servant in livery. He waited on ladies and gentlemen. He booked appointments with their children and even their pets, as he did in the fall of 1788, when he attended "2 dog[s] of Mr. Maclin."[14]

The sitter books also contain many entries, a handful every year, that read simply, "Infant." No parents, no servants, no family name, just "infant." Who were these babies? Art historians offer one answer: they were the subjects not of portraits—portraits have patrons, and patrons, even child-patrons, have surnames—but of Reynolds's "fancy pictures," little genre paintings like *Cupid as a Link Boy* (1774) and the kitschy allegory, *The Infant Academy* (1782). I'm as curious about fancy pictures and their buyers as the next scholar of the period. But the sometime novelist wanted to know something quite different: Dear God, who were these babies?

A different collection in the Royal Academy, the letters of Reynolds's apprentice and later biographer James Northcote, offers a tantalizing clue. "[C]oncerning drawing from naked women [it] is really true," he told his brother, "this is much disapproved of by some good folks."

> miss Reynolds says it is a great pitty that it should be a necessary part in the education of a painter but she draws all her figures cloath'd except infants which she often paints from life[,] some begger womans child[,] which is laid naked on a pillow or in the mothers arms.[15]

"Miss Reynolds" was Sir Joshua's younger sister, a 42-year-old spinster at the time of this exchange with Northcote. An ambitious painter in her own right, Fanny Reynolds could have been Shakespeare's sister, in Virginia Woolf's terms. That is, her gender defined the expression of her talents. Women couldn't study life drawing, which severely hampered their training in anatomy, and thus their chances at commercial success. Hers is a poignant story, versions of which feminist art historians have told.[16]

I have never read a line about the babies. "Some begger womans child ... laid naked on a pillow or in the mothers arms." What might the pious, well-fed Miss Reynolds have offered a beggar woman to induce her to step inside the Reynolds's Leicester Square manse in the icy December of 1771? Was a farthing a fair price, or a cup of broth, or did the mother make the trade for warmth alone? These are, perhaps, a novelist's questions. But they deserve a historian's answers, answers leading to a richer, more nuanced portrait of the complex economy of culture.

9. Only Connect

"Only connect!" runs E. M. Forster's famous epigraph in *Howard's End*. The novel elaborates: "Only connect the prose and the passion, and both will be exalted, and human love will be seen at its height. Live in fragments no longer."[17]

For decades, scholars have generally followed the opposite impulse: only distinguish, only divide. Forster is out; L. P. Hartley is in—at least in the form of one remembered line from this forgotten author's forgotten novel, *The Go-Between*: "The past is a foreign country: they do things differently there."[18] We have honed our skepticism of broad claims about the so-called human condition on the whetstone of poststructuralism and its descendants. Tired of wholeness, we like the cutting edge; we ask our students to live and work along it. And to be sure, it has its virtues. Newly sensitive to the social construction of elements of life once considered fundamental to our species (when they were considered at all), we have discovered the impress of history and culture upon the emotions, the mind, the body, the self itself.

Trained at the very height of the poststructuralist moment, I cast my lot with the skeptics. I wouldn't, couldn't have it any other way. Yet the recovering novelist in me worries that we've thrown out the humanistic baby—that beggar woman's baby, posed naked on a pillow by Sir Joshua Reynolds's fireside—with the Enlightenment bathwater. Whither the sympathy in our science?

The past is a foreign country, yes, and we who study the paltry remains of various days are but curious travelers along its broadest byways. Yet like all good tourists, we would do well to remember that the past is not just a place where we pause to gawk while loading up on souvenirs. Real people lived there, people who resembled us in some ways, if not in others.

History is not a séance. Groping like drunks in the dark, we're doomed to get people wrong, as that great twentieth-century American historian Philip Roth laments: "You get them wrong before you meet them, while you're anticipating meeting them; you get them wrong while you're with them; and then you go home to tell somebody else about the meeting and get them all wrong again." But what's the alternative? Precisely "what are we to do about this terribly significant business of other people?"[19]

The writer, the painter, the scholar: all of us make a living pressing that terribly significant business into two dimensions. My season as an accidental novelist reawakened the futile, insatiable hunger for a third.

16

Sorting Fact from Fiction

A Novelist Researches the Lapérouse Expedition

Naomi J. Williams

I own a small collection of antique maps. The most interesting among these was a gift from my husband twenty years ago (Fig. 16.1). We were still living in San Francisco then, and the well-known and established Bay Area map seller who sold the map to my husband told him it was a late-eighteenth-century map of San Francisco Bay.

It is not.

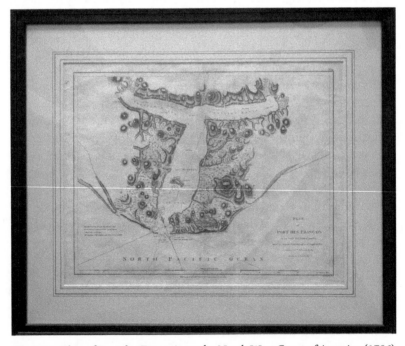

Fig. 16.1 Plan of Port des Français on the North West Coast of America (1786)

Naomi J. Williams, *Sorting Fact from Fiction: A Novelist Researches the Lapérouse Expedition*. In: *Historical Fiction Now*. Edited by Mark Eaton and Bruce Holsinger, Oxford University Press. © Naomi J. Williams (2023). DOI: 10.1093/oso/9780198877035.003.0017

I didn't know this at first, although I should have. Roughly 2 feet wide and 1 foot high, and oriented with its upper-left corner pointing north, the map depicts a narrow, T-shaped bay and surrounding land masses, an image that rather uncomfortably resembles the female reproductive system. The bottom of the bay's T empties into the "North Pacific Ocean," while its vertical stem is labeled "The Harbour" and its left and right arms, respectively, "Western Basin" and "Eastern Basin." A "Cenotaph Island" appears in the middle of the bay. And on the map's lower right are seven lines of imperfectly proofread text:

PLAN

of

PORT DES FRANÇAIS

on the North West Coast of America

in 58° 37′ Latitude North and 139° 50 of Longitude West

Discovered^{nd} July 1786, by the

Boussole & Astrolabe.

None of this particularly puts one in mind of San Francisco Bay. But I was pleased to have such an old and curious object, and we hung it in the hallway of our Mission District apartment. Occasionally I would stop and examine it, wondering at the discrepancies between the map and what I knew about the local geography and its history. The bay was so misshapen, the Golden Gate oddly narrowed, and Cenotaph Island ... was that supposed to be *Alcatraz?* As for "Port des Français"—surely "San Francisco" was meant to honor St. Francis, not a group of Frenchmen. Hadn't *Spaniards* been the first Europeans to sail into the bay, well before 1786? Also, whoever drafted this map had not explored the waterway with any seriousness. Even two centuries of climate change could not account for the "glaciers" and "grottoes of ice" marked in the bay's interiors. Then the coordinates: 58° 37′ Latitude North. If I'd had any sense whatsoever, I would have realized immediately that this was somewhere much, much further north than San Francisco Bay.

It embarrasses me to confess that I owned this map for several months before I really questioned its identity. The predisposition to believe what you're told—especially if the person telling you purports to be an expert; if, in fact, that person's livelihood depends on your trust of that expertise; and most especially if you, or your spouse, in this case, has put down good money based on that trust—the predisposition to believe, I submit, turns out to be quite strong.

But eventually I took the map down from the wall and flipped it over. Affixed to the back was a description I'd previously ignored. It identified the map as coming from the Lapérouse[1] expedition, a French voyage of exploration led by Jean-François de Galaup de Lapérouse (1741–?1788), which left Brest in August of 1785, charged with circumnavigating the globe for the advancement of science and economic opportunities for France.

I had never heard of this expedition before, but a few keystrokes into a search engine solved the mystery: "Port des Français" was not San Francisco Bay at all, of course. It was the French name for Lituya Bay, a remote, challenging place in southeast Alaska. The "Français" of the Lapérouse Expedition sailed into the bay in July of 1786 and were, indeed, the first Europeans to explore the place. The distinction cost them dearly. An outing to take soundings of the bay—soundings for this very map—led to the deaths of twenty-one men when a freak tidal current swamped their boats and drowned them. It would be only the first of the expedition's tragedies. They would go on to lose another twelve crew members in a violent melee with islanders in Samoa, then begin to lose men one by one to accident and disease. And then the expedition disappeared altogether, their fate one of the great mysteries of European navigation for nearly forty years.

It was several hours before I climbed out of this Internet rabbit hole. "What a sad and compelling story," I thought. "What a perfect subject for historical fiction! Someone should write a book."

Then the sensible thing would have been to return the map sold to my husband—let us say, *in error*, rather than *fraudulently*—and enjoyed the refund in some way. Instead, I dove back into that rabbit hole and wrote a novel. *Landfalls*, my reimagining of the Lapérouse expedition, appeared after nearly a decade of meticulous historical research and writing. But the project sprang, ironically, from a fiction: a map of a remote Alaskan bay masquerading as a map of San Francisco.

***

The map seller's "mistake" feels like an apt jumping-off point for considering some questions about responsible and ethical uses of history. For this initial misstatement of cartographic fact would turn out to be only the first of many not-quite-true things I would encounter while conducting research for *Landfalls*.

Take, for instance, an oft-repeated anecdote about Louis XVI (1754–93), who authorized the Lapérouse expedition and took an active personal interest in it.[2] Lapérouse and his men had been expected to return to France by

July of 1789. They did not, and although folks in France were distracted by other matters at that point, the National Assembly did eventually authorize a search for the missing frigates.[3] By the time Louis XVI was executed in January of 1793, however, no sign of the missing explorers had turned up. And it is said, in many, many, *many* sources about the expedition, that before the deposed king ascended the scaffold, he stopped and asked, "A-t-on des nouvelles de Lapérouse?" (Is there any news of Lapérouse?)

This is an almost irresistible moment for a novelist, and in fact, the first version of my book succumbed to the temptation of this scene. The manuscript opened with a prologue about Louis XVI, beginning with his lifelong interest in geography and ending with him on the scaffold, reflecting, not on the guillotine that was about to decapitate him or what would become of his country or his family, or even the state of his immortal soul, but what might have happened to the Lapérouse expedition he'd sent out eight years earlier. And then you were supposed to turn the page and get swept up into what *I* imagined might have happened during that long-ago voyage.

This prologue did not survive the years of revision and rewriting that followed, and it's just as well. The whole thing was a bit hokey. But I'd also lost interest in the "A-t-on des nouvelles de Lapérouse?" episode because I became convinced it had never happened. And when I told people I'd jettisoned my Louis XVI prologue, they all had the same response: "So what if it never happened? You're a fiction writer."

So what if it never happened? As a philosophical matter and in an ideal world, I agree that fiction writers are free to do as they please and are not bound by historicity. In fact, I used to say that I believed writers of historical fiction had no obligation to accuracy and that my own decision to hew as closely as I could to known facts was a stylistic choice, that being as factually correct as possible offered interesting narrative challenges, and that I saw it the way a poet might regard composing a Shakespearean sonnet, committing myself to a set of constraints inside of which my imagination might creatively wander.

It's true that hewing to known facts makes for interesting narrative challenges. But otherwise this position now strikes me as naïve. For we *don't* live in an ideal world. We live in a world in which education, scholarship, and journalism are routinely devalued, even reviled. A world in which demonstrably false assertions that benefit bad actors are embraced and touted as "alternative facts." A world in which important histories are ignored and erased. In this "real" world, I was dismayed by the way the story about Louis

XVI, as well as others about the expedition, a few of which I will share below, had acquired the patina of "truth" simply through repetition. I didn't want to participate in the maintenance of *bad* conventional wisdom, not even for a tragedy two centuries old. And while I don't insist that fiction writers stick with known or knowable "facts," I do prefer it from people who call themselves historians or nonfiction writers, and I was not willing to dignify shoddy scholarship by turning it into "art."

This story about Louis XVI is *everywhere*: on the French and English Wikipedia pages for Lapérouse,[4] in books and articles,[5] on websites and blog posts,[6] and in museum study guides devoted to the expedition.[7] Although some sources are careful to note that *it is said that* or *a possibly apocryphal tale relates that* Louis XVI posed this question right before he died, even scholarly sources state it as a fact. Notable in this regard is New Zealand historian John Dunmore, a leading expert on the expedition, who has seen fit to repeat this anecdote, attestation-free, in both English and French.[8]

Where the story is notably absent is in accounts of the life and death of Louis XVI. I consulted numerous studies of the king for whom Lapérouse sailed, especially texts that focused on the circumstances surrounding his execution, including reference-heavy scholarly accounts, contemporaneous accounts in the press, and interviews with or later recollections of eyewitnesses.[9] Some sources detail everything the doomed monarch supposedly did and said and even ate in his final days,[10] while others engage freely in their own, often self-exculpatory, historical fictions.[11] Not one of these sources makes mention of the king asking after Lapérouse.

The only place I can find this anecdote, in other words, is in accounts of the Lapérouse expedition. I have not succeeded in tracking down who first told this story, but clearly it has endured because so many people have circulated it, no questions asked.

***

A similar mechanism appears to be at work with another much-repeated story about the voyage, a marvelous tidbit that was my Plan B for a prologue. Having lost the Louis XVI episode, my novel was going to open instead with a moody young cadet at the École militaire in Paris crushed to learn that his application to join an important voyage of exploration has been denied. He suspects bitterly that it's because his family has neither wealth nor connections. Worse, he's not even properly French. He speaks the language with an accent. The other cadets make fun of him. He'll show them, he thinks. One day they won't be laughing when they hear his name. A friend tries to console him. "Cheer up, Bonaparte," he'll say, and the reader would experience a jolt of recognition and that special frisson generated by contemplating a great "what-if" of history.

This anecdote about the young Napoleon usually appears as an established fact. But there's nothing "established" about it. This case also illustrates the way repetition and the accumulation of small embellishments over time can shape what passes as "true." And it exposes a phenomenon I've taken to calling "citation theater"—the use of references to create a *semblance* of credibility rather than establishing *actual* credibility.

Let's start with the Wikipedia page for Lapérouse. This is where the average person curious about the expedition would first go. I've wanted to clean up this article for years, but I appreciate its value in demonstrating some of the points I'm making. Here's the paragraph that relates the Napoleon story:

> One of the men who applied for the voyage was a 16-year-old Corsican named Napoléon Bonaparte.[15] Bonaparte, a second lieutenant from Paris's military academy at the time, made the preliminary list but he was ultimately not chosen for the voyage list and remained behind in France. At the time, Bonaparte was interested in serving in the navy rather than army because of his proficiency in mathematics and artillery, both valued skills on warships.[12]

As you can see, a Wikipedia editor has included a citation for this passage, which takes you to Robert W. Kirk's 2012 book *Paradise Past: The Transformation of the South Pacific, 1520–1920*. I duly tracked down this book, where I found the following:

> An ambitious and energetic Corsican lad named Napoleon Bonaparte (1769–1821) had offered to use his precocious mathematical ability to further La Pérouse's objectives. For unknown reasons, La Pérouse rejected the application of the 16-year-old to sail with him. Turned down, young Bonaparte became an army officer. Had he vanished in the Pacific with La Pérouse, Europe might have been spared sixteen years of brutal warfare and hundreds of thousands of deaths.[13]

Indeed. Quite apart from the somewhat debatable conclusion that if only Napoleon had perished with Lapérouse, there would have been peace in Europe, one might note that this passage says nothing about Napoleon making a short list of candidates, as is claimed in the Wikipedia article.

Kirk, for his part, provides two sources for his version of the story.[14] The first is Gavan Daws's 1968 *Shoal of Time*, a work of popular history about the Hawaiian Islands that briefly alludes to this Napoleon story in the context of history's tantalizing "near misses."[15] Daws, in turn, cites the English-language translation of Paul-Émile Victor's 1962 *Man and the Conquest of the Poles*.[16] Monsieur Victor, a French ethnologist and an explorer in his own right, casually and citation-lessly mentions the Napoleon anecdote in a chapter that's actually about the doomed Franklin expedition in North America.[17] Meanwhile, Kirk's *second* source for the Napoleon story? A 2001 Lonely Planet guide to Tonga, an island that Lapérouse, never mind Napoleon, never visited. This may be an excellent guide book. But it hardly counts as a credible source for biographical information about Napoleon.

Not one of these texts cites a primary source or even a source that is primarily—or even *secondarily*—concerned with Napoleon. These citations may indicate where the writers in question *encountered* the anecdote; they don't *verify* it. While I'm not surprised to find a Wikipedia citation isn't up to snuff, it both surprised and disappointed me to discover equally un-rigorous, basically performative citation efforts in so many published histories.

Just as I did with Louis XVI, I pored through one biographical treatment of Napoleon after another, looking for evidence that he'd applied to join the expedition.[18] (I *really* wanted this new prologue.) What I found was that although there are contradictory accounts of his early years, and it seems Napoleon may indeed have initially wanted to pursue a naval career, scholars tend to agree that by the time he entered the École militaire in Paris in the fall of 1784, less than a year before Lapérouse left France, Napoleon was already committed to joining the artillery branch of the army. I could find only one biographer who repeated this tale: Frank McLynn in his 2002 work, *Napoleon: A Biography*.[19] Yet not one of the sources he cites for these pages corroborates the legend,[20] while one quite specifically contradicts it.[21]

This tenacious bit of apocrypha seems to have arisen because of the young Napoleon's proximity to three members of the doomed expedition: Roux d'Arbaud, a fellow cadet at the École militaire, and the astronomers Joseph Lepaute Dagelet and Louis Monge, who were instructors there. It owes much to the somewhat shaky recollections of one Alexandre des Mazis (1768–1841), a friend of Napoleon's from the École. In des Mazis's memoirs, written late in life but not published till 1954,[22] he relates that Dagelet regaled the students with such wonderful stories about his time serving on a previous voyage of exploration that he inspired great enthusiasm for the sea among the cadets, including Napoleon.[23] And here's what he says about the Lapérouse expedition:

> Bonaparte would have liked to have had the opportunity to deploy his energies toward such a fine enterprise, but only Darbaud was chosen; no more pupils could be admitted, and Darbaud left with Dagelet and Monge in 1784.[24]

Factual errors abound in des Mazis's text, including, in this very quote, the year (Darbaud would have left with his astronomy teachers in 1785, not 1784).[25] But even if we take the general gist of des Mazis's recollections as factual, it still falls well short of asserting that Napoleon formally applied for a place on the expedition or that he made any sort of short list, much less that Lapérouse himself turned the lad down or that this was why Napoleon ended up an army man rather than a naval officer.[26]

It's not hard to imagine how this account, repeated and embroidered over the years, could turn into the story I kept encountering. It also bears mentioning that almost none of the sources that repeat this Napoleon story mention des Mazis. Nearly all, even supposedly "serious" sources, do little better than the Wikipedia article I began with: one person simply repeating and often embellishing another person's repetition and embellishment.

So much for Plan B of my prologue.

***

Perhaps no real harm is done if we imagine that Louis XVI inquired on the scaffold about his missing explorers. Or that a teenage Napoleon had a near-miss with a famous expedition gone missing. But some exaggerations, half-truths, and fabrications can be injurious, especially if they contribute to the othering or dehumanization of individuals or groups. Let's look, for example, at accounts of what eventually became of the Lapérouse expedition.

No one in the West knew what happened to the *Boussole* or the *Astrolabe* or their men until 1826, when Peter Dillon (1788–1847), an Irish trader based in Sydney, went to the Melanesian island of Tikopia and found islanders in possession of numerous items of obvious European manufacture, including knives, sword guards, and glass beads. They told Dillon the objects had come from the neighboring island of Vanikoro, today part of the Solomon Islands, where two ships had come to grief years before, when the oldest islanders were children. Dillon, who knew his maritime mysteries, guessed he'd stumbled on evidence of the lost Lapérouse voyage and eventually made his way to the island in question.[27]

In his 1829 memoir, Dillon relates the scenario he pieced together from the Tikopians' testimony and, later, from the Vanikorans themselves.[28] The frigates had likely foundered on the reefs offshore during a storm. Most of the men had drowned with the wrecks or, if they made it to shore, had been killed by islanders. A Tikopian who claimed to have lived for a time in Vanikoro told Dillon that some sixty European skulls were on display in a temple on the island, but no Vanikoran would confirm this, and Dillon never found such a site or any recognizably European remains.[29]

This account was largely corroborated by the report of Jules Dumont-d'Urville (1790–1842), a French naval officer who arrived in Vanikoro just a few months after Dillon.[30] Dumont-d'Urville suspected the islanders had kept French skulls as trophies. But when asked, the islanders told him the remains had long since been buried or thrown into the sea. One member of the expedition, Gaimard, was taken to a "spirit house" (*maison des esprits*) where he believed skulls were kept but found no human heads there at all. When he offered axes and red cloth in exchange for European skulls, the islanders insisted, with poetic good sense, that the ocean possessed the shipwrecked men.[31]

Both Dillon and Dumont-d'Urville also learned that a group of survivors had managed to remain alive on the island for a few months before sailing away on a boat made from timber salvaged from the wreckage. They also reported that several survivors had apparently remained behind on Vanikoro but had since died or left.[32] These elements form the basis of my own fictionalized treatment of the shipwreck in *Landfalls*.

***

Somehow between these early accounts of the discovery of the Lapérouse wrecks and the end of the long nineteenth century, however, narratives about the expedition began to include stories about cannibalism—specifically, that the men who'd managed to swim or float away from the frigates and reach the island had been murdered and then *cannibalized* by the Vanikorans.

How did this shift in the story occur? It seems due in part to a kind of "guilt by narrative association." Dillon himself is the worst culprit in this regard. Although his account never identifies the Vanikorans as cannibals or suggests that Lapérouse's men might have been cannibalized, the book is replete with stories of cannibalism. Indeed, it begins with a grisly and not-at-all credible tale of how Dillon barely escaped becoming a main course at a cannibal feast in Fiji some years before his adventures in Vanikoro, and the pages that follow are peppered, as it were, with references to cannibalism.[33]

This juxtaposition of the Lapérouse story with cannibalism continues with Dumont-d'Urville, who rarely introduces a group of native people without indicating whether or not they are known to be "cannibales" or "anthropophages."[34] He too finds no evidence of cannibalism in Vanikoro, specifically noting that the Vanikorans deny over and over that they eat human flesh.[35] One wonders what the South Pacific islanders of this period must have made of these white men who, for all their impressive ships and weaponry, were so obsessed by the prospect of being eaten by other people.

It took some Victorian-era missionaries and their chroniclers to turn this association about cannibalism into a "fact" about the fate of the Lapérouse shipwreck survivors. First, of course, the Vanikorans themselves had to be recast as cannibals. For this we can thank John Coleridge Patteson (1827–71), missionary and first Anglican bishop of Melanesia. He landed very briefly on Vanikoro in 1856 while conducting a tour of the area on the *Southern Cross*, a 70-ton schooner built for the purpose.[36] In his journals, he records that they saw no one on the island, then adds:

> That there *are* people we had sad proof, for close under those very trees I smelt some most offensive and violent smell, and the Maori boy who was with us turning up the ground disclosed human bones with the flesh still hanging to them, and close by was the oven in wh. they had been cooked. Here we had indisputable proof of the existence and character of the people.[37]

Let us ignore for the moment the above-referenced accounts of earlier European visitors who actually interacted with Vanikorans, yet failed to find evidence of cannibalism despite rather assiduously looking for it. Let us also ignore a missionary's predisposition to find proof that his target population is in grave need of the "civilizing" influence of Christianity. We'll further allow that Patteson's account may indeed be a faithful record of what he experienced during his few minutes on a Vanikoran beach. One is still tempted to suggest that what's really "indisputable" here is that a white man had a native child desecrate a burial site.

Disseminating and embellishing the scant evidence of this journal entry fell to the popular English writer Charlotte Yonge (1823–1901), a distant cousin of Patteson and the Melanesian Mission's most prominent and generous financial backer.[38] After Patteson was killed on the tiny island of Nukapu in 1871, Yonge wrote a biography of her "martyred" relative. Her description of Patteson's visit to Vanikoro begins with a brief and generally factual introduction to the Lapérouse expedition and its sad history. When she relates the story of Dillon's discoveries, however, she avers, counterfactually, the existence of the temple containing "sixty European skulls." Then she goes on to describe Patteson's brief landing and its "proof" of Vanikoran cannibalism.[39]

Predictably, many subsequent writers either reported these statements nearly verbatim[40] or transitively conflated these claims such that, if the Vanikorans were cannibals and the Lapérouse expedition was wrecked in Vanikoro, it followed that Lapérouse and his men must have been cannibalized. In his 1900 *History of the Melanesian Mission*, for example, E. S. Armstrong writes of Vanikoro:

> Here two French vessels commanded by Count La Pérouse were wrecked, and the unfortunate crews devoured by sharks and by the natives. Of the latter there still remained the *conclusive evidence* of sixty European skulls in a temple [emphasis added].[41]

Some of this conflation reached fulsome and silly proportions, as in this passage from an 1885 book about famous shipwrecks:

> To perish so far away! ... When, O Pérouse, it seemed so much glory awaited thee on thy return! To perish, perhaps devoured by monsters with the semblance of humanity, whom thou hadst visited to endow them with the benefits of civilisation, and, it may be, after having seen all thy comrades—whom thou didst look upon as thy brothers—carried, one after the other, in bleeding morsels to the horrid orgies of cannibals![42]

"Alternative facts," once they get a toehold, are hard to shake. I've found this unfortunate implication of Vanikoran cannibalism in even quite recent sources about the Lapérouse expedition. It appears, for instance, in an otherwise quite nuanced and beautifully rendered piece in the late W. S. Merwin's 2005 essay collection, *The Ends of the Earth*.[43] It also informs the premise of *Vanikoro*, a movie project that French horror director Xavier Gens has reportedly had in the works for some years. One film-related website describes the planned film as one "about a group of shipwrecked guys on an island full of cannibals."[44] Is it possible that a film pitting beleaguered white "guys" against dark-skinned "cannibals" might avoid manifestly racist depictions of the South Pacific islanders, who have long had to contend with the exhausting legacy of fallacious allegations of cannibalism in their cultures?[45] The outré conceptual graphics for the project, complete with tiki torches, topless island women, and chieftains bedecked with feathers and skulls, suggest not.[46]

**

Hilary Mantel has said that there isn't really a "code of good practices" for writers of historical fiction, and suggests we should at least seek to avoid circulating the errors and prejudices of the past.[47] This is a helpful baseline. Of course, the more challenging work begins after we've finally left the library and find ourselves alone before our writing implements, striving to weave together, from all that we've learned—and *un*learned—a tale at once truthful and compelling. We will inevitably make errors of our own. We harbor prejudices we cannot see even when we look for them. In future years, if we're lucky enough to be read and remembered and discussed, some critic might inveigh against our own inadequate research or blinkered worldview. In the meantime, however, if we can help upend some bad conventional "wisdom" or counter prejudicial thinking, we may avoid perpetrating harm and may even prove useful. Often that means questioning our initial understandings. Sometimes we need to take the map down from the wall and see what's printed on the other side.

17

Am I Chinese Enough to Tell This Story?

Kirstin Chen

After my first novel was published, I flew back home to Singapore for the Singapore Writers Festival. I'd been asked to read an excerpt at my panel. It was a simple request; I'd given countless readings in the preceding months, always alternating between the same three passages. This time, however, when I flipped through my book, I felt a new trepidation. *Soy Sauce for Beginners* is set in contemporary Singapore and filled with Singaporean characters, and yet, I'd spent little time considering how a Singaporean audience would receive it. The sentences had been composed in Boston and San Francisco, revised from feedback offered by my American graduate school classmates and agent and editor, and read mainly by American readers. What if Singaporeans thought I'd been away in the United States for too long? That despite what my passport said, I wasn't Singaporean enough to tell this story?

I wondered if I should temper my American accent with some British pronunciations, since British English was what was taught in school. Perhaps I should choose a passage without any Singlish lines (the local English creole) to avoid unnecessary judgment. Or perhaps I should read solely in Singlish to prove my bona fides.

In the end, because I could not find a better excerpt of the right length, I read the passage I always read—the one at the beginning of the book, with the single line of Singlish dialogue. And when I read that line, I felt the festival tent stir. I thought I saw heads turn and glances exchanged. But maybe I'd imagined it all.

What I didn't imagine, though, was the encounter with the woman in the book-signing line after the panel.

"I'm looking forward to reading your novel," she said, "but I don't think you've spent enough time in Singapore to speak Singlish."

Still smiling, I said, "I grew up here. My parents live here. I moved away for school when I was 15."

Kirstin Chen, *Am I Chinese Enough to Tell This Story?*. In: *Historical Fiction Now*. Edited by Mark Eaton and Bruce Holsinger, Oxford University Press. © Kirstin Chen (2023). DOI: 10.1093/oso/9780198877035.003.0018

"Fifteen still too short, lah," she said. "Must at least be 18."

***

Back in my apartment in San Francisco, I turned my attention to my new novel. The idea for it began with an unforgettable story a friend had told me about a relative who was left behind in early Maoist China. When my friend's father was a boy in the 1950s, he'd witnessed his grandmother defacing the portrait of Chairman Mao with a hammer and reported her to the authorities. The family decided to flee to Hong Kong, but when they attempted to procure the necessary exit permits, they were forced to leave one child behind as proof of their intention to return. As a result, my friend's aunt—his father's younger sister—had to remain in China. I can no longer recall what compelled my friend to reveal this part of his family history, but I do remember my reaction, the chills that shot down my spine, the thudding of my heartbeat. I leaned in and asked question after question: How old was your aunt? Whom was she left with? Did she eventually get out of China? Where does she live now?

After my interaction back in Singapore, however, I had doubts as to my ability to write this next novel. If there were readers out there who believed I didn't have the right to tell a story set in Singapore—the land of my birth, the only home I knew—who was I to embark on this novel, set in a part of southern China that I'd only visited twice, during a time period that I knew almost nothing about? While I am Chinese, my family hasn't lived in China for several generations. My relatives live in Singapore, Hong Kong, or the United States. English is my first language, and my years in America have chipped away at my ability to read Chinese. If I wasn't Singaporean enough to tell a Singaporean story, then how could I possibly be Chinese enough to tell a Chinese one?

I studied essays on cultural appropriation by writers I admired, like Kaitlyn Greenidge and Viet Thanh Nguyen, searching for guidance, clarifying my own views. Like them, I take it for granted that "a writer has the right to inhabit any character she pleases—she's always had it and will continue to have it," as Greenidge writes in the *New York Times*. At the same time, one can't simply ignore history, particularly when writing characters of a different race. "The sensitivity over culture cannot be understood in isolation from deeply entrenched histories of colonization, exploitation and inequality," Nguyen writes in the *LA Times*.

All of this made sense when thinking about white writers writing minority characters, but how did this apply to me, a Singaporean Chinese with

Filipino-Singaporean-Chinese parents, who had lived in America for over half her life, and was writing a Maoist Chinese story?

***

Research seemed like the only way to fight back my doubts. If I didn't yet have a right to this story, I would earn it through sheer hard work. I read novels and memoirs, history and economic texts. I watched narrative and documentary films. I pored over glossy pictures of propaganda posters. Still, every day I added to the already long list of questions to which I could not find answers. Each time I sat down to write I imagined my words being picked apart—in the *New York Times Book Review*, why not?—by some famous historian of modern China.

Somehow I completed a draft of *Bury What We Cannot Take*. I could no longer put off tackling my list of unanswered questions, and since my books and the Internet had failed me, I turned to my father's oldest sister, the only member of my immediate family with in-depth, first-hand knowledge of the setting and time period of my novel.

Bury What We Cannot Take is set on the tiny island of Drum Wave Islet, located just across the channel from the city of Xiamen, in 1957. As a young child, my aunt had lived on Drum Wave Islet (more commonly known by its Chinese name, Gulangyu) for several years, before moving to the Philippines with her family in the 1940s. The year she turned 15, she took the money meant for school fees and ran away from home to join the wave of overseas Chinese students returning to China to rebuild the fatherland. She ended up back in Xiamen.

I was not close to this aunt. I saw her every couple of years at family reunions, but aside from hugging hello and goodbye, we'd barely spoken. Still, she welcomed me into her home and made me lunch and asked, "What do you want to know?"

She shared her childhood memories of living on Gulangyu: how, during the war, her family had been so hungry that her mother had slaughtered the family dog and made soup; how my aunt and her older brother had launched a protest to voice their anger and had refused to eat the soup, only to be held down and force fed by the grown-ups.

She shared later memories, too, of the famine of 1960: how as a young and pregnant reporter, sent to write about a rural village, she got so hungry and exhausted that she simply lay down by the side of the road and slept until she gained the strength to keep going.

From the day she ran away from home, two decades would pass before she saw her parents and siblings again.

In truth, very few of these memories actually made it into the book. My aunt had given me something even more valuable: insight into the resiliency of family. How do members of a family probe and stretch the limits of familial love? How does a family recover from the profoundest of traumas? These are the questions I ask in *Bury What We Cannot Take*; these are the questions I now ask of my own family. I'd spent all these years on research in order to fully render my characters, but in the end my characters had revealed my family to me.

***

Now, in hindsight, I see how I'd managed to sidestep the issue of cultural appropriation altogether. My aunt had bestowed upon me the right to this story, which had given me the confidence to tell it the best way I knew how. But what if, instead of my aunt, I had interviewed a stranger? What if, instead of being a Chinese writer, I was white? If a white writer had done the same research and spoken to the same people and ended up with the same novel, would she have earned a right to it?

I picture my book cover with a new name under the title, say, Mary Smith. I turn the pages and imagine Mary typing these phrases and descriptions and scenes. When she writes of the husband losing his temper and striking his wife, is she guilty of promoting the stereotype of the stern and remote Asian patriarch? When she describes the cruelty of the Maoist government official, has she villainized him to the point of caricature?

To be fair, these are concerns that I, too, considered, before concluding that each of these character's motivations and fears allowed him to transcend type. Still, it's possible that Mary would be asked to justify her portrayals more than I've been asked to (so far); it's possible that some critics would even assert that no amount of research could give Mary Smith the right to tell this Chinese story. And while I disagree with that perspective, I welcome the full spectrum of criticism, especially from the formerly silenced. All fiction writers, regardless of our cultural backgrounds, must acknowledge the privileges and responsibilities that come with the job. If I'd never questioned my right to tell the story of *Bury What We Cannot Take*, I might not have sought out my aunt. I might have believed that all the information I'd needed was in my research texts, and my novel would have suffered for it. Instead, I never forgot what a privilege it was to be able to share this history, this region, and these characters with a mainly Western, English-speaking audience—and the profound responsibility I had to get the details right.

Afterword

I Met a Man Who Wasn't There

Hilary Mantel

Recently, *BBC History* magazine asked me a bald question: What advice I would give to historical novelists. My first thought was that there are so many different kinds of historical fiction that it's impossible to say anything useful. But I thought I must contribute something, and so I said, "If you are writing about real people, make sure you pick a character you don't understand."

The old adage says, "Write what you know." I am going to *talk* about what I know, this evening—about how my Wolf Hall trilogy has evolved—and I trust you won't mind if I filter general thoughts through my own process: because Thomas Cromwell fills my horizon at present. But I am dubious about the advice, "Write what you know." I've always thought that, in any type of fiction, you write to find out; not even to settle an answer, but to pose the most acute questions. If everything yields to the eye at first glance, you will bore yourself and the reader. Better have a puzzle, a mystery, and don't count on solving it.

When I say a puzzle, I don't mean a puzzle as in a detective story. And I don't just mean a subject or theme that is intricate, but one that is complex, layered. I mean a puzzle that is human, and thus never solved, because you never arrive at perfect understanding even of the people you live with, let alone those who are dead and gone. A historical novel isn't usually a quick project. If I were going to work for a number of years on a topic, I would want to feel it would exhaust me before I exhausted it.

I began writing fiction a long time ago, when I was just out of university, though I wasn't published till my mid-thirties. My first book was about the French Revolution: I saw myself making a career as a historical novelist, and I thought, when the Revolution's over, Thomas Cromwell is next.

My career didn't work according to my master-plan, and the first novels I published were contemporary. But Cromwell was always lurking in the half-dark of my intentions.

Hilary Mantel, *Afterword: I Met a Man Who Wasn't There.* In: *Historical Fiction Now.* Edited by Mark Eaton and Bruce Holsinger, Oxford University Press. © Hilary Mantel (2023). DOI: 10.1093/oso/9780198877035.003.0019

It was like that old rhyme.

> As I was going up the stair
> I met a man who wasn't there.
> He wasn't there again today:
> I wish, I wish, he'd go away.

Luckily for me, he didn't. For a decade now, he has offered a constant challenge to my ingenuity, and I still wake up, some days, feeling I know less about him than ever I did.

I am fascinated by how novelists and biographers select their subjects: by how they meet. It's like dating—first impressions count, but then you may be surprised what ensues. Before I began looking at the sources, my view on Thomas Cromwell was conventional. I supposed he was a bad man—as the books said so. But I thought, surely, he must be interesting? He must be, because of his story arc, which cuts straight through the layers of society—from obscurity to fame, from brewer's son to earl. Cromwell rose with the help of a powerful patron, Cardinal Wolsey: but he rose without an affinity, without a great family to back him, and launched his public career with the money he made himself.

Medieval and early modern England was stratified and status conscious, but it wasn't static. It was possible for a poor boy to get on, if he was bright—but usually he did it by entering the church, which rendered him classless: so Thomas Wolsey, the butcher's son, could talk to princes as their equal, once he had risen to be a cardinal. But Cromwell didn't take that route—so what was going on here? How did he become the second most powerful person in England, after his master Henry: how did he become a force in Europe, so that foreign courts hung on his word?

I'm not someone who believes in genius running in families. But it's a fact that Oliver Cromwell was descended from Thomas's sister, and I think it's interesting that this obscure and ordinary family gave us two men who redrew the map of their country. Thomas was born around 1485—we can't be sure, but it's seemed convenient to the tidy minds of historians to situate him at the supposed end of the Middle Ages, and have him born in the first Tudor year, the year of Henry VII's victory over Richard III at Bosworth: though it's worth remembering that the importance of that year is our construction, not theirs: no one who was then living said to themselves, "Thank the Lord, that's the end of the York v. Lancaster wars!": and in fact, it wasn't, as Henry VII was back on the battlefield within two years, and had to struggle throughout his reign with pretenders to his title.

But in any event, as the Tudor era began, the Cromwells were nobodies: small businesspeople living in Putney, west of London, on the river.

They were not poor. Thomas's father, Walter, had a number of trades— brewer, blacksmith, fuller—and he had respectable connections: but for the townsfolk he was the neighbor from hell, and every year he was fined for adulterating the ale he brewed—it seems he was impervious to public opinion, paid his fine and carried on poisoning folk.

So Walter's existence makes a faint mark on the historical record—he's fined for drunkenness and assault and general unpleasantness, and there are some business and property dealings that leave traces. Otherwise we would know nothing about Thomas's background. It was he who later began systematic records of baptisms, marriages, and deaths. But he didn't record himself—so we don't even know the name of his mother. He once told the Spanish ambassador that she was 52 when he was born. Impossible to be sure, because he used to tease the ambassador. But if it was true, she may not have been much of a figure in his life at all. There's no record of his education. It's believed he got away from Putney early—he seems to have been abroad by his late teens, serving in the French army, and going with them on campaign to Italy.

From the historical point of view, these are his missing years. But interestingly, they're not missing in fiction. There was an Italian monk called Matteo Bandello, whose writings provided Shakespeare with some of his plots—and he wrote up the young Englishman's adventures in Italy, in a highly fantastical form. So only twenty years after his death, he was a character in a story.

Then we find stories about him in John Foxe, in the *Book of Martyrs*— *Acts and Monuments*, as it's properly called. Foxe was writing a generation later—but he got his information from people who had known Cromwell. In some of his anecdotes Cromwell is a kind of trickster figure—which picks up on the version of him in Bandello's tales. In Shakespeare's *Henry VIII*, he is a more sober character, confidant to Wolsey. He's the hero in a chaotic Elizabethan play, *Thomas, Lord Cromwell*, which starts with him as a boy in Putney in Walter's forge: you know young Thomas is destined for great things because the blacksmiths speak prose, but he speaks verse. Early in the seventeenth century, in a long poem by Michael Drayton, he comes back from the dead to confront his accusers and put the record straight about his career.

But at the hands of modern writers he's done less well. For twentieth-century historians, it was Geoffrey Elton who defined his central role in the making of Henry's new England. The details of Elton's interpretation are now often disputed—he is the father of modern Tudor studies, and of course, historians have to murder their fathers. But for academics, Elton wrote Cromwell's name right at the top of any consideration of religion and government and finance in his era. Now, Elton believed that Cromwell was "unbiographable," and when you look at what biographers have done so far, you suspect he was right.

For a novelist trying to get a grounding in an era, an armful of biographies of the major figures is usually a good starting point—but in Cromwell's case the accounts were one-note—not just judgmental but also muddled and confusing. Early in the twentieth century there was a biographical study by a Harvard historian called Roger Bigelow Merriman, who also edited Cromwell's letters. Merriman was unremittingly hostile, apt to put the worst construction on everything Cromwell did or said. He had an enormous influence on later commentators, and where he made mistakes, or simply aired a prejudice, they rolled on unchallenged.

It's not hard to understand the difficulties of the biographer. It's not just Cromwell's missing years that hamper them: it's the fact that when Cromwell achieved power, he was Minister of Everything—on any given day, the entire business of England might cross his desk. The detail can be overwhelming, and everything seems to happen at once, and challenge your command of the narrative. The few weeks after Anne's Boleyn's death contain five years' worth of events. You could sink under the weight of Cromwell's paperwork. And the archive, though it's huge, is one-sided—by and large, we have his in-tray, but not his out-tray. And his letters out, of course, went all over Europe, so it's chance whether the original survives.

It's easy enough to write a study of one aspect of his policy or activities. It seems impossible, though, to capture any sense of his whole life. Inside the Cromwell biographies there is analysis, information, data of all kinds, but no living man. Without readable accounts of a life it's difficult for the general reader to get a grasp on a character in history: in popular perception, I found he was a caricature. I thought, is this a case where a novelist might actually make herself useful?

What I saw very clearly was that the story has an archetypal force. It's the story of the boy who leaves home and can't go back, so must push on into hostile territory, equipped with a strong nerve and an agile brain. He's like a boy in a fairytale who, by cunning, makes himself necessary to a giant—in this case, Henry VIII. The giant is very strong but lonely and needy and a bit slow to maneuver. The boy is nimble, and always has an original solution to a giant's troubles. The giant rewards him, munificently—till one day he turns around and stamps on his head.

There is enough fiction about the reign of Henry VIII to fill a library. Not the wildest imagination could invent Henry. He outdoes anything in *Game of Thrones*—a king who has six wives, and beheads two of them—it's irresistible. In this vast library of fiction, Cromwell is marginal or stereotyped or both. But more than one generation was influenced by Robert Bolt's play, *A Man for All Seasons*, and the subsequent film—a wonderful film, but unpersuasive to me in its portrait of Thomas More as a 1960s liberal. Cromwell comes badly out of it—less subtle in performance, in fact, than Bolt made him on the page. It's an illustration of the sticking power of historical fiction. I have had difficulty in persuading the general public that my version of More is actually derived from the record—that he is not an invention of mine, driven by my supposed grudges against Roman Catholics.

So what I saw was a black space in popular imagination, where Thomas Cromwell might be. And I started to paint into it. Most subjects have gaps in their story. For the biographer, these are deep, muddy trenches where you haul yourself around, from one dubious speculation to another. To the novelist, they are airy spaces in which your imagination swings on its flying trapeze.

I haven't tried to fill in Cromwell's missing years—his youth in Italy, his early twenties in the Low Countries. *Wolf Hall* takes a huge chronological jump: we meet him at 15, and in chapter 2, he's 40-odd. I felt that no conjecture of mine would have sufficient power to stand up. I thought it would detract from the authority of what I might write when I began to work with the historical record. But what I do, through the three books, is to revisit the missing years through fragmentary memories, often images rather than narrative—these dart in and out of the main story. So we do gradually build a picture of his early life, and we find out what happened the night before the action of the first novel begins.

Before *Wolf Hall* there were basically two views of him in fiction: desiccated bureaucrat, or thug. Neither of these works with the contemporary evidence. He was a very clever man, with a huge appetite for work and life. Then and now, his abilities were admired even by his worst enemies. But even his best friends were frightened of him. Andrew Boorde, the traveler and physician, wrote to him, "There is no creature living that I do love and fear you so much as you."

I don't deny he had his share of single-minded ruthlessness—like his master Henry and his companions in government. But what I soon realized was that Cromwell past and present is trapped in a set of constructions, like literary tropes, about how an ordinary man would behave if he got power. In this context, "noble" does not simply imply a family pedigree: it has the full connotation of seemly, dignified, godly behavior, which—in theory—only men of pedigree exhibit. And Cromwell, by definition, was ignoble. Even in twentieth-century texts we find references to the king's "low-born" advisor—so we are allowing our vocabulary and view to be colored by the values of Henry's more gently bred courtiers. Meanwhile the idea has got around that Henry VIII's England was something like Stalin's Russia—a notion that can easily be disproved by facts and figures. But people find it easier to embrace the black legend, and Cromwell is part of it.

I began proper work on my novels around 2005: I was still thinking, "bad man, but interesting." But there comes a moment when you find you are standing in your man's boots. Passing judgment ceases to be the point.

Also, I started relishing his company. There's a letter Cromwell wrote to a friend abroad, in 1523, when he was still a lawyer making his way. That year he was a member of Parliament—parliaments then were called irregularly, usually when a king needed to raise money—and they were frequently brief because everybody had a job to get back to. When Parliament was dissolved, Cromwell wrote:

> I amongst others have endured a parliament which continued by the space of 17 whole weeks. Where we communed of war, peace, strife, contention, debate, murmur, grudge, riches, poverty, penury, truth, falsehood, justice, equity, deceit, oppression, magnanimity, activity, force, attempraunce, treason, murder, felony, conciliation, and also how a commonwealth might be edified and continued within this our realm. Howbeit, in conclusion we have done as our predecessors have been wont to do—that is to say, as well as we might, and left where we began. (Summer 1523, letter to John Creke)

It was when I read that letter I thought, "I want to come and work with you." His biographers have made much of it, usually to his disadvantage—he's an irredeemable cynic, they say, years before he comes into government. It immediately struck me as funny—and it was shared with a friend to whom he's passing on the London gossip ("Mr. Woodall is merry without a wife," he says—which strikes me as a compacted novel). So he is coming to life—he's no longer made of paper.

Then as you explore, you quickly find Cromwell seen through the eyes of his friend and antagonist, the Spanish ambassador in London—who knows he should stay away from Cromwell, but somehow can't, because of the fascination of his talk, and magnificent hospitality, his carefully calculated diplomatic indiscretions, and his subtle mind, and his jokes. Cromwell's face lights up, the ambassador says, in conversation: and he describes how when Cromwell says something particularly cogent or sharp, he flicks his eyes sideways. That's where I position my reader—the recipient of the sideways glance.

Cromwell himself doesn't help you out. If you think about his contemporary, Thomas More: More was really interested in himself, and he was always telling you what you should think of him; while he was still successful and in excellent health (1532) he wrote his own epitaph; he was going to control the rights in himself, even beyond the grave. As far as one can tell, Cromwell was not at all interested in his image. There's a Holbein miniature, and also the major portrait that hangs in the Frick, opposite to Thomas More. More looks as if he's going to step down and start an argument—his face, his posture, suggest vulpine intelligence, swiftness, intensity. Cromwell seems to be looking into the next room. He is the nearest thing to a blank wall.

He is that most intriguing object—a man who resists representation. So I have thought a lot about that portrait. In my novels I return to it again and again—wondering about the effects of being portrayed by an artist, and then being copied, reproduced. In *Wolf Hall* I talk about the lost group picture of Thomas More and his family. In the third book, I watch Henry being painted—the Henry who is the body politic, his magnificence hiding the beginnings of decay: and I will write about the king's search for wife number four, when Holbein was sent trotting around Europe with drawing materials, to capture the likeness of all princesses who were free and willing.

I also talk about Martin Luther, whose face was famous through Europe thanks to the dissemination of engravings. This was new—people knowing the face of a public man—not as a stylized image like that on a coin, and not idealized, like the portrait of the donor in a religious picture—but recognizable and life-like—so you would know Luther if you saw him in the street. In effect, that is the trick I have worked for Cromwell through my fiction: I hope you could spot him in a crowd.

When I began writing, and I'd tell people who I was working on, they'd say, "You mean Oliver?" Now Thomas is firmly placed in the general imagination—of politicians, as well as the reading public. Though in my third novel, he says it's a bad idea to lose your anonymity—he doesn't want it to happen to him. It only makes you more attractive to assassins.

In life, it's made him more attractive to a new crop of biographers. And now there is hope. A young scholar called Michael Everett recently published a study of his early career, and that's possibly a way to do it; to slice it up. Diarmaid Macculloch, who is an expert on the Reformation, is writing a full biography—and if any modern historian has the will and the expertise to make it work, he is the one.[1] So soon the picture of an amoral Machiavellian will be replaced by something much truer and more original.

Tudor historians have been, on the whole, hospitable to me, so Diarmaid Macculloch and I check in with each other. Our pictures of the man are congruent as far as I can tell, but of course our methods are quite different. Last year I asked Diarmaid where he was up to, and he said something like, "20 May 1530, 2 o'clock in the afternoon." When people ask me where I am up to, I can only say, several different places. Even if you are one of those writers who begins at the beginning and works straight through, your narrative moves around in time and space, as you fold in flashbacks, stories inside stories, stories beneath stories. The nature of memory is one of my concerns, and the interpenetration of today's consciousness by our past experiences. The title, *The Mirror and The Light*, is drawn from a letter of Cromwell's, and it is a guide to the structure and function of the novel: a mirror is held up to the past, and new light is cast on previous events.

Diarmaid's answer made me think how historians and novelists handle time differently. When a historian writes, for example, about the execution of Anne Boleyn, the head falls, and a chapter closes. New page. New chapter. But human experience isn't like that. Those who are still alive wake up next day, confused, frightened. There has been a wave of arrests, but are they over? Is Anne's execution the end of something or the beginning of something? We know. They didn't. By trying to reimagine the continuity of human experience, rather than draw a line and turn a page, I have, I hope, been able to cast some light back on the last weeks of the life of Anne and her circle. I haven't made any discoveries. I'm just writing it differently, because I'm reading it humanly.

***

No kind of writer has to explain herself as much and as often as the writer of historical fiction. No matter how much "creativity" is praised, we are brought up to distrust imagination, as an inferior function, ethically dubious. So novelists feel, from the first, accused. It's in the paratext—the author's note, and so on—that we begin our apology: forgive me, for making things up. This is where we stress, with touching anxiety, that we take our research seriously:

and to prove it, some novelists publish bibliographies: "Oh, what a good girl am I!" We are keen to stress that we intend to entertain, but not mislead. We are not *all that* imaginative—just imaginative enough.

We have to stop apologizing, I believe. Historians, in their role as public communicators, are also in the narrative game. To make a narrative that works, a historian must edit, highlight, select, omit. Unless you're very skillful and very committed, you oversimplify, and next you distort. These are the problems all storytellers have in common. The difference is one of transparency. The reading public assumes historians to be free from bias, without an agenda. In fact, the historian's text seethes with *ad hominem* communications. Wars are fought in footnotes, unnoticed by the general reader. Pressure to publish, academic fashion, the need—as I mentioned earlier—to mark out original territory, or at least prove that some great predecessor has made a mistake—these drives and imperatives are invisible to the reader, who takes the narrative to be coming from the hand of God.

Back in the eighteenth century, William Godwin said that novelist should hold their heads high—they have the moral high ground, because they admit to invention. Invention, of course, must be grounded in context, it must have some foundation in the evidence—or else we lose that high ground, and can be charged with telling lies for money, like other novelists. There are so many different types of historical fiction that you can't hope to come up with a code of good practice, but at minimum we should aim at intelligent engagement with research and new thinking—we shouldn't circulate the errors of past generations, or their prejudices. And we all, historians and novelists, have to join an honesty project, to help the public understand that history is not simply a body of knowledge, but an interpretive skill. We must try to push the reader toward questioning the basis of our trade, and into understanding the partial, patchy, often encoded nature of evidence—to think about what can be known, and how, and what kind of thing can never be known, only imagined.

And we must be clear in saying that the historical novelist is not an inferior kind of historian. Our texts are not made of other texts—they are not made out of history books, or even out of source documents. The kind of knowledge we seek is different. We need to know as much as historians do, and tell a *little* of it—and then we have to add value. What we are presenting is the inner experience of our subjects. We know that inner experience exists, however hard to access. We access it through our familiarity with the age we are writing about—something which is not quickly achieved. If we're going to imagine, we have to be equipped to do it thoroughly. Our characters have to come onto the page with a hinterland—what they read, what music they listened to, the metaphors that govern their lives, the tales they heard as children. And we learn about them by listening and looking as well as reading: by rearranging our senses, if we have to, and certainly rearranging our ethical framework, and questioning our assumptions about human nature—if indeed such a thing exists.

I think that whether you are using real people in real situations, or just using the past as a backdrop, you are obliged, as a novelist, to accuracy, and fairness—but not to neutrality. That's for the historian. We bring our biases, our opinions, and we are open about them. As novelists, we're not repudiating subjectivity, we're seeking it—it's what we bring to the table. Good historical fiction is self-conscious, like a painting where the brush-strokes are visible. Our characters are representations in a chain of representations, and those representations have their own natural history. In writing the Thomas Cromwell books, I am carrying forward Holbein's portrait, and Matteo Bandello's romances, and John Foxe's clever and humane Cromwell, and Cromwell as Elizabethan hero, as well as the bad man trapped in the airless pages of all those biographies; and, of course, I am also listening to his own voice in the letters he wrote: and listening between the lines of those letters.

All I ever have is a negotiating position. I can't imagine Thomas Cromwell stopping to write his epitaph. I can't imagine him *stopping*. He behaved as if he would never die, his workload always increasing, his reach longer. The sign-off to his letters often ran: "by the hasty and leisureless hand of your servant Thomas Cromwell."

My hasty and leisureless hand hopes to deliver the final novel next year. Diarmaid Macculloch knows where he's up to with his biography, but doesn't know when he will be done. He says Thomas Cromwell is like Macavity the Mystery Cat.

> Macavity, Macavity, there's no one like Macavity,
> He's broken every human law, he breaks the law of gravity.
> His powers of levitation would make a fakir stare,
> And when you reach the scene of crime—Macavity's not there!

For me he represents the dream subject, the unfinishable sentence. I shall scramble through and present a version of a work in progress—knowing there is no last word. The moment he is dead he will leap up again, and reprocess himself, on screen, in the theatre.

I think in the end it will be like his friend Thomas Wyatt's verse:

> I am as I am and so will I be
> But how that I am none knoweth truly.
> Be it evil, be it well, be I bound, be I free,
> I am as I am and so will I be ...
>
> But how that is I leave to you.
> Judge as ye list, false or true.
> Ye know no more than afore ye knew.
> Yet I am as I am whatever ensue.

List of Credits

Notes

Introduction

1. Augusto Roa Bastos, *I the Supreme*, trans. Helen Lane (New York: Vintage, 1974), 3–4.
2. György Lukács, *The Historical Novel*, trans. Hannah and Stanley Mitchell (Lincoln, NE and London: University of Nebraska Press, 1962), 17.
3. Perry Anderson, "From Progress to Catastrophe: Perry Anderson on the Historical Novel," *London Review of Books* 33, no. 15 (July 28, 2011).
4. See especially Alison Light, *Forever England: Femininity, Literature and Conservatism between the Wars* (New York and London: Routledge, 1991), esp. ch. 4; and Diana Wallace, *The Women's Historical Novel: British Women Writers, 1900–2000* (New York: Palgrave, 2005).
5. Linda Hutcheon, *A Poetics of Postmodernism: History, Theory, Fiction* (New York and London: Routledge, 1988).
6. Jonathan Lee, "For Literary Novelists the Past Is Pressing," *New York Times Book Review* (Sunday, June 13, 2021), 19.
7. Kurt Thometz, "Fran Lebowitz on Reading," The Private Library (March 27, 2012), https://www.the-private-library.com/2012/03/27/fran-lebowitz-on-reading-2/ (accessed July 12, 2021).
8. Richard Lea, "Make It Now: The Rise of the Present Tense in Fiction," *The Guardian* (November 21, 2015), https://www.theguardian.com/books/2015/nov/21/rise-of-the-present-tense-in-fiction-hilary-mantel (accessed July 12, 2021).
9. Cited in Lea, "Make It Now."
10. George Eliot, *Romola* (New York: Harper and Brothers, 1863), 9.
11. Hilary Mantel, *Wolf Hall* (New York: Picador, 2009), 3.
12. Doris Sommer, *Proceed with Caution When Engaged by Minority Writing in the Americas* (Cambridge, MA: Harvard University Press, 1999), x.
13. Quoted in Katherine Clay Bassard, "Imagining Other Worlds: Race, Gender, and the 'Power Line' in Edward P. Jones's 'The Known World'," *African American Review* 42 (2008): 409.

Chapter 2

1. Hilary Mantel, *The Mirror and the Light* (London: 4th Estate, 2020), 298.
2. Mantel, *The Mirror and the Light*, 299.
3. Mantel, *The Mirror and the Light*, 505.

4. Mantel, *The Mirror and the Light*, xiii.

5. Though all three instalments of the trilogy feature a Cast of Characters, *The Mirror and the Light* is the only one in which Mantel distinguishes five characters (Jenneke, Christophe, Mathew, Bastings, and Martin) as wholly fictional. They are marked out by the parenthetical tag "(Invented character)"—an intriguing designation, since it implies strongly that the other characters are *not* invented.

6. Sir Philip Sidney, "A Defence of Poesy," in *Renaissance Literature: An Anthology of Poetry and Prose*, ed. John C. Hunter (Oxford: John Wiley & Sons, 2009), 530.

7. Georg Lukács, *The Historical Novel*, trans. Hannah and Stanley Mitchell, int. Fredric Jameson (Lincoln, NE: University of Nebraska Press, 1983), 38.

8. Ann Rigney, *Imperfect Histories: The Elusive Past and the Legacy of Romantic Historicism* (Ithaca: Cornell University Press, 2018), 19.

9. Rigney, *Imperfect Histories*, 15.

10. Eileen Pollard and Ginette Carpenter, "What Cannot be Fixed, Measured, Confined: The Mobile Texts of Hilary Mantel," in *Hilary Mantel: Contemporary Critical Perspectives* (London: Bloomsbury Academic, 2018), 1–11, 1.

11. Starkey originally used this wording in an interview with Radio 5 Live, which has been widely quoted across news media. A clip of the interview is available at https://www.bbc.co.uk/programmes/p02hpw19 (accessed August 28, 2020).

12. Simon Caldwell, "Bishops Criticise 'Perverse' Depiction of St Thomas More in Wolf Hall," *Catholic Herald* (February 2, 2015), https://catholicherald.co.uk/bishops-criticise-perverse-depiction-of-st-thomas-more-in-wolf-hall/ (accessed August 28, 2020).

13. Mark Brown, "Students Take Hilary Mantel's Tudor Novels as Fact, Says Historian," *The Guardian* (Wednesday, May 31, 2017), https://www.theguardian.com/books/2017/may/31/students-take-hilary-mantels-tudor-novels-as-fact-hay-festival (accessed August 28, 2020).

14. Mark Eaton, "Teaching Historical Fiction: Hilary Mantel and the Protestant Reformation," in *Teaching Narrative*, ed. Richard Jacobs (London: Palgrave Macmillan, 2018), 103–21; Peter Iver Kaufman, "Dis-Mantel-ing More," *Moreana* 47: 179–80, 165–93.

15. Staffan Nyström, "Names and Meaning," in *The Oxford Handbook of Names and Naming*, ed. Carole Hough (Oxford: Oxford University Press, 2016), 39–51, 39–40.

16. Richard Steele, no. 61 (August 30, 1709), in *The Tatler*, ed. Donald F. Bond, 3 vols. (Oxford: Clarendon Press, 1987), 3: 221.

17. Jonathan Swift, "The Importance of the Guardian Considered," in *Jonathan Swift, Political Tracts, 1713–1719*, eds. Herbert Davis and Irvin Ehrenpreis (Oxford: Basil Blackwell, 1953), 14–15.

18. See Andrew Bricker, "Libel and Satire: The Problem with Naming," *ELH* 81, no. 3 (Fall 2014): 889–921, 904.

19. *Knuppfer* v. *London Express Newspaper* [1944] AC 116. I am grateful to Nick McKerrell for directing me toward several key legal cases concerning naming and defamation.

20. Gerhard Eis, "Über die Namen im Kriminalroman der Gegenwart," in Gerhard Eis, ed., *Vom Zauber der Namen. Vier Essays* (Berlin: Erich Schmidt, 1970), 59–92. Translated in Birgit Falck-Kjällquist, "Genre-Based Approaches to Names in Literature," in *The Oxford Handbook of Names and Naming*, 330–43, 332.

21. Alastair Fowler, *Literary Names: Personal Names in English Literature* (Oxford: Oxford University Press, 2012).

22. Fowler, *Literary Names*, 4.

23. *Hulton* v. *Jones* [1910] AC 20.

24. Catherine Gallagher, *Nobody's Story: The Vanishing Acts of Women's Writing in the Marketplace, 1670–1920* (Berkeley, CA: University of California Press, 1994).

25. "Publish and Be Damned: Giles Fights Back for Revie and Clough," *The Independent* (November 13, 2010), http://www.independent.co.uk/sport/football/news-and-comment/publish-and-be-damned-giles-fights-back-for-revie-and-clough-2132719.html (accessed August 28, 2020). See also Jerome de Groot, *The Historical Novel* (London: Routledge, 2009), 9.

26. When Mantel published her short story "The Assassination of Margaret Thatcher," a former advisor to Thatcher called for a criminal investigation. See Zachary Davies Boren, "Hilary Mantel 'Should Be Investigated by Police' over Margaret Thatcher Assassination Story, Says Lord Bell," *The Independent* (September 21, 2014), https://www.independent.co.uk/news/people/news/hilary-mantel-should-be-investigated-by-police-over-margaret-thatcher-assassination-story-says-lord-9746747.html (accessed August 28, 2020).

27. Hilary Mantel, *Wolf Hall* (London: 4th Estate, 2009), 3. For useful accounts of Cromwell's pronouns, see Renate Brosch, "Reading Minds: Wolf Hall's Revision of the Poetics of Subjectivity," in Pollock and Carpenter, *Hilary Mantel*, 57–72, 57, and Leigh Wilson, "Reality Effects: The Historical Novel and the Crisis of Fictionality in the First Decade of the Twentieth Century," in *The 2000s: A Decade of Contemporary British Fiction*, eds. Nick Bentley, Nick Hubble, and Leigh Wilson (London: Bloomsbury, 2015), 145–73.

28. Mantel, *Wolf Hall*, 6, 7.

29. Mantel, *Wolf Hall*, 17.

30. Mantel, *Wolf Hall*, 18.

31. Mantel, *Wolf Hall*, 68.

32. Mantel, *Wolf Hall*, 71.

33. Mantel, *Wolf Hall*, 201.

34. Mantel, *Wolf Hall*, 205.

35. Mantel, *Wolf Hall*, ix.

36. Hilary Mantel, *Bring Up the Bodies* (London: 4th Estate, 2014), ix.

37. Mantel, *Bring Up the Bodies*, 53.

38. Mantel, *Bring Up the Bodies*, 77.

39. Mantel, *Bring Up the Bodies*, 200.

40. Mantel, *Bring Up the Bodies*, 141.

41. Mantel, *The Mirror and the Light*, 4.

42. Mantel, *The Mirror and the Light*, 770.

43. Mantel, *The Mirror and the Light*, 216.

44. Mantel, *The Mirror and the Light*, 199.
45. Mantel, *The Mirror and the Light*, 209.
46. Mantel, *The Mirror and the Light*, 240.
47. Mantel, *The Mirror and the Light*, 313.
48. Mantel, *The Mirror and the Light*, 581, 785, 787.
49. Mantel, *The Mirror and the Light*, 302.
50. Mantel, *The Mirror and the Light*, 344.
51. Mantel, *The Mirror and the Light*, 83.
52. Mantel, *The Mirror and the Light*, 168.
53. Mantel, *The Mirror and the Light*, 313.
54. Mantel, *The Mirror and the Light*, 460.
55. Mantel, *The Mirror and the Light*, 689.
56. Mantel, *The Mirror and the Light*, 608.
57. Mantel, *The Mirror and the Light*, 613.
58. Mantel, *Bring Up the Bodies*, 99, and *Wolf Hall*, 17.
59. Mantel, *The Mirror and the Light*, 805.
60. Mantel, *The Mirror and the Light*, 813.
61. Mantel, *The Mirror and the Light*, 813.
62. Hayden White, "The Historical Text as Literary Artifact," in *The Norton Anthology of Theory and Criticism*, 2nd ed. (New York and London: W. W. Norton & Co., 2010), 1533–53, 1537.
63. Patricia Parker, "What's in a Name: And More," *Sederi* 11 (2002): 101–49. I am grateful to Helen Pringle for suggesting sources addressing More's punning.
64. This was part of a broader understanding of the divine origin of language. Robert Essick offers a valuable overview of the "myth of the motivated sign, the word or gesture or image bearing more than an arbitrary relationship to its referent" in *William Blake and the Language of Adam* (Oxford and New York: Oxford University Press, 1989), 28–32.
65. Stephen Wilson, *Means of Naming: A Social History* (London: Psychology Press, 2000), 191.
66. See Sophie Coulombeau, "'The Knot, that ties them fast together': Personal Proper Name Change and Identity Formation in English Literature, 1779–1800" (Ph.D. thesis, University of York, 2014), http://etheses.whiterose.ac.uk/6694/ (accessed August 28, 2020).

Chapter 4

1. Olga Tokarczuk, "I Believe in the Novel," in Michael Lackey, *Conversations with Biographical Novelists: Truthful Fictions across the Globe* (New York and London: Bloomsbury Academic, 2019), 237.
2. Colm Tóibín, *The Master* (New York: Scribner, 2004), 317.
3. Colm Tóibín, "The Anchored Imagination of the Biographical Novel," in Lackey, *Conversations with Biographical Novelists*, 228.

4. James, Letter to Sarah Orne Jewett, October 5, 1901, in *The Selected Letters of Henry James*, ed. Leon Edel (New York: Farrar, Straus and Cudahy, 1955), 202–3.

5. Colum McCann, "Interview with Robert Birnbaum," in *Conversations with Colum McCann*, ed. Earl Ingersoll (Jackson, MS: University of Mississippi Press, 2017), 71.

6. Colum McCann, "Do What Is Most Difficult," in *Conversations with Colum McCann*, 181.

7. Javier Cercas, "Resisting the 'Dictatorship of the Present' in the Biographical Novel," in Lackey, *Conversations with Biographical Novelists*, 49.

8. Joanna Scott, "A Roundtable Forum with Joanna Scott," in *Conversations with Joanna Scott*, ed. Michael Lackey (Jackson, MS: University Press of Mississippi, in press).

9. Friedrich Nietzsche, "On the Uses and Disadvantages of History for Life," in *Untimely Meditations*, ed. Daniel Breazeale (Cambridge: Cambridge University Press, 1997), 95–96.

10. Atwood, "In Search of *Alias Grace*: On Writing Canadian Historical Fiction," *American Historical Review* 103, no. 5 (December): 1516.

11. Atwood, "In Search of Alias Grace," 1516.

12. Malcolm Bradbury, "'Preface' from *To the Hermitage*," in Michael Lackey, *Biographical Fiction: A Reader* (London and New York: Bloomsbury, 2017), 55.

13. Russell Banks, "The Truth Contract in the Biographical Novel," in Michael Lackey, *Truthful Fictions: Conversations with American Biographical Novelists* (London and New York: Bloomsbury Academic, 2014), 45.

14. Banks, "The Truth Contract," 50.

15. Banks, "The Truth Contract," 51.

16. Banks, "The Truth Contract," 51.

17. Banks, "The Truth Contract," 47.

18. Banks, "The Truth Contract," 47–8.

19. Banks, "The Truth Contract," 51.

20. Banks, "The Truth Contract," 51.

21. Nietzsche, "On the Uses and Disadvantages of History for Life," 95.

22. Georg Lukács, *The Historical Novel* (Lincoln, NE and London: University of Nebraska Press, 1983), 60.

23. Lukács, *The Historical Novel*, 35.

24. Friedrich Nietzsche, *Ecce Homo*, in *On the Genealogy of Morals* and *Ecce Homo*, trans. Walter Kaufmann and R. J. Hollingdale (New York: Vintage, 1989), 326.

25. Nietzsche, *Ecce Homo*, 328.

26. Oscar Wilde, "Historical Criticism," in *Criticism: Historical Criticism, Intentions, The Soul of Man*, ed. Josephine M. Guy, Vol. IV of *The Complete Works of Oscar Wilde* (Oxford: Oxford University Press, 2007), 28.

27. Wilde, "Historical Criticism," 10.

28. Wilde, "Historical Criticism," 30.

29. Wilde, "Historical Criticism," 28.

30. Josephine M. Guy, "Introduction," in Wilde, *Criticism*, xix.

31. Oscar Wilde, "Critic," in *Criticism*, 143–44.

32. Lukács, *The Historical Novel*, 35.

33. Oscar Wilde, "Epistola: In Carcere et Vinculis," in *De Profundis and "Epistola: In Carcere et Vinculis,"* ed. Ian Small, Vol. II of *The Complete Works of Oscar Wilde* (Oxford: Oxford University Press, 2005), 126.

34. Oscar Wilde, "Decay," in *Criticism*, 79.

35. Wilde, "Decay," 92.

36. Bruce Duffy, "In the Fog of the Biographical Novel's History," in Lackey, *Truthful Fictions*, 113.

37. Sabina Murray, "Complex Psychologies in the Biographical Novel," in Lackey, *Conversations with Biographical Novelists*, 182.

38. Murray, "Complex Psychologies," 182.

39. Murray, "Complex Psychologies," 182–83.

40. Chika Unigwe, "Biographical Fiction and the Creation of Possible Lives," in Lackey, *Conversations with Biographical Novelists*, 255.

41. Unigwe, "Biographical Fiction," 255.

42. Rosa Montero, "Speculative Subjectivities and the Biofictional Surge," in Lackey, *Conversations with Biographical Novelists*, 164.

43. Montero, "Speculative Subjectivities," 167.

44. Montero, "Speculative Subjectivities," 167.

45. Montero, "Speculative Subjectivities," 167.

46. Bertolt Brecht, "Writing the Truth: Five Difficulties," in *Galileo*, ed. Eric Bentley and trans. Charles Laughton (New York: Grove Press, 1966), 137.

47. David Ebershoff, "The Biographical Novel as Life Art," in Lackey, *Conversations with Biographical Novelists*, 101.

48. David Ebershoff, "Author's Note," in *The Danish Girl* (New York: Penguin Books, 2001), 271.

49. David Ebershoff, "A Conversation with David Ebershoff," in *The Danish Girl*, 8.

50. David Ebershoff, "The Biographical Novel as Life Art," in Lackey's *Conversations with Biographical Novelists*, 99.

Chapter 6

1. Pauline E. Hopkins, *Contending Forces: A Romance Illustrative of Negro Life, North and South* (1900; reprint: Schomburg Library of Nineteenth-Century Black Women Writers, New York: Oxford University Press, 1988). Pauline E. Hopkins, *The Magazine Novels of Pauline Hopkins* (reprint: Schomburg Library of Nineteenth-Century Black Women Writers, New York: Oxford University Press, 1988). Frances E. W. Harper, *Iola Leroy, or Shadows Uplifted* (1892; reprint: Schomburg Library of Nineteenth-Century Black Women Writers, New York: Oxford University Press, 1990). Frances Smith Foster, ed., *Minnie's Sacrifice, Sowing and Reaping, Trial and*

Triumph, Three Rediscovered Noves by Frances E. W. Harper (Boston, MA: Beacon, 1994).

2. Octavia E. Butler, *Kindred* (1979; reprint: Boston, MA: Beacon, 2004).

3. Tiya Miles, *The House on Diamond Hill: A Cherokee Plantation Story* (Chapel Hill, NC: University of North Carolina Press, 2010). Also see Tiya Miles, "Showplace of the Cherokee Nation: Race and the Making of a Southern House Museum," *Public Historian* 33, no. 4 (November 2011): 11–34.

4. For a detailed description of my experience of writing fiction as a way of doing public history as well as the anxieties, risks, and fallout involved, see Tiya Miles, "Edges, Ledges, and the Limits of Craft: Imagining Historical Work beyond the Boundaries," National Council on Public History Keynote Address 2015, *Public Historian* 38, no. 1 (February 2016): 8–17.

5. Rowena McClinton, ed., *The Moravian Springplace Mission to the Cherokees, Vols. I and II, 1814–1821* (Lincoln, NE: University of Nebraska Press, 2007). Also see Rowena McClinton, ed., *The Moravian Springplace Mission to the Cherokees, Abridged* (Lincoln, NE: University of Nebraska Press 2010).

6. For more on my research on the historical figure of Mary Ann Battis, see Tiya Miles, "The Lost Letter of Mary Ann Battis: A Troubling Case of Gender and Race in Creek Country," Notes from the Field, *Native American and Indigenous Studies* 1, no. 1 (spring 2014): 88–98.

7. For this "Author's Note" on sources as well as a "Readers' Guide" and book club questions, see the paperback edition, Tiya Miles, *The Cherokee Rose: A Novel of Gardens and Ghosts* (Winston-Salem, NC: John F. Blair, Publisher, 2016).

8. In draft form, I had titled the novel "Our Mothers' Gardens," inspired, of course, by Alice Walker's classic work of womanist theory. My literary agent, Deirdre Mullane, suggested the new title of "The Cherokee Rose," also fitting and more immediately explanatory for readers regarding the subject matter. Alice Walker, *In Search of Our Mothers' Gardens* (New York: Harcourt, Brace, Jovanovich, 1983).

9. *The Cherokee Rose*, though imperfect, was named "A Book All Georgians Should Read" by the Georgia Center for the Book. It was a finalist for a Lambda Literary Award in the category of Lesbian Fiction, and a winner of a Bronze Medal in Multicultural Fiction, Independent Publisher Book Awards.

Chapter 9

1. "Richelieu," in Balzac, *Œuvres Complètes*, Vol. 22 (Paris: Maison Michel Lévy Frères, 1879), 88; cited in Bruce Tolley, "Balzac and the *Feuilleton des Journaux Politiques*," *Modern Language Review* 57 (1962): 513.

2. "Hernani ou l'Honneur Castillan," in Balzac, *Œuvres Complètes*, Vol. 22, 52; cited in Tolley, "Balzac and the *Feuilleton*," 512.

3. Seth Lerer, *Error and the Academic Self: The Scholarly Imagination, Medieval to Modern* (New York: Columbia University Press, 2003), 2.

4. Lerer, *Error and the Academic Self*, 2.

5. For a perceptive account of this passage and the incident to which it refers, see Frank Grady, "Gower's Boat, Richard's Barge, and the True Story of the *Confessio Amantis*: Text and Gloss," *Texas Studies in Literature and Language* 44 (2002): 1–15.

6. Susanne Alleyn, *Medieval Underpants and Other Blunders: A Writer's (& Editor's) Guide to Keeping Historical Fiction Free of Common Anachronisms, Errors, & Myths*, 3rd ed. (Albany, NY: Spyderwort Press, 2013).

7. Alleyn, *Medieval Underpants*.

8. Cited in Nigel Saul, *Richard II* (New Haven, CT: Yale University Press, 2008), 340.

9. Saul, *Richard II*, 340.

10. Cicero, *De inventione* vii, trans. Charles Duke Yonge, *The Orations of Marcus Tullius Cicero*, Vol. 4 (London: George Bell & Sons, 1890), 248.

11. On Rykener's life and its documentation, see Carolyn Dinshaw, *Getting Medieval: Sexualities and Communities, Pre- and Postmodern* (Durham, NC and London: Duke University Press, 1999), esp. 101–10.

12. Rita Felski, *The Limits of Critique* (Chicago, IL: University of Chicago Press, 2015), 86.

13. R. G. Collingwood, *The Idea of History* (Oxford and London: Oxford University Press, 1946), 215.

14. Both statements quoted in Aaron Blake, "Kellyanne Conway's 'Bowling Green Massacre' Wasn't a Slip of the Tongue. She Has Said It Before," *Washington Post* (February 6, 2017), https://www.washingtonpost.com/news/the-fix/wp/2017/02/06/kellyanne-conways-bowling-green-massacre-wasnt-a-slip-of-the-tongue-shes-said-it-before/ (accessed July 5, 2021).

15. Donna Haraway, *Primate Visions: Gender, Race, and Nature in the World of Modern Science* (New York and London: Routledge, 1989), 4.

16. Friedrich Nietzsche, *The Will to Power: A New Translation*, trans. Walter Kaufmann and R. J. Holingdale (New York: Random House, 1967), par. 481.

17. Judith Butler, *Gender Trouble: Feminism and the Subversion of Identity* (New York: Routledge, 1990), 115.

18. Carlos Maza, "KellyAnne Conway's Interview Tricks, Explained," *Vox* (February 13, 2017), https://www.vox.com/videos/2017/2/13/14597968/kellyanne-conway-tricks (accessed July 5, 2021).

19. A typical statement of this charge can be found in Alan Sokal and Jean Bricmont, *Fashionable Nonsense: Postmodern Intellectuals' Abuse of Science* (New York: Picador, 1999), 51–52.

20. In Nathan Howard, Jr., *Practice Reports in the Supreme Court and Court of Appeals of the State of New York*, Vol. 19 (Albany, NY: William Gould, 1860), 236.

21. A. J. Villiers, statement in *Haydenrych v. Colonial Mutual Life Assurance Society Ltd*, 1920 CPD 67 at 70–71.

22. Paul Michael Lisnek and Eric G. Oliver, *The Complete Litigator: Reality, Perception, and Persuasion in and Out of Court* (Wayne, PA: Andrews Publications, 1994), 103.

23. Cited and discussed in Anne H. Stevens, "Learning to Read the Past in the Early Historical Novel," in Kate Mitchell and Nicola Parsons, eds., *Reading Historical Fiction: The Revenant and Remembered Past* (New York: Palgrave, 2013), 22.

24. The review is printed in F. R. Leavis, ed., *A Selection from Scrutiny*, Vol. 2 (Cambridge: Cambridge University Press, 1968), 258.

25. On this enlistment, see David Lipscomb, "Caught in a Strange Middle Ground: Contesting History in Salman Rushdie's *Midnight's Children*," *Diaspora* 1, no. 2 (1991): 163–89.

26. Pat Barker, *Regeneration* (New York: Random House, 1991), 1. On the interweaving of fact and fiction in the trilogy, see Greg Harris, "Compulsory Masculinity, Britain, and the Great War: The Literary-Historical Work of Pat Barker," *Critique* 39 (1998): 290–304.

27. See this volume's introduction, above, for discussion of some of these techniques and modes (e.g. historiographic metafiction).

28. The letter has been reprinted many times. See, for example, Rapin de Thoyras's *History of England*, trans. M. Tindal (London: James, John, and Paul Knapton, 1732), Vol. 5, 811.

29. See the account of what can be known about Cromwell's visits to the Tower in Alison Weir, *The Lady in the Tower: The Fall of Anne Boleyn* (New York: Ballantine, 2012), 174–75.

30. Hilary Mantel, *Bring Up the Bodies* (New York: Henry Holt, 2012), 345.

Chapter 10

1. Details about the Hart kidnapping and the Thurmond and Holmes lynching are drawn from James P. Delgado, "The Facts behind John Steinbeck's 'The Lonesome Vigilante,'" *Steinbeck Quarterly* 16, no. 3–4 (1983), 70–77; Brian McGinty, "Shadows in St. James Park," *California History* 57, no. 4 (Winter 1978–9), 290–307; and Ken Gonzales-Day, *Lynching in the West: 1850–1935* (Durham, NC: Duke University Press, 2006), 105–11.

2. Steinbeck letter to Tom Collins, 1938, quoted in Jackson J. Benson, *John Steinbeck, Writer: A Biography* (New York: Penguin, 1990), 205.

3. The letter to Otis was during the writing of the destroyed early draft, "L'Affair Lettuceberg," in Elaine Steinbeck and Robert Wallsten, eds., *Steinbeck: A Life in Letters* (New York: Penguin, 1989), 162.

4. John Steinbeck, *Working Days: The Journals of The Grapes of Wrath*, ed. Robert DeMott (New York: Viking, 1989), 25.

5. Steinbeck later writes to Roosevelt to thank her for the comment. See Benson, *John Steinbeck*, 422.

6. See Yi-Ping Ong, *The Art of Being: Poetics of the Novel and Existentialist Philosophy* (Cambridge, MA: Harvard University Press, 2018), especially 23–45.

7. Ong, *The Art of Being*, 171, 174.

8. John Steinbeck, "The Vigilante," in *The Grapes of Wrath and Other Writings, 1936–1941*, ed. Robert DeMott (New York: Library of America, 1996), 87. See Delgado, "The Facts," 75.

9. Delgado traces these various parallels ("The Facts," 75–76).

10. The Long Valley ledger, Martha Heasley Cox Center for Steinbeck Studies, San Jose State University.

11. Gonzales-Day, *Lynching*, 206.

12. John Steinbeck, "Flight," in *The Grapes of Wrath and Other Writings, 1936–1941*, ed. Robert DeMott (New York: Library of America, 1996), 34, 47.

13. My transcription of Steinbeck's notes in the Long Valley ledger, 80.

14. Ernest Hemingway, "Soldier's Home," *The Short Stories* (New York: Scribner, 1995), 145–53.

15. The conversations on this topic between Doc Burton and the other characters in Steinbeck's *In Dubious Battle* (1936) is another good example.

16. Steinbeck, "Case History," Long Valley ledger, 82.

17. In "Case History," the victim of the lynching is accused of kidnapping and murder, as were Thurmond and Holmes.

18. Steinbeck, "Case History," Long Valley ledger, 81–82, 85.

19. Steinbeck's note in the Long Valley ledger, 126.

20. In the ledger version of "The Vigilante" we read "on south 10th between Jones and Santa Rosa" (124); the actual streets would be John and Santa Clara.

21. We learn that the bar Mike visits closes at midnight; the actual lynching took place at 11.15 p.m.

22. See Delgado, "The Facts," 74.

23. Steinbeck, "The Vigilante," 87.

24. Take for example the exhibition that became James Allen's *Without Sanctuary: Lynching Photography in America* (Santa Fe, NM: Twin Palms Publishers, 2000).

25. Steinbeck, "The Vigilante," 87.

26. See Gonzalez-Day, *Lynching*, 97; Shawn Michelle Smith, "The Evidence of Lynching Photographs," in Dora Apel and Shawn Michelle Smith, *Lynching Photographs* (Berkeley, CA: University of California Press, 2007), 14.

27. Dora Apel, "On Looking: Lynching Photographs and Legacies of Lynching after 9/11," *American Quarterly* 55, no. 3 (September 2003), 458.

28. According to Gonzales-Day, someone produced a multi-card set of images depicting the journey from prison cell to hang tree (*Lynching*, 115).

29. See Brian McGinty, "Shadows in St. James Park," *California History* 57, no. 4 (Winter 1978–9), 304. McGinty also notes that the community had effective law enforcement.

30. Steinbeck's ideas often resonate in curious ways with those of the philosophers Gilles Deleuze and Félix Guattari, who were fascinated with states of becoming and "pack" action—for example, the move toward assemblage that they describe as the war machine: "a pure and immeasurable multiplicity, the pack, an irruption of the ephemeral and the power of metamorphosis." See Gilles Deleuze and Félix Guattari, *A Thousand Plateaus: Capitalism and Schizophrenia*, trans. Brian Massumi (Minneapolis, MN: University of Minnesota Press, 1987), especially 351–423.

31. Gonzales-Day, *Lynching*, 108.
32. Jacqueline Goldsby, *A Spectacular Secret: Lynching in American Life and Literature* (Chicago, IL: University of Chicago Press, 2006), 281.
33. John Steinbeck, The Pearl, in *Novels 1942–52*, ed. Robert DeMott (New York: Library of America, 2001), 298.
34. Steinbeck, "The Vigilante," 86.
35. Goldsby, *Spectacular Secret*, 231. Goldsby observes that black men were photographed to display the full extent of their wounding and humiliation.
36. See Walter White, *A Man Called White: The Autobiography of Walter White* (New York: Viking, 1948), 166–67.
37. Kate Flint, *Flash!: Photography, Writing, and Surprising Illumination* (Oxford: Oxford University Press, 2017), 173, 170.
38. Dora Apel, "Lynching Photographs and the Politics of Public Shaming," in Apel and Smith, *Lynching Photographs*, 58. For the young flirting couple in the Marion photograph, writes Apel, "it is as though the myth of the hypersexed black male, now safely controlled, has now become an invisible erotic power haunting their relation" (58).
39. Steinbeck, "The Vigilante," 89.
40. Susan Stewart, *On Longing: Narratives of the Miniature, the Gigantic, the Souvenir, the Collection* (Durham, NC: Duke University Press, 1993), 135, 133, 136. Goldsby also draws from Stewart in her description of lynching souvenirs (*Spectacular Secret*, 275–76).
41. Steinbeck, "The Vigilante," 91, 87. See Stewart, *On Longing*, 136, on experiences being "not for sale."
42. Stewart, *On Longing*, 136.
43. See Goldsby, *Spectacular Secret*, 20–21, 25.
44. Steinbeck, "The Vigilante," 89.
45. Edgar Allan Poe, "Twice-told Tales," *Graham's Magazine* 20, no. 5 (May 1842), reprinted in John L. Idol, Jr. and Buford Jones, eds., *Nathaniel Hawthorne: The Contemporary Reviews* (Cambridge: University of Cambridge Press, 1994), 63–68.
46. Eudora Welty, "Where Is the Voice Coming From?" in *The Collected Stories of Eudora Welty* (New York: Harcourt Brace Jovanovich, 1980), 603–7.
47. Eudora Welty, *One Time, One Place: Mississippi in the Depression, A Snapshot Album* (Jackson, MS: University Press of Mississippi, 1996), 4.
48. Julio Cortázar, "Some Aspects of the Short Story," in Charles E. May, ed., *The New Short Story Theories*, 245–55. Cortázar writes that short stories/photographs are thus capable of acting on their viewer/reader beyond the visual/literary anecdote they embody.
49. Nadine Gordimer, "The Flash of Fireflies," in May, *Short Story Theories* (Athens, OH: Ohio University Press, 1978), 178–81.
50. Roland Barthes, *Camera Lucida: Reflections on Photography* (New York: Hill & Wang, 2010), 119.

51. Susan Sontag describes photographs as reinforcing a "view of social reality as consisting of small units" in *On Photography* (New York: Picador, 1990), 22.
52. "Photographed images do not seem to be statements about the world so much as pieces of it," writes Sontag in *On Photography*, 4.
53. Sontag, *On Photography*, 74, 10.

Chapter 12

1. Catherine Gallagher, *Telling It Like It Wasn't: The Counterfactual Imagination in History and Fiction* (Chicago, IL: University of Chicago Press, 2018), 3.
2. Gallagher, *Telling It Like It Wasn't*, 147.
3. Alexandra Alter, "Steven King's New Monster," *Wall Street Journal* (October 28, 2011). In fact, the most prolific writer of alternate-history novels is probably Robert Conroy, who published more than fifteen titles from 1995 until his death in 2014.
4. This is consistent with recent scholarship on slavery, which chronicles the shameful afterlife of slavery during Reconstruction and beyond: see Douglas A. Blackmon, *Slavery by Another Name: The Re-enslavement of Black Americans from the Civil War to World War II* (New York: Anchor, 2009); and Michelle Alexander, *The New Jim Crow: Mass Incarceration in the Age of Colorblindness* (New York: The New Press, 2010).
5. Paul K. Saint-Amour, "Counterfactual States of America: On Parallel Worlds and Longing for the Law," *Post-45* (September 20, 2011).
6. Catherine Gallagher, "War, Counterfactual History, and Alternate-History Novels," *Field Day Review* 3 (2007): 53.
7. Gallagher, "War, Counterfactual History, and Alternate-History Novels," 61.
8. Gallagher, "War, Counterfactual History, and Alternate-History Novels," 61.
9. Philip K. Dick, *The Man in the High Castle* (Boston, MA: Houghton Mifflin Harcourt, 1962), 68–69.
10. Dick, *The Man in the High Castle*, 119.
11. Dick, *The Man in the High Castle*, 131.
12. Dick, *The Man in the High Castle*, 133.
13. Dick, *The Man in the High Castle*, 244–45.
14. Dick, *The Man in the High Castle*, 244–45.
15. Brian Ladd, *Autophobia: Love and Hate in the Automotive Age* (Chicago, IL: University of Chicago Press, 2008), 109.
16. Dick, *The Man in the High Castle*, 245–46.
17. Dick, *The Man in the High Castle*, 246.
18. Saint-Amour, "Counterfactual States of America."
19. Gallagher, "War, Counterfactual History, and Alternate-History Novels," 64.
20. Gallagher, "War, Counterfactual History, and Alternate-History Novels," 64.
21. Gallagher, "War, Counterfactual History, and Alternate-History Novels," 64.
22. Saint-Amour, "Counterfactual States of America."

23. In an early essay titled "Writing American Fiction" (1961), Roth famously observed, "The American writer in the middle of the twentieth century has his hands full in trying to understand, describe, and then make credible much of American reality. It stupefies, it sickens, it infuriates, and finally it is even a kind of embarrassment to one's meager imagination. The actuality is continually outdoing our talents, and the culture tosses up figures almost daily that are the envy of any novelist." Philip Roth, "Writing American Fiction," in *Reading Myself and Others* (New York: Vintage, 2001), 167–68.

24. Philip Roth, *The Plot Against America* (Boston, MA: Houghton Mifflin, 2004), 52–53.

25. Richard Brody, among other critics, has noted similarities to Donald Trump's electoral college victory in 2016. See Richard Brody, "The Frightening Lessons of Philip Roth's *The Plot Against America*," *New Yorker* (February 1, 2017). For his part, Roth himself has disavowed any links. "My novel wasn't written as a warning," he insists. "I was just trying to imagine what it would have been like for a Jewish family like mine, in a Jewish community like Newark, had something even faintly like Nazi anti-Semitism befallen us in 1940, at the end of the most pointedly anti-Semitic decade in world history. I wanted to imagine how we would have fared, which meant I had first to invent an ominous American government that threatened us. As for how Trump threatens us, I would say that, like the anxious and fear-ridden families in my book, what is most terrifying is that he makes everything possible, including, of course, the nuclear catastrophe." Judith Thurman, "Philip Roth E-mails on Trump," *New Yorker* (January 30, 2017).

26. Philip Roth, "The Story behind *The Plot Against America*," *New York Times* (September 19, 2004).

27. Roth, *The Plot Against America*, 232–33.

28. J. M. Coetzee observes that the title perhaps inadvertently echoes the terrorist attacks on 9/11. See J. M. Coetzee, "What Philip Knew," *New York Review of Books* (November 18, 2004); rpt. in J. M. Coetzee, *Inner Workings: Literary Essays 2000–2005* (New York: Viking, 2007), 229.

29. Roth, *The Plot Against America*, 364.

30. Roth, *The Plot Against America*, 364.

31. Roth, *The Plot Against America*, 387–88.

32. Roth, *The Plot Against America*, 13.

33. A. Scott Berg, *Lindbergh* (New York: Putnam, 1998), 394.

34. Roth, *The Plot Against America*, 14.

35. Roth, *The Plot Against America*, 166.

36. Luther Huston, "Bund Activities Widespread," *New York Times* (February 26, 1939): 6E.

37. Catherine Gallagher, "Telling It Like It Wasn't," *Pacific Coast Philology* 45 (2010): 24.

38. Roth, *The Plot Against America*, 176–77.

39. Roth, *The Plot Against America*, 176.

40. Roth, *The Plot Against America*, 301.
41. Roth, *The Plot Against America*, 316.
42. Roth, *The Plot Against America*, 305.
43. Roth, *The Plot Against America*, 354.
44. Sinclair Lewis, *It Can't Happen Here* (New York: Signet Classics, 2014), 160.
45. Lewis, *It Can't Happen Here*, 158.
46. Lewis, *It Can't Happen Here*, 219.
47. Lewis, *It Can't Happen Here*, vi.
48. Roth, *The Plot Against America*, 177.
49. Saint-Amour, "Counterfactual States of America."
50. Roth, *The Plot Against America*, 319–20.
51. Terry Gross, "Colson Whitehead's 'Underground Railroad' Is a Literal Train to Freedom," *Fresh Air*. National Public Radio. August 8, 2016.
52. Colson Whitehead, *The Underground Railroad* (New York: Doubleday, 2016), 161.
53. Whitehead, *The Underground Railroad*, 161, 172.
54. Whitehead, *The Underground Railroad*, 162–63.
55. Whitehead, *The Underground Railroad*, 163.
56. Whitehead, *The Underground Railroad*, 165.
57. Jason Parham, "Colson Whitehead on Writing, Slavery, and the True Origins of America," *Fader* (August 17, 2016).
58. Sven Beckert, "Slavery and Capitalism," *Chronicle Review* (December 12, 2014). See also Walter Johnson, *River of Dark Dreams: Slavery and Empire in the Cotton Kingdom* (Cambridge, MA: Harvard University Press, 2013); Edward E. Baptist, *The Half Has Never Been Told: Slavery and the Making of American Capitalism* (New York: Basic Books, 2014); Sven Beckert, *Empire of Cotton: A Global History* (New York: Alfred A. Knopf, 2014); Caitlin Rosenthal, *Accounting for Slavery: Masters and Management* (Cambridge, MA: Harvard University Press, 2018).
59. Whitehead, *The Underground Railroad*, 215.
60. Whitehead, *The Underground Railroad*, 215.
61. Orlando Paterson, *Slavery and Social Death: A Comparative Study* (Cambridge, MA: Harvard University Press, 1982).
62. Valerie Babb, *A History of the African-American Novel* (Cambridge: Cambridge University Press, 2017), 234.
63. Whitehead, *The Underground Railroad*, 91.
64. Whitehead, *The Underground Railroad*, 113.
65. Whitehead, *The Underground Railroad*, 121–22.
66. Whitehead, *The Underground Railroad*, 127.
67. Henry Friedlander, *The Origins of Nazi Genocide: From Euthanasia to the Final Solution* (Chapel Hill, NC: University of North Carolina Press, 1995); Dieter Kuntz and Susan Bachrach, eds., *Deadly Medicine: Creating the Master Race* (Washington, DC: United States Holocaust Memorial Museum, 2004).
68. Whitehead, *The Underground Railroad*, 143.

69. Whitehead, *The Underground Railroad*, 153.

70. Whitehead, *The Underground Railroad*, 154.

71. Whitehead, *The Underground Railroad*, 157.

72. Whitehead, *The Underground Railroad*, 156.

73. Whitehead, *The Underground Railroad*, 166.

74. Whitehead, *The Underground Railroad*, 166.

75. Whitehead, *The Underground Railroad*, 90.

76. Parham, "Colson Whitehead on Writing."

Chapter 15

1. Hilary Mantel, *Wolf Hall* (New York: Henry Holt, 2009), 25.

2. The *Journal of American History* has published a lively round table on "The Senses in American History." See *Journal of American History* 95 (2008): 378–451. On the return to phenomenology in historical scholarship more broadly, see Geoff Eley, *A Crooked Line: From Cultural History to the History of Society* (Ann Arbor, MI: University of Michigan Press, 2005).

3. Marcel Proust, *Swann's Way* [1913] (New York: Dover Thrift Edition, 2002), 37–40.

4. Jeffrey L. Pasley, *"The Tyranny of Printers": Newspaper Politics in the Early American Republic* (Charlottesville, VA: University Press of Virginia, 2001), 25.

5. Adam Hochschild, *Bury the Chains: Prophets and Rebels in the Fight to Free an Empire's Slaves* (New York: Houghton Mifflin, 2005), 96.

6. John McPhee, *A Sense of Where You Are* (New York: Farrar, Strauss & Giroux, 1965), 22.

7. Of course, the discourse and expression of emotions, too, are historical; see, e.g., Sarah A. Knott, *Sensibility and the American Revolution* (Chapel Hill, NC: University of North Carolina Press, 2008); Nicole Eustace, *Passion Is the Gale: Emotion, Power, and the Coming of the American Revolution* (Chapel Hill, NC: University of North Carolina Press, 2008); and too many volumes by Peter N. Stearns.

8. Nicholson Baker, *The Mezzanine* (New York: Grove Press, 1988), 3, 135, 130.

9. Jane Kamensky and Jill Lepore, *Blindspot* (New York: Random House, 2009), 139, 411.

10. A young David Hackett Fischer labeled our tendency toward "misplaced temporal literalism" the "chronic fallacy." I like to think this is a double entendre. See David Hackett Fischer, *Historians' Fallacies* (New York: Harper & Row, 1970), 152–54.

11. Kierkegaard's diary, quoted in Michael J. Strawser, *Both/And: Reading Kierkegaard—From Irony to Edification* (New York: Fordham University Press, 1996), 17.

12. Richard Scarry, *What Do People Do All Day?* (New York: Random House, 1968), 6.

13. Philip Roth, *American Pastoral* (Boston, MA: Houghton Mifflin, 1997), 4, 24, 27.

14. Reynolds sitter books, Royal Academy, London. REY 1/25 (1788), entries for 9/29.

15. James Northcote to Samuel Northcote, December 21, 1771, Northcote Papers, Item 7, Royal Academy, London.

16. See, e.g., Angela Rosenthal, "She's Got the Look! Eighteenth-Century Female Portrait Painters and the Psychology of a Potentially 'Dangerous Employment,'" in Joanna Woodall, ed., *Portraiture: Facing the Subject* (Manchester: Manchester University Press, 1997), 147–66.

17. E. M. Forster, *Howard's End* (New York: Knopf, 1921), 214.

18. L. P. Hartley, *The Go-Between* [1953] (New York: NYRB Classics, 2002), 17. Cultural historian David Lowenthal took Hartley's line as the title to his powerful book about the historical construction of history and memory. See David Lowenthal, *The Past Is a Foreign Country* (Cambridge: Cambridge University Press, 1986).

19. Roth, *American Pastoral*, 35.

Chapter 16

1. This name is variously spelled Lapérouse and La Pérouse. Cogent arguments support both. I have chosen to go with the single-word spelling throughout this essay, except where I quote someone who renders it otherwise.

2. John Dunmore, ed. and tr., introduction to *The Journal of Jean-François de Galaup de la Pérouse 1785–1788*, Vol. 1 (London: The Hakluyt Society, 1994), xx–xxx, and Catherine Gaziello, *L'Expédition de Lapérouse 1785–1788, Réplique française aux voyages de Cook* (Paris: Comité des travaux historiques et scientifiques, 1984), 73–77.

3. Dunmore, introduction to *The Journal*, ccvii–ccxix.

4. "Jean-François de Galaup, comte de Lapérouse," *Wikipedia*, last modified September 29, 2020, en.wikipedia.org/wiki/Jean-François_de_Galaup,_comte_de_Lapérouse (accessed March 1, 2023); "Jean-François de La Pérouse," *Wikipédia*, last modified September 14, 2020, *fr.wikipedia.org/wiki/Jean-François_de_La_Pérouse* (accessed March 1, 2023).

5. John Dunmore, *Where Fate Beckons: The Life of Jean-François de la Pérouse* (Fairbanks, AK: University of Alaska Press, 2007), 252, 275; Claudine Wéry, "What News of Lapérouse?" *The Guardian* (April 8, 2005), theguardian.com/theguardian/2005/apr/08/guardianweekly.guardianweekly11 (accessed March 1, 2023); Garrick Hitchcock, "The Mystery of the La Pérouse Expedition Survivors: Wrecked in Torres Strait?" *The Conversation* (August 30, 2017), theconversation.com/the-mystery-of-the-la-perouse-expedition-survivors-wrecked-in-torres-strait-81901 (accessed March 1, 2023); and Aaron Walker, "Finding La Pérouse," *ANU Reporter* 48, no. 3 (Australian National University), reporter.anu.edu.au/finding-la-pérouse (accessed August 20, 2020).

6. "La Pérouse," Napoleon: Revolution to Empire, National Gallery of Victoria, 2012, ngv.vic.gov.au/napoleon/exploration-and-discovery/la-perouse.html (accessed August 27, 2020); "La Pérouse's Story," *La Collection La Pérouse*, 2016, collection-laperouse.fr/en/history#3 (accessed August 27, 2020); Catherine

Delors, "Lapérouse, explorer extraordinaire, at the Musée de la Marine," *Versailles and More* (blog), blog.catherinedelors.com/laperouse-explorer-extraordinaire-at-the-musee-de-la-marine/ (accessed August 20, 2020),; Nimah Koussa, "Following in the Footsteps of James Cook: The Adventures of the Count of La Pérouse," in "10 People in History Who Decided to Explore the Unknown," Grand Luxury Hotels (blog), blog.grandluxuryhotels.com/2020/04/10-people-in-history-who-decided-to-explore-the-unknown-part-2-of-3/ (accessed August 20, 2020).

7. "Visite-atelier: A-t-on des nouvelles de Monsieur de Lapérouse?" *Musée national de la Marine* (Brest, 2012), musee-marine.fr/sites/default/files/11_fe_at-ton_des_nouvelles_de_monsieur_de_laperouse_.pdf (accessed August 20, 2020).

8. John Dunmore, introductions to *The Journal of Jean-François de Galaup de la Pérouse*, xxx, and to *La Peyrouse dans l'Isle de Tahiti* (Cambridge: MHRA, 2006), 9.

9. Arthur Isak Applbaum, "Professional Detachment: The Executioner of Paris," *Harvard Law Review* 109, no. 2 (1995): 458–86, JSTOR, jstor.org/stable/1341979; Daniel Arasse, *The Guillotine and the Terror*, trans. Christopher Miller (London: Allen Lane, Penguin, 1989), ch. 2, archive.org/details/guillotineterror00aras; "Anecdote très-exacte sur l'exécution de Louis Capet," *Thermomètre du Jour* (February 13, 1793), no. 410: 356, retronews.fr/journal/thermometre-du-jour/13-fevrier-1793/1657/2881263/4 (accessed August 20, 2020); Jean-Baptiste Cléry, *A Journal of Occurrences at the Temple, During the Confinement of Louis XVI, King of France*, trans. R. C. Dallas (London: Baylis, 1798), books.google.com/books?id=pUsuAAAAMAAJ; "Détails sur la mort du ci-devant roi," *Thermomètre du Jour* (January 23, 1793), no. 389: 186–88, retronews.fr/journal/thermometre-du-jour/23-jan-1793/1657/2881335/1; Henry Essex Edgeworth de Firmont, *Memoires of the Abbé Edgeworth; containing his narrative of the last hours of Louis XVI*, ed. C. S. Edgeworth (London: Rowland Hunter, 1815), hdl.handle.net/2027/nyp.33433069323719; Victor Hugo, *The Memoirs of Victor Hugo*, trans. John W. Harding (London: William Heinemann, 1899), ch. 1, books.google.com/books/about/The_Memoirs_of_Victor_Hugo.html?id=ahpAAAAAYAAJ; Simon Schama, *Citizens: A Chronicle of the French Revolution* (New York: Alfred A. Knopf, 1989), chs. 15–16.

10. David P. Jordan, *The King's Trial: Louis XVI vs. the French Revolution* (Berkeley, CA: University of California Press, 1979), chs. 11–13, archive.org/details/kingstrial00davi.

11. *Memoirs of the Sansons from Private Notes and Documents*, ed. Henry Sanson, Vol. 1 (London: Chatto and Windus, 1876), 281–85, books.google.com/books?id=iMIBAAAAYAAJ; see Applbaum, "Professional Detachment," 461, for lack of credibility of this family memoir.

12. "Jean-François de Galaup, comte de Lapérouse," *Wikipedia*.

13. Robert W. Kirk, *Paradise Past: The Transformation of the South Pacific, 1520–1920* (Jefferson, NC: McFarland, 2012), 206.

14. Kirk, *Paradise Past*, 269.

15. Gavan Daws, *The Shoal of Time: A History of the Hawaiian Islands* (Honolulu, HI: University of Hawaii, 1968), 28.

16. Daws, *The Shoal of Time*, 420.

17. Paul-Émile Victor, *Man and the Conquest of the Poles*, trans. Scott Sullivan (London: Hamish Hamilton, 1964), 95.

18. David Bell, *Napoleon: A Concise Biography* (Oxford: Oxford University Press, 2015); Arthur Chuquet, *La Jeunesse de Napoléon*, Vol. 1: *Brienne* (Paris: Armand Colin, 1897), books.google.com/books?id=Ic5CAAAAYAAJ; Vincent Cronin, *Napoleon Bonaparte: An Intimate Biography* (London: Penguin, 1988 rpt.), archive.org/details/napoleon0000cron; Geoffrey Ellis, *Napoleon*, 2nd ed. (New York: Routledge, 2000); Alan Forrest, *Napoleon: Life, Legacy, Image*, (New York: St. Martin's Press, 2011); August Fournier, *Napoleon I, A Biography*, Vol. 1, trans. Margaret Bacon Corwin and Arthur Dart Bissell (New York: Henry Holt, 1903), books.google.com/books?id=jI0aAAAAMAAJ; Maurice Hutt, *Napoleon* (Englewood Cliffs, NJ: Prentice-Hall, 1972), archive.org/details/napoleon0000maur_m7e9; Paul Johnson, *Napoleon: A Life* (New York: Penguin, 2006); Harold T. Parker, "The Formation of Napoleon's Personality: An Exploratory Essay," *French Historical Studies* 7, no. 1 (1971): 6–26, jstor.org/stable/286104; William Milligan Sloane, *The Life of Napoleon Bonaparte*, Vol. 1 (London: The Times Book Club, 1911), archive.org/details/in.ernet.dli.2015.553517; Timothy Wilson-Smith, *Napoleon: Man of War, Man of Peace* (London: Constable, 2002).

19. Frank McLynn, *Napoleon: A Biography* (New York: Arcade Publishing, 2002), archive.org/details/napoleonbiograph00mcly, 23.

20. Alexandre Assier, *Napoléon 1ᵉʳ à l'École royale militaire de Brienne: d'après des documents authentiques et inédits, 1779–1784* (Paris: Champion, 1874), hdl.handle.net/2027/hvd.hx86hm; Francois Gilbert de Coston, *Biographie des prèmieres années de Napoléon Bonaparte*, Vol. 1 (Paris: Librairie de Marc Aurel Frères, 1840), books.google.com/books?id=dsVBAAAAcAAJ; Jean-Lambert-Alphonse Colin, *L'Éducation militaire de Napoléon* (Paris: Librairie militaire R. Chapelot et Co., 1900), books.google.com/books?id=sQkKAAAAIAAJ; Robert Laulan, "La chère à l'École Militaire au temps du Bonaparte," *Revue de l'Institut Napoléon* (1959): 18–23.

21. Robert Laulan, "Que valent les 'Cahiers' d'Alexandre des Mazis?" *Revue de l'Institut Napoléon* (1956): 56–57.

22. Laulan, "Que valent?" 54.

23. Des Mazis, "Les Cahiers d'Alexandre des Mazis," qtd. in *Napoléon Bonaparte—L'épopée impériale* (August 11, 2007), napoleonbonaparte.wordpress.com/2007/08/11/les-cahiers-alexandre-des-mazis-ecole-militaire-1/.

24. Des Mazis, qtd. in Laulan, "Que valent?" 56. My translation.

25. Laulan, "Que valent?" 55–59.

26. Dunmore believes Napoleon may have wished to join the expedition but that his formidable mother had already decided his career path for him. (See Dunmore, introduction to *The Journal of Jean-François de Galaup de la Pérouse*, lxx.)

27. Dunmore, introduction to *The Journal*, ccxx.

28. Peter Dillon, *Narrative and Successful Result of a Voyage in the South Seas, Performed by Order of the Government of British India, to Ascertain the Actual Fate of La Pérouse's Expedition* (London: Hurst, Chance, and Co., 1829), google.com/books/edition/Narrative_and_Successful_Result_of_a_Voy/GbUBAAAAYAAJ, 39–41, 194–95, 215–19.

29. Dillon, *Narrative and Successful Result of a Voyage in the South Seas*, 119, 120, 159, 168, 217.

30. Jules Dumont-d'Urville, *Voyage de la corvette l'Astrolabe Executé par Ordre du Roi, pendant les années 1826-1827-1828-1829, sous le commandement de M. J. Dumont D'Urville, capitaine de vaisseau*, Vol. 5 (Paris: J. Tastu, 1833), google.com/books/edition/Voyage_de_la_corvette_l_Astrolabe_ex%C3%A9cu/NGBHAAAAYAAJ.

31. Dumont-d'Urville, *Voyage de la corvette l'Astrolabe*, 154, 159, 329.

32. Dillon, *Narrative and Successful Result of a Voyage in the South Seas*, 41–42, 195, 401; Dumont-d'Urville, *Voyage de la corvette l'Astrolabe*, 154, 161.

33. Dillon, *Narrative and Successful Result of a Voyage in the South Seas*, 1, 6, 8, 14–23, 92–93, 185, 222–224, 255–256, 433.

34. Dumont-d'Urville, *Voyage de la corvette l'Astrolabe*, 113, 167, 234, 344, 412.

35. Dumont-d'Urville, *Voyage de la corvette l'Astrolabe*, 217.

36. *The Island Mission: Being a History of the Melanesian Mission from Its Commencement. Reprinted from "Mission Life"* (London: William Macintosh, 1869), ch. 9, anglicanhistory.org/oceania/island_mission1869/.

37. John Coleridge Patteson journal, August 1856, "Patteson's Correspondence 1856," Melanesia Diocese 1838–1958, Bodleian Library, microform.digital/boa/documents/2110/pattesons-correspondence-1856, img 231.

38. Charlotte Mary Yonge, *Life of John Coleridge Patteson, Missionary Bishop of the Melanesian Islands* (London: Macmillan and Co., 1874), 199, hdl.handle.net/2027/uc2.ark:/13960/t9t15430z; Georgina Battiscombe, *Charlotte Mary Yonge, The Story of an Uneventful Life* (London: Constable and Co., 1943), 90, archive.org/details/in.ernet.dli.2015.62485/; "Melanesian Mission Accounts. 1862-3," Appendix to "Lecture on the Melanesian Mission, by the Reverend R. H. Codrington, M.A.," *Project Canterbury*, 17, anglicanhistory.org/oceania/codrington_lecture1863.pdf.

39. Yonge, *Life of John Coleridge Patteson*, 280–81.

40. W. C. O'Ferrall, *Melanesia: Santa Cruz and the Reef Islands* (London: The Church House, 1908), anglicanhistory.org/oceania/oferrall_santacruz1908/.

41. E. S. Armstrong, *History of the Melanesian Mission* (London: Isbister & Co. Ltd., 1900), 28. See also Mathurin Dondo, *La Perouse in Maui* (Wailuku, HI: Maui, 1959), 29–32, hdl.handle.net/2027/uc1.b2808123.

42. *Stories of the Sea in Former Days: Narratives of Wreck and Rescue* (London, Blackie & Son, 1885), 162.

43. W. S. Merwin, *The Ends of the Earth: Essays* (Berkeley, CA: Counterpoint, 2005), 265.

44. Caffeinated Clint, "Xavier Gens Doing *Vanikoro* Next," *MovieHole* (November 12, 2007), moviehole.net/xavier-gens-doing-vanikoro-next/.

45. See, for example, Michael Pickering, "Cannibalism in the Ethnographic Record," *The International Encyclopedia of Anthropology*, Wiley Online Library (September 29, 2017), doi.org/10.1002/9781118924396.wbiea1993; and Gananath Obeyesekere, *Cannibal Talk: The Man-Eating Myth and Human Sacrifices in the South Seas* (Berkeley, CA: UC Press, 2005).

46. Arnaud Bordas, "Vanikoro: Le Rêve de Xavier Gens," *Capture Mag* (August 13, 2012), capturemag.net/analyse-this/vanikoro-le-reve-de-xavier-gens/.

47. Hilary Mantel, "I Met a Man Who Wasn't There" (Ridge Lecture, Huntington Library, San Marino, CA, May 11, 2017).

Afterword

1. *Thomas Cromwell: A Life* by Diarmaid Macculloch was published in 2018. *The Mirror and the Light* by Hilary Mantel was published in 2020.

Index

For the benefit of digital users, indexed terms that span two pages (e.g., 52–53) may, on occasion, appear on only one of those pages.